Working with Paradata, Marginalia and Fieldnotes

Working with Paradata, Marginalia and Fieldnotes

The Centrality of By-Products of Social Research

Edited by

Rosalind Edwards

Department of Sociology, Social Policy and Criminology, University of Southampton, UK

John Goodwin

Department of Sociology, University of Leicester, UK

Henrietta O'Connor

Department of Sociology, University of Leicester, UK

Ann Phoenix

Thomas Coram Research Unit, Department of Social Sciences, UCL Institute of Education, UK and Helsinki Collegium for Advanced Studies, University of Helsinki, Finland

 Edward Elgar
PUBLISHING

Cheltenham, UK • Northampton, MA, USA

Published by
Edward Elgar Publishing Limited
The Lypiatts
15 Lansdown Road
Cheltenham
Glos GL50 2JA
UK

Edward Elgar Publishing, Inc.
William Pratt House
9 Dewey Court
Northampton
Massachusetts 01060
USA

A catalogue record for this book
is available from the British Library

Library of Congress Control Number: 2016953905

This book is available electronically in the **Elgar**online
Social and Political Science subject collection
DOI 10.4337/9781784715250

ISBN 978 1 78471 524 3 (cased)
ISBN 978 1 78471 525 0 (eBook)

Typeset by Servis Filmsetting Ltd, Stockport, Cheshire
Printed and bound in Great Britain by TJ International Ltd, Padstow

Contents

Contributors

Karen Bell is ESRC Future Research Leaders Fellow at the School for Policy Studies, University of Bristol. Her teaching, research and publishing interests and accomplishments have spanned poverty, inequality, political economy and environmental and social justice, as well as social research methods.

Janet Boddy is Professor of Child, Youth and Family Studies at the University of Sussex, where she is also Director of the Centre for Innovation and Research in Childhood and Youth (CIRCY). Her research is concerned with family lives and with services for children and families, in the UK and internationally. Her recent research includes European studies concerned with young people in out-of-home care, and an ESRC National Centre for Research Methods study of family lives and the environment in India and the UK (working with Ann Phoenix and others within the NOVELLA Node; see www.novella.ac.uk). Janet also has a long-standing interest in research ethics and governance, including advisory work for ESRC and ERC, and wrote the chapter on Research Ethics in the latest edition of the methods handbook *Researching Social Life* (Sage).

Robert G. Burgess is the former Vice-Chancellor of the University of Leicester. He currently chairs the Boards of NatCen Social Research and GSM London. As a sociologist he researched and wrote extensively on qualitative research and education.

Gabriele B. Durrant is Associate Professor (Reader) in Social Statistics in the Department of Social Statistics and Demography, School of Social Sciences at the University of Southampton. She is Deputy Director of the ESRC National Centre for Research Methods (NCRM), Director of NCRM Training and the lead researcher of the NCRM work package 1. She is also Co-Investigator of the Administrative Data Research Centre for England (ADRCE). Her research interests are in the areas of paradata, interviewer effects, non-response in sample surveys, measurement error, and statistical modelling in the social sciences, in particular multilevel modelling. More recently she also developed an interest in using linked data sources, particularly in the area of energy use and environmental attitudes.

Rosalind Edwards is Professor of Sociology, a co-director of the ESRC National Centre for Research Methods and Social Sciences Director of Research and Enterprise at the University of Southampton. She is also an elected member of the Academy of Social Sciences. Rosalind has a methodological interest in micro-level historical comparative research and qualitative longitudinal research, and her area of substantive expertise is family studies. She is a co-author of a much-downloaded review paper: *How Many Qualitative Interviews is Enough?*: http://eprints.ncrm. ac.uk/2273/; and her recent book publications include *Understanding Families Over Time* (ed. with J. Holland, 2014, Palgrave), *What is Qualitative Interviewing?* (co-author with J. Holland, 2013, Bloomsbury), and *International Perspectives on Racial and Ethnic Mixing and Mixedness* (ed. with S. Ali, C. Caballero and M. Song, 2012, Routledge).

Heather Elliott is a researcher at the Thomas Coram Research Unit, at University College London's (UCL) Institute of Education. She has interests in mothering and work, marginalia and in children's imaginaries. Recent projects, funded by ESRC and UCL, have involved research on mothers' online representations of family life and entanglements of mothers' and children's digital practices. She uses, and writes about, narrative, psychosocial, archival and longitudinal qualitative methodologies.

Eldin Fahmy is Senior Lecturer and Centre Head for the Study of Poverty and Social Justice in the School for Policy Studies at the University of Bristol. His main research interests include the measurement and analysis of poverty and social exclusion, and the applications of mixed methods designs in poverty research. Dr Fahmy was a member of the *2012 UK Poverty and Social Exclusion Survey* research team with lead responsibility for survey development work. He is co-editor of the *Journal of Poverty and Social Justice* published by The Policy Press.

John Goodwin is a Professor of Sociology at the University of Leicester. As a sociologist John has a broad range of research interests including education to work transitions, sociological research methods and the history of sociology (particularly 'classic' British empirical studies post-1940). He is a recognised expert on the life and sociology of Pearl Jephcott and he also has a significant interest in the works of Norbert Elias and C. Wright Mills. In terms of his sociological practice John has expertise in qualitative secondary analysis, restudies, biographical methods and the use of unconventional data sources in sociological research. He has long-standing interest in the UK Birth Cohort Studies.

H.J. Jackson, Emeritus Professor of English at the University of Toronto, is the author of two books about readers' notes in books: *Marginalia* and

Romantic Readers. Her most recent book, on the subject of literary fame, is *Those Who Write for Immortality* (Yale, 2015).

Daniel Kilburn is a Geography Teaching Fellow at UCL. His research explores individual and collective experiences of dwelling, the political economy of housing, and social research methodology, with disciplinary groundings in both Human Geography and Sociology. He recently co-edited a special issue of the *International Journal of Social Research Methodology* on the teaching and learning of social research methods. He has also presented on the potential for substantive analyses of paradata at the UK *Housing Studies Association Conference* and convened a session on advances in research with paradata for the *7th ESRC Research Methods Festival, 2016*.

Olga Maslovskaya is a Senior Research Fellow at the National Centre for Research Methods, the University of Southampton. She is currently working on the project 'Data Collection for Data Quality'. Her primary research interests are in the field of survey methodology, social statistics and quantitative research methods. Specific areas include paradata, interviewer effects in sample surveys, non-response, web surveys and use of mobile devices, and statistical modelling in social sciences. She has recently published articles in the *Journal of Survey Statistics and Methodology*, the *Journal of Epidemiology and Community Health*, the *Journal of Biosocial Science*, and *Health Promotion International*.

Henrietta O'Connor is Professor of Sociology in the Department of Sociology at the University of Leicester. Her research interests focus on the sociology of work, youth employment and gender. She also has an active interest in research methods ranging in scope from her early work on online research methods to more recent research based around the secondary analysis of qualitative data, qualitative longitudinal research and community restudies.

Ann Phoenix is Professor of Psychosocial Research at the Thomas Coram Research Unit, UCL Institute of Education, University of London and, from 2016 to 2018, she is the Erkko Visiting Professor in Studies on Contemporary Society at Helsinki Collegium for Advanced Studies, University of Helsinki, Finland. Her research is mainly about social identities and the ways in which psychological experiences and social processes are linked. It focuses on intersectionality; racialised and gendered identities and experiences; mixed-parentage, masculinities, consumption, young people and their parents; the transition to motherhood; and narrative research.

William H. Sherman is Director of Research and Collections at the Victoria and Albert Museum, where he is leading the development of the V&A Research Institute, and Honorary Professor at the University of York, where he was Director of the Centre for Renaissance & Early Modern Studies. He has published widely on the history of books and readers, the plays of Shakespeare and his contemporaries and the interface between word and image. His recent publications include *Used Books: Marking Readers in Renaissance England*, an edition of Ben Jonson's *Alchemist*, and a special issue of the *Journal of Medieval and Early Modern Studies* on *Renaissance Collage*.

Marginalia

Sometimes the notes are ferocious,
skirmishes against the author
raging along the borders of every page
in tiny black script.
If I could just get my hands on you,
Kierkegaard, or Conor Cruise O'Brien,
they seem to say,
I would bolt the door and beat some logic into your head.

Other comments are more offhand, dismissive –
'Nonsense.' 'Please!' 'HA! !' –
that kind of thing.
I remember once looking up from my reading,
my thumb as a bookmark,
trying to imagine what the person must look like
who wrote 'Don't be a ninny'
alongside a paragraph in The Life of Emily Dickinson.

Students are more modest
needing to leave only their splayed footprints
along the shore of the page.
One scrawls 'Metaphor' next to a stanza of Eliot's.
Another notes the presence of 'Irony'
fifty times outside the paragraphs of A Modest Proposal.

Or they are fans who cheer from the empty bleachers,
Hands cupped around their mouths.
'Absolutely,' they shout
to Duns Scotus and James Baldwin.
'Yes.' 'Bull's-eye.' 'My man!'
Check marks, asterisks, and exclamation points
rain down along the sidelines.

And if you have managed to graduate from college
without ever having written 'Man vs. Nature'
in a margin, perhaps now
is the time to take one step forward.

We have all seized the white perimeter as our own
and reached for a pen if only to show
we did not just laze in an armchair turning pages;
we pressed a thought into the wayside,
planted an impression along the verge.

Even Irish monks in their cold scriptoria
jotted along the borders of the Gospels
brief asides about the pains of copying,
a bird singing near their window,
or the sunlight that illuminated their page –
anonymous men catching a ride into the future
on a vessel more lasting than themselves.

And you have not read Joshua Reynolds,
they say, until you have read him
enwreathed with Blake's furious scribbling.

Yet the one I think of most often,
the one that dangles from me like a locket,
was written in the copy of Catcher in the Rye
I borrowed from the local library
one slow, hot summer.
I was just beginning high school then,
reading books on a davenport in my parents' living room,
and I cannot tell you
how vastly my loneliness was deepened,
how poignant and amplified the world before me seemed,
when I found on one page

A few greasy looking smears
and next to them, written in soft pencil –
by a beautiful girl, I could tell,
whom I would never meet –
'Pardon the egg salad stains, but I'm in love.'

'Marginalia' from *Picnic, Lightning*, by Billy Collins, © 1998. Reprinted by permission of the University of Pittsburgh.

Foreword

The shape, substance and style of the field of social research methodology have undergone considerable change in the last 60 years. In the 1950s the term 'social research' was synonymous with the conduct of social surveys and major texts paid little attention to other methods of social investigation apart from a brief mention of observational methods. It was not until the 1980s that we witnessed the development of ethnographic or field methods as an alternative to the social survey – in part a reflection of the changing intellectual problems that the research set out to investigate. Among the problems that emerged was the way in which some research practitioners and their students erroneously began to divide the social world into a sharp division of quantitative and qualitative styles of social investigation – a situation that researchers now readily appreciate is a false dichotomy. Accordingly, the field has been reshaped further with the use of 'mixed methods' that appropriately bring together quantitative and qualitative data to better understand the social situation under study whereby quantitative and qualitative research data complement each other.

While these general developments occurred in social research, other trends can be identified in the teaching of research methodology. First, it was no longer sufficient for the field to rely on the teaching of research techniques. Second, the shape of methodology teaching was developed not only by those who might describe themselves as 'methodologists' but also by active researchers who began talking and writing about the research process that took us well beyond the world of research techniques. Furthermore, it emphasised how research could not be reduced to a set of standard procedures. Instead, researchers became engaged in discussing various aspects of research including: designing projects, collecting data, analysing data and research writing. The result was that reflections on the research process covered what researchers experienced when doing research.

But the reader might reasonably ask how these trends and developments relate to this volume on *Working with Paradata, Marginalia and Fieldnotes*.

First, the chapters in this volume extend the terrain of 'social research methodology' by broadening out what counts as methodology. Second, as the choice of chapters illustrates, the editors and authors have not confined their attention to quantitative or qualitative studies. Third, the authors examine the work of others through an analysis of quantitative *and* qualitative studies, some of which are research classics such as Peter Townsend's volume on poverty, as well as empirical work conducted by key figures in British sociology including Norbert Elias and Pearl Jephcott. However, the focus is not on the substantive material but on an under-recognised aspect of methodology.

By looking at paradata, the authors extend the field of research methodology by examining not only the by-products of data collection but also the interpretation and analysis of data. As a consequence, this takes us closer to the research experience and illustrates how researchers can draw upon a variety of materials that have the potential to deliver an increased understanding of the research process as well as the substantive field of investigation. So we might ask: what could be included in this research material? In attempting to address this issue the following examples can be included (in no particular order):

- Grant applications that might include handwritten notes by the applicant.
- Research correspondence that can include letters, memos and notes between researchers and sponsors as well as the letters and notes that may be written by members of a research team to each other. These days email correspondence has the potential to shed much light on the research process as notes written between team members can be used to analyse the development of the research study.
- Photographs may be taken of research locations or of respondents and research team members (subject to their permission).
- Letters that include handwritten comments by the writer as well as responses generated by the recipient.
- Diaries kept by the researcher that provide additional insights into the research process by focusing on methodological, theoretical and substantive issues.
- Informants Diaries that may be commissioned by the research team.
- Fieldnotes that can include detailed observations recorded by the researcher and may take many forms, including notes on the conduct of a social survey interview as well as the substantive material that may contribute to an ethnographic study.

The list could be endless, and will prompt researchers to think about the paradata that may be gleaned from existing research materials. In this respect, they contribute not only to data collection but also to data analysis and have the potential to highlight strengths and weaknesses in an investigation as well as providing a greater understanding of the different ways principal researchers may work and the various ways in which members of a large field force engage with respondents and handle research questions. Altogether, this opens up opportunities for a reanalysis of the conduct of some classic studies, as illustrated in several of the chapters in this volume. However, there are a number of other issues that are raised by the discovery of paradata and their use in social research. We might ask:

- Did researchers intend their comments on interview schedules to be used for further investigations? Did they really consider that their notes describing the research location, the respondents and their families, might be quoted directly and used by researchers?
- Is research correspondence appropriate research material? Who owns it, the writer or the recipient?
- Do photographs provide research insights or are they socially constructed depending on the position of the researcher, the angle of the camera lens and so on?
- Are diaries public documents? Were they written for the public domain or are they private intimations for the writer alone?

In short, these questions point to some of the ethical dilemmas that researchers may need to confront in using paradata, marginalia and field-notes in the course of an investigation.

The researcher may therefore face many of the problems shared with other forms of social research. Yet it may encourage the researcher to revisit particular methods to see if their use has been maximised in particular research studies to gain further insights into the research process.

The beauty of this volume is that it has the potential to introduce the reader to a relatively new field in methodology and to provide insights not only into methodology but also into the substantive field of investigation. These chapters clearly illustrate the way in which social research treats all data as having the potential to develop our understanding of the social world. The collection also has the potential to broaden our understanding of social research that is not to be confined in a methodological strait-jacket but opened up for the richness that can be generated by researchers who think creatively about using different approaches to social research.

On this basis we might ask, who are the audiences for this volume? First, it is appropriate for the beginning student who will be assisted to take a wide-ranging approach to social research and to methodology. Second, the experienced researcher may read these chapters with benefit as they point to a range of data that is on the margins of social research methods and which can augment traditional styles of collecting, analysing and writing up data. Third, research teams may be encouraged to use this volume to consider ways in which they may correspond with each other in order that further data can become available in the research process and the way in which researchers work. Finally, those members of the public who participate in social research may also be encouraged to read this volume to obtain a greater insight into social research and the methodologies used.

Overall, the editors and authors have extended the research repertoire and the contours of social research methodology. This has the potential to invigorate the way in which social research methodology is developed and used to extend our understanding of the social world.

Robert G. Burgess

1. Introduction: working with paradata, marginalia and fieldnotes

John Goodwin, Henrietta O'Connor,
Ann Phoenix and Rosalind Edwards

INTRODUCTION

While research areas do not just 'appear', the genesis of academic interests and specialities is neither straightforward nor always clear. How we come to be interested in specific areas is often tied up with individual research histories, career trajectories or even chance discoveries and accidental encounters. It may also be the case that while we may think we are working in niche or even obscure fields of enquiry sometimes serendipitous meetings, conversations or exchanges reveal shared interests, common ground and opportunities for future productive collaborations. Indeed, this volume, like many others, has origins in niche areas, chance discoveries and fortuitous encounters. Its roots lie in two separate sets of joint research experiences coming together to form a shared interest for the four editors in what is a burgeoning and emergent field. That interest is in research that treats the by-products of an activity as data and of research interest in itself: paradata, marginalia and fieldnotes. Yet how did we get here?

Ros Edwards' interest in by-products was sparked by listening to survey methodologists who were co-members of the ESRC National Centre for Research Methods (NCRM), discussing the 'paradata' created by delivering surveys (for example Turner et al., 2014). Her colleagues' reference to the useful information that could be gained by analysis of keystrokes and other electronic aspects of computer-aided surveys, prompted Ros to realise that the notes scribbled by fieldworkers on the paper copies of Peter Townsend's old poverty survey booklets (from the *1967–68 Poverty in the UK* Study) that she had spotted stored in the basement of a data archive could also be considered useful paradata. Chatting about this material with Ann Phoenix, whose Novella narrative analysis project was attached to the NCRM, together they conceived a project that investigated the possibilities for analysing the interviewer notes. This was the start of a fascination with paradata and marginalia, and, together with other colleagues, conducting research that analysed these by-products as data (initially funded by NCRM and later by an additional grant from the ESRC).

For John Goodwin and Henrietta O'Connor interest in the 'by-products' of research was sparked by the rediscovery of interview schedules from a lost research project on the transitions from school to work in 1960s Leicester (see Goodwin and O'Connor, 2006, 2015a; O'Connor and Goodwin, 2010) and the detailed interviewer notes that accompanied them. Knowing little about the origins of the lost project, Goodwin and O'Connor had to visit relevant archives and reconstruct the project using any research materials, by-products and ephemera that they could find. However, while the rediscovered interview schedules contained important data, there was a realisation that all of these research by-products (letters, correspondence, notes, interviewer notes and so forth) were valuable data in and of themselves that could also be subject to sociological analysis in their own right (see O'Connor and Goodwin, 2010). This research led them, along with colleagues, to revisit a number of past studies (*The Established and the Outsiders*; Young Adults in the Labour Market; and The Changing Structure of Youth Labour Markets), long forgotten researchers (Pearl Jephcott) and the contributions of well-known sociologists (C. Wright Mills) using paradata, marginalia and fieldnotes as the subject and object of their analyses (for example, see Goodwin and O'Connor, 2015).

These two strands of work came together in 2012 when Henrietta made a chance discovery of an article in an NCRM newsletter in which Ann and Ros had asked the question 'what can we do with marginalia, notes and letters?' (see Phoenix et al., 2012). The question resonated and it was clear that all four editors were grappling with the same issues. After a brief exchange of correspondence at the end of 2012 (John with Ann and Henrietta with Ros) the idea for collaboration and a one-day conference gradually emerged.

> A collaborative event focusing on working with microparadata and marginalia . . . Presentations could include our team on working with written microparadata in the late '60s *Poverty in the UK* booklets, our colleagues at Bristol . . . on working with audio-recorded microparadata for the contemporary Poverty and Social Exclusion project . . . and of course yourself and John Goodwin on your work with Elias's early 1960s study and/or the analysis of the '80s material.
> (Ros Edwards to Henrietta O'Connor, June 2013)

The conference – *Working with Paradata, Marginalia and Fieldnotes: The Centrality of By-Products of Social Research* – was held at the University of Leicester in January 2014 and was jointly organised by the NCRM and members of the Department of Sociology at the University of Leicester. The key issue addressed by speakers at the conference, in line with the central problem considered in the chapters of this book, was how do we as social scientists make the very best use of the 'by-products' of social research? Through the conference, we sought to bring together colleagues working in this area for a 'dialogue' across disciplines and research paradigms: across the social sciences and humanities, historical and contemporary data, primary and secondary sources, and quantitative and qualitative approaches. The intention was exploring, learning and sharing our research practices, as there are no established conventions for using such data. This dialogue, and the opportunities to share and exchange afforded by the one-day conference, we considered to be crucial given that it is only very recently that social science researchers have begun to recognise the value of such data. This recent turn contrasts directly with other disciplinary areas. For example, if we consider marginalia there has been a rich tradition in the arts and literary criticism of exploring the 'histories' of books, manuscripts and documents through the inscriptions, notes, augmentations and marginalia recorded within them. As Orgel (2015) suggests:

> inscriptions were so ubiquitous and marginalia not unusual; it is a rare book that remained unmarked in some way, even if only by an owner's name.
>
> (Orgel, 2015: 19)

This quotation, from Orgel's (2015) *The Reader in the Book*, is useful in that it not only neatly captures the prevalence of such marginalia in ancient manuscripts but also points to the potential analytical value that such inscriptions can have for contemporary understandings of those texts. Orgel's (2015) interest is the history of the book via an 'archaeology of the use of margins and other blank spaces, a sociology of reading and writing in relation to ownership' (Orgel, 2015: 2). Much can be revealed about the ownership of, and engagement with, texts via an analysis of what has been 'added to' those texts whether directly related to the substantive context of the book or otherwise. So how would the approach advocated by Orgel (2015), amongst others (see, for example, Sherman, 2008, and also this volume) translate for the social sciences? How could an analysis of marginalia, paradata and fieldnotes complement the 'standard' methodologies and data sources across the social sciences? It is the case that those engaged in creating and analysing large-scale survey data are increasingly turning their attention to paradata, the context in which questionnaires are completed and the observations made during interviews as well as those factors which impact upon the recruitment and retention of participants. Likewise, for those researchers undertaking secondary analysis of existing datasets, there is analytical value in examining paradata and marginalia in the form of fieldnotes, fieldworker comments in the 'margins' of interview schedules, as well as the ephemera created during the research process. This is especially important given their potential to cast light on those otherwise usually hidden aspects of research in the field. As such, and by organising the conference, we were signalling, and remain convinced, that a discussion relating to the systematic use of the by-products of social research, by researchers themselves, is long overdue.

MOVING FORWARD: TOWARDS A TYPOLOGY OF SOCIAL RESEARCH 'BY-PRODUCTS'

In recent years, two methodological innovations have led researchers to attend to features of their research beyond the data collected. On the one hand, rising costs and falling response rates have led survey researchers to find ever-more sophisticated ways of understanding and improving survey quality and costs. Couper (1998) coined the term 'paradata' to refer to the by-products of data collection in survey research at either macro (the whole survey) or micro (survey case) level. 'Paradata' analysis is becoming well established in the quantitative field. The main focus has been on automatically captured audit trails from computer keystrokes such as the order of completion and revisions of answers; use of the help window; call records; non-response; and measurement error. The term is expanding, however, to include the context in which questionnaires are completed; interviewer-generated observations about the process of data collection; as well as the neighbourhood, housing unit, interviewee and interview (Kreuter and Casas-Cordero, 2010). These paradata have been collected and analysed in various surveys, with a view to improving recruitment and retention in large-scale datasets. Nicolaas (2011) has identified the methodological benefits of 'paradata' as improved understanding of data collection processes and evaluation and monitoring, including quality control. On the other hand, many qualitative researchers now analyse fieldnotes in order to better understand how research accounts are co-constructed between researchers and participants, allowing psychosocial, interpretivist or interactionist insights into the identities of both research participants and interviewers. In parallel with the use of fieldnotes in qualitative research, paradata allow interrogation of the place of the researcher in the data-gathering process. Both paradata and fieldnotes are, therefore, simultaneously methodology and productive of substantive data. Questions of analytic approach to fieldnotes and paradata are currently receiving research attention (e.g. Bell et al., 2014; Hollway, 2015), but require further work.

However, amongst the key issues explored during the conference, and again reflected upon in this volume, were definitional issues around what is actually meant by paradata, marginalia and fieldnotes. At first sight, these may appear to be disparate and different 'types' of data, all of which may be defined differently by scholars from different traditions, depending upon their epistemological proclivities. For example, the term 'marginalia' was coined in 1832 by Samuel Taylor Coleridge (Jackson, 2001) to describe a practice that was already current since 1700, of reader alterations to books, including marginal notes, underlining, highlighting and dog-earing (Jackson, 2001). People would sometimes write in books for one another in ways that Anderson (2011: 46) suggests was 'a kind of slow-motion, long-form Twitter, or a statusless, meaning-soaked Facebook, or an analog, object-based G-chat'. Many researchers report a plurality of reasons for the production of marginalia, including better comprehension of meanings, conversing with other potential readers and engagement with the text, often intertextually (Fajkovic and Björneborn, 2014; Jackson, 2001; Sherman, 2008; Wagstaff, 2012). As with fieldnotes, marginalia, because it 'is unguarded, meant only as an aide-memoire, . . . can accidentally reveal much about the person writing it' (Moran, 2011). In much the same way, it is clear that while paradata analyses and social survey research appear to give minimal place to the identities, creativity and agency of researchers, these are still a central part of the data collection process (Bell et al., 2014). Used in this way, as data to add meaning to the data collection process, the main characteristic that all these different types of data have in common is that they can all be considered 'by-products', accompaniments or augmentations to broader research processes. So by imagining these paradata, marginalia, fieldnotes as 'by-products' we can include the whole, and vast array, of materials created and co-created during the research process (such as notes, files, annotations, keystrokes, observations, letters and correspondence, diaries and even photographs). These materials have major analytical value and can potentially add considerable depth to our understanding of the research process.

In Table 1.1 we outline a typology of paradata, marginalia and fieldnotes, as by-products of the research process. The examples we provide are not exhaustive and are not mutually exclusive. For example, letters and correspondence can be both paradata in the sense that they are by-products of the research process with the potential to offer insights but they may also contain marginalia that is interesting analytically in its own right. They can also be differentiated, in some respects, by the 'level of observation'. Paradata may be 'macro' and created at the level of the research design,

Table 1.1   A typology of 'by-products' of social research

By-Products	Examples
Paradata (macro)	Keystrokes, respondent details, 'contextual' data, access information, duration of data collection, research instrument properties, respondent refusals and non-responses (see Figure 1.1)
(micro)	Letters, correspondence, photographs, images, notes, observations, research ephemera (see Figures 1.2 and 1.3)
Fieldnotes	Fieldnotes, interviewer notes, recorded observations, research diaries (see Figure 1.3)
Marginalia	Annotations and augmentations to research instruments, books, book proofs, letters and correspondence (see Figures 1.4 and 1.5)

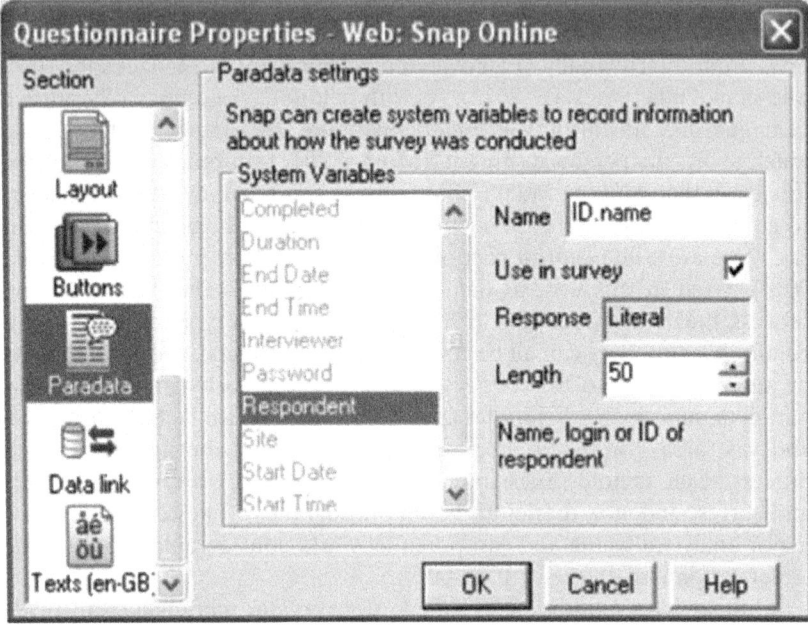

Figure 1.1   Paradata (macro) – screen shot of paradata creation software

research programme or research instruments or it could be more 'micro' and pertain to individual respondents or groups of respondents. Visual illustrations of the by-products of social research are provided and the first of these, Figure 1.1, is an example of macro paradata which shows the

Person interviewed (comment) widow, widower, divorced sep etc details:

Mother. - sugg. see father during day.

Date: 30|5|61   Time of day: 4-40 p.m   Length: 25 mins.

Situation (doorstep, kitchen, front room etc)

living room. She said 'Come in'. before she knew what we were calling for. Young daughter present joined in with information about the school. Turned T.V. sound down but left picture on.

Source: From unpublished study by Dennis Marsden, ACE Parents and Education 1960–1961 [unprocessed study]. Colchester, Essex: UK Data Archive [distributor], SN: 6224.

Figure 1.2   Paradata (micro) – survey fieldnotes

detailed information collected when surveys are conducted. The menu on the left-hand side of the box includes a paradata icon revealing the extent to which this by-product of survey research has become integrated with the process of data collection.

Figure 1.2 is an example of micro paradata collected as part of an historical study on parental school choice. The interview schedule included questions designed to capture elements of micro paradata that may have impacted on the interview encounter, such as the date, time, length and location of the interview.

Figure 1.3 is an example of the interviewer notes section in Norbert Elias's *Adjustment of Young Workers to Adult Roles* project interview schedule. Here the interviewers were encouraged to record some of the factual information relating to the interview, as in Figure 1.2. From the figure we can see they also recorded their own reflections and impressions of the interview and any problems connected with work, family and leisure. The completed notes vary in length with some fieldworkers recording basic information whereas others recorded full and frank observations or detailed accounts of their impressions of the respondents and their surroundings.

Figure 1.4 is an example of more literary marginalia, a much more widespread, commonplace and familiar by-product; the notes made by readers in the margins of printed books. It illustrates clearly how marginalia is used to augment and add to existing texts to create additional meaning or note interpretations of the texts. Here we can see the author of the marginalia engaging directly with the author of the text, questioning and seeking a form of reflexive clarification of the actions, emotions and sentiments

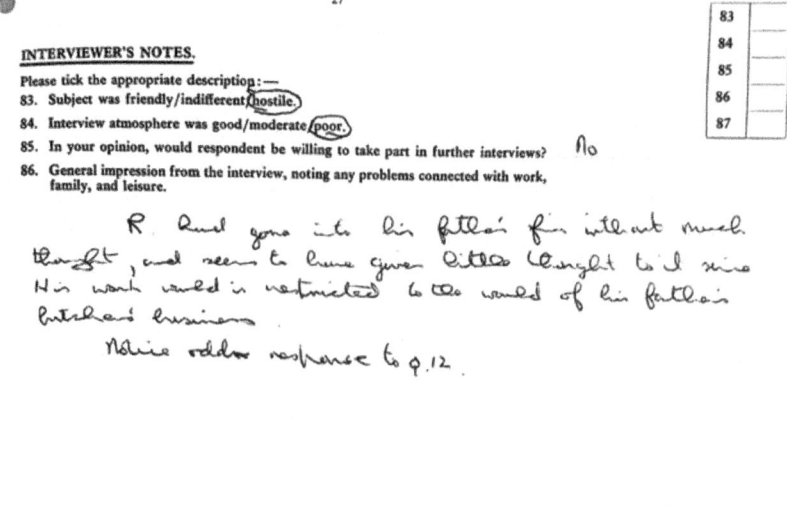

INTERVIEWER'S NOTES.

Please tick the appropriate description:—
83. Subject was friendly/indifferent/hostile.
84. Interview atmosphere was good/moderate/poor.
85. In your opinion, would respondent be willing to take part in further interviews? No
86. General impression from the interview, noting any problems connected with work, family, and leisure.

R. had gone into his father's firm without much thought, and seems to have given little thought to it since His work would is restricted to the world of his father's butcher's business.

Notice odder response to q.12.

87. Any other comment.

R. was either stupid, or unwilling to make the effort

Figure 1.3   Fieldnotes – from adjustment of young workers to adult roles, 1962–1964

implied by the text. Such marginalia offer clear insight into the reader's interpretations.

Figure 1.5 is Pearl Jephcott's own proof copy of her book *Time of One's Own* (1967). Jephcott herself has annotated the front cover, made corrections, additions and alterations. In this sense marginalia may not only be about seeking clarification or documenting interpretation, but can also be revelatory regarding the writing process itself. It offers insight into how texts emerge, how writing and expression becomes refined or where the author has changed their mind. Such marginalia are instructive as they provide evidence that the writing process never ends but is a continually evolving practice.

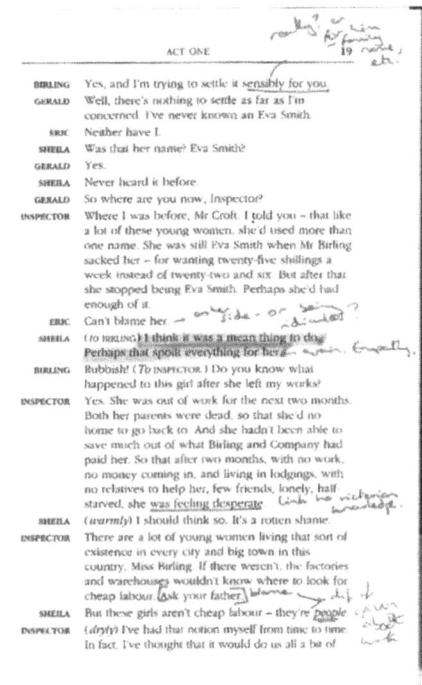

*Figure 1.4   Marginalia – annotations, augmentations and additions
(with thanks to Sarah Read)*

THE ANALYTIC POTENTIAL OF 'BY-PRODUCT' MATERIAL

It would be remiss of us not to acknowledge those within the history of our disciplines who have actively encouraged the use of marginalia and paradata and who recognised, early on, the centrality of such material to the 'practice' of social science research. Most notable of these was the American sociologist C. Wright Mills. Mills was both an active creator of marginalia and paradata and a passionate advocate for the use of these 'by-products' in research practice as well as being one of the most innovative social scientists of the mid-twentieth century. The continual creation of marginalia was central to Mills's own sociological imagination. For example, in his letters and autobiographical writings Mills reveals something of how he developed his ideas and crafts his writings, outlining his working practices in *To Tovarich: Specimen Days of My Life, Summer 1960*. This was a letter to an

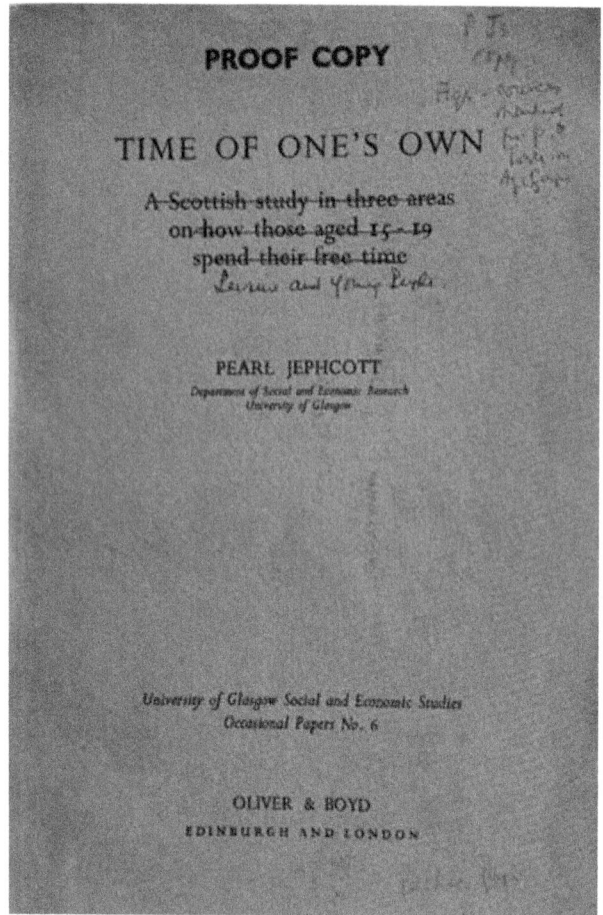

Source: Printed with permission of the estate of Pearl Jephcott.

Figure 1.5   Marginalia – writing process and corrections

imaginary Russian academic in which Mills sketches his working routines and how writing in the 'margins' was central to his creative process.

> While the coffee is making, I go out to the road and get the New York Times. Then, with the paper and the coffee, I go up to my study . . . Usually, it takes between twenty and forty minutes to read the paper, lying on the couch, marking it for clipping later. Sometimes I begin to write on the margins of the paper, spilling over onto one of the variously sized pads lying around.
>
> (Mills, 1960 in Mills and Mills, 2000: 292)

This approach is documented elsewhere and, in an interview for Pacifica Radio about Mills shortly after his death, the publisher Ian Ballantine points to the vast array of materials that Mills had assembled and the centrality of marginalia to Mills's sociological writing. Ballantine (1962) suggests that Mills:

> had a Danish filing system in his den or office and everything in each drawer was all in good order. And there were several hundred drawers. He clipped a lot, relying heavily on the New York Times. He would write little remarks to himself in the margins of the story.
>
> (Ballantine, 1962)

The remarks to himself in the margins, the constant 'clipping' of newspapers, books, magazines, articles, all retained in files in his Danish filing system, provided the stock of knowledge as well as the inspiration for Mills's own writing. In 2011, one of the editors of this volume (John Goodwin) visited the archived Mills papers housed at the University of Texas, Austin. From viewing the files, it is clear that Ballantine's observations were accurate – Mills carefully recorded and retained everything, keeping files of notes, clippings and various other research 'by-products' on every topic he encountered and became interested in. The files included full correspondence, notes, ephemera, pictures, letters, everything from a single word on a scrap of paper through to notations for lectures that Mills had given or was going to give. These marginalia, fieldnotes, paradata were central to his sociological practice and helped fuel his sociological imagination.

Mills also preaches what he practised himself and viewed the active creation of such materials as key to the research craft. He invites us to work as he worked, positioning paradata, marginalia, fieldnotes and the like as a very necessary part of developing and maintaining the 'sociological imagination'. For example, in the appendix to *The Sociological Imagination* (1959), titled *On Intellectual Craftsmanship*, Mills set out an agenda for sociological research practice designed to encourage the development of 'good habits' for research and the continual cultivation of ideas through systematic and repeated observing, recording and reflection. Mills encourages us to:

> set up a file, which is, I suppose, a sociologist's way of saying: keep a journal. Many creative writers keep journals; the sociologist's need for systematic reflection demands it. In such a file as I am going to describe, there is the joined personal experience and professional activities, studies under way and studies planned. In this file, you, as an intellectual craftsman, will try to get together what you are doing intellectually and what you are experiencing as a

person ... It also encourages you to capture 'fringe-thoughts': various ideas
which may be by-products of everyday life, snatches of conversation overheard
on the street, or, for that matter dreams.

(Mills, 1959: 196)

Here, Mills advocates the active creation of paradata, marginalia and
fieldnotes and that such data should be placed in files. The process of creating a file and the constant reflection, re-ordering and mixing up of these
materials, these by-products of everyday life, Mills suggests, are one way
to 'invite imagination' (Mills, 1959: 212). This systematic process clearly
worked for him.

Yet despite both the established tradition of literary and humanities
scholars of using such materials, and the clear advice offered by Mills
(1959) of using such materials for cultivating the sociological imagination,
there remains no such established tradition (or even a consistent approach)
within the social sciences for using the by-products of research. Nor has
there been any sustained discussion as to the value of such 'additions' for
social science research or how such materials could be used by social scientists. We can speculate as to why this may be and perhaps there are many
reasons for this.

First, there is the dominance of a natural science view within the social
sciences that primary data collection and analysis is the 'gold standard'
approach to research. Why spend time examining the by-products of
research when we should be concerned with more formal data types and
collection methods? Why be concerned with what those working in the
field recorded in their notes or focus on supplementary materials in relation to keystrokes, data entry, access to respondents or the research context
more generally? As Hughes (2013) suggests, data such as this may suffer
from dominant notions of empirical legitimacy and political alignment
that impact on what we research, how we research it and which approaches
and research areas are legitimised and privileged as compared to others.

Second, the privileging of types of data extends to data that are seen to
be in the 'foreground' (the formal empirical data collected as part of the
survey, interviews or observations directly from the field), as compared to
data in the 'background' (paradata, marginalia, fieldnotes, photographs
and ephemera) with the latter easily dismissed as merely 'context'. Do
we need to analyse this contextual material when we cannot exhaust the
analytic potential of this other, formally collected data? Why bother with
contextual, background or supplementary materials? If we follow writers
such as Elias, who advocated a 'holistic' approach to analysis, considering
'whole' processes or phenomenon (see, for example, Elias and Scotson,
1965; Goodwin and Hughes, 2011) then it becomes difficult, even arbi-

trary, to make such an artificial distinction between data types and privilege one form of data (background, foreground, formal, informal and so forth) over another. We cannot use paradata, marginalia and fieldnotes as if they were somehow separate from, or incidental to, the more 'formal' data collection process. Paradata, marginalia and fieldnotes *are* data and are created as part of the data collection or analysis process. For example, one can only speculate as to what is in the research files, relating to issues of concern and projects underway, of those who adhered to the advice from Mills (1959). It is with some conjecture that we ask what paradata, marginalia and fieldnotes exist, perhaps stored away in attics, offices and archives. However, for those interested in the history of the social sciences, or in revisiting 'classic' research of the recent past (see Chapters 4, 5 and 6) then such paradata, marginalia and fieldnotes offer significant analytical value for a holistic understanding.

Third, and again a related point, a significant reason why paradata and fieldnotes may not be commonly used in the social sciences could be due to problems of access. One of the attractive features of marginalia is that they are available and can be found in books and written documents. Indeed, most public libraries have books on their shelves that someone at some point has thought fit to annotate, augment or even illustrate. However, the same may not be said for paradata and fieldnotes. While the formal data collected as part of a research project may be deposited in official archives, the paradata, marginalia and fieldnotes may not always accompany them, given the perceived secondary status and the personal nature of much of the by-products. Researchers may also retain their own research materials, given their personal investment in the research.

OVERVIEW OF THE CHAPTERS

As suggested above, the inspiration for this volume emerged from a one-day conference held at the University of Leicester in January 2014. The resultant volume is, we believe, rich in its interdisciplinarity. We have deliberately included contributions from a range of writers to enable us to highlight the importance of marginalia, paradata and fieldnotes in the arts, humanities and in the social sciences. The book is loosely structured into three sections. It begins with contributions from quantitative social science in the form of two chapters that explore the role of paradata in large-scale contemporary survey-based research. The next section comprises three chapters each of which focus on more qualitative aspects of social research and each of which are concerned with reusing historical datasets primarily from the 1960s but with a nod to the 1980s. All the authors of these three chapters were involved in the secondary analysis of large-scale sociological projects and had, independent of each other, become fascinated with the marginalia present in each of the studies and the richness that was added to the main data by notes that had previously been largely ignored. Finally, the last two chapters are from the humanities and explore the notion of marginalia that is perhaps best known – that of notes made by readers in the margins of books and manuscripts.

The collection begins then with two contributions which focus on the creation and use of numerically-based paradata in survey research. The first of these (Chapter 2), by Durrant and Maslovskaya explores the notion of paradata that is generated as a by-product of computer-assisted survey administration. Their interest is in investigations on nonresponse in social surveys that are administered face-to-face, via telephone or online and the insight that survey designers can gain from examining data on aspects such as call record data, interviewer observations and the length of question and answer sequences. Although initially this type of data was collected unintentionally it has become increasingly relevant in understanding aspects of survey administration such as non-response behaviours and thus feeds into the development of survey design. This, in turn can reduce costs and improve the quality of the data generated. Durrant and Maslovskaya use examples from their own research to demonstrate the use of paradata for interviewer-administered interviews. They end with practical suggestions for survey research design focused on understanding nonresponse through statistical modelling based on paradata, and working out which respondents to continue to follow up and when survey administrators should stop calling.

The third chapter is from Fahmy and Bell who provide an account of their use of paradata generated when collecting data for the UK Poverty and Social Exclusion Survey (2012 PSE-UK). The authors use their experience of collecting these recent data as a basis for identifying means of improving the quality of survey design. They argue that the use of paradata, in this case the analysis of actual interviewer and respondent interactions, can better improve survey design than the more traditional approach of survey pre-testing. Their interest lies specifically in the area of behaviour coding which is a technique used to identify issues affecting questionnaire administration that stem from the behaviours of the respondents and the fieldworker. Using an example from their own experience of collecting data for 2012 PSE-UK they show how paradata collected from interview transcripts can provide survey designers with valuable information enabling the identification of problems with questions and so helping to improve future survey design and enhance the quality of data collected in survey-based research.

The next three contributions have a very different focus and take us in a slightly different direction. The authors of these three chapters have all revisited past empirical studies from the social sciences and use historical material to explore the importance of paradata, marginalia and field-notes. The first, written by Phoenix, Boddy, Edwards and Elliott, uses Townsend's renowned *Poverty in the UK* Study 1967/68 (PinUK). Rather than focusing on the extensive data collected by Townsend's team in the original survey research, Phoenix et al.'s attention became absorbed by the detailed handwritten notes they came across on the questionnaires themselves and it is this that they draw attention to here. The team used 69 annotated questionnaires from the original study and developed a typology of marginalia. This consisted of seven different categories that enabled them to analyse the comments made by the interviewers as amplifications, justifications and explanations of codes and evaluations of responses made by participants. The examples they draw upon in the chapter provide the reader with rich, descriptive accounts of the domestic lives of the respondents who took part in the study. Phoenix et al.'s account reveals much about the research process and the ways in which the researchers used marginalia as a way of making sense of research encounters. They also draw out the importance of marginalia as a means of adding depth and meaning to the quantitative nature of much of the coded data collected in the main survey.

Kilburn's chapter makes a different use of the same historical dataset, Townsend's *Poverty in the UK* Study, as used by Phoenix et al. in the previous chapter. He focuses on the housing conditions of interviewees and draws our attention to how informants' housing conditions were coded during survey interviews. In keeping with the Phoenix et al. chapter, Kilburn makes use of qualitative data that were not intended to be part of the main study. His interest arose from reading the marginalia and notes that fieldworkers made in spaces in the interview schedule, sometimes not more than a few words but in other cases filling a number of pages. Kilburn explores, in particular, responses and comments in the margin to the question of whether or not respondents believed they had a serious housing problem. Often responses to this question were contested – inhabitants did not consider that they had a housing problem, yet the marginalia reveal interviewers' accounts of very poor quality housing and overcrowding, making living circumstances intolerable. Thus, it was only through the marginalia that the true extent of poor housing conditions, central to the study, were revealed. Kilburn highlights here the insufficiency of coded, quantitative data made apparent by the interviewers' use of qualitative amplifications to the coded data in order fully to represent the housing conditions.

The last of these three chapters is from O'Connor and Goodwin who use a range of by-products of social research, from a number of projects, to draw out the importance of focusing attention on material which is often not considered as data yet provides rich insight to the research process. Focusing on three different projects, the authors show that marginalia, fieldnotes and ephemera from historical social science research projects are of great value to the secondary analyst and help to shed light on research from the past. They begin by exploring fieldnotes from Norbert Elias's 1960s project on youth employment. The marginalia and fieldnotes generated by the original research team have much in common with the data used by Phoenix et al. and Kilburn in the earlier two chapters. From extensive descriptive and very evocative fieldnotes they were able to gain insights into the lives of young people in Leicester in the 1960s – details that do not emerge from the more formal project data. Following on from this they turn to two other restudies on youth employment in the 1980s where again it is through additional notes in the margin and, as with Phoenix et al.'s and Kilburn's chapters, amplifications to the coded data, that the experience of school leavers in the 1980s really comes to life. Last but not least they turn to very different forms of research by-products and examine the importance of materials often stored in archives such as letters, photographs and research notebooks in providing invaluable additional, contextual information to the often over-sanitised published accounts of research projects. In this part of the chapter they explore letters written by the sociologist Norbert Elias to Ilya Neustadt, his Head of Department for the duration of the 1960s research project and to the notebooks and photographs of the sociologist Pearl Jephcott, a prolific researcher whose work is often forgotten by contemporary social scientists.

In the final two chapters of the book the focus shifts to the more traditional locus of marginalia – literary history. Jackson is a leading authority in the field and this chapter begins with a theme that is carried forward in Sherman's final chapter. Jackson explains how the custom of writing in books is frequently discountenanced and viewed as an act of defacing rather than enhancing a particular volume. However, the reader's attention is drawn to the fact that marginalia created by some individuals is actually highly valued and it is only the notes made by unknown readers that are frowned upon. By contrast marginalia created by famous historically significant individuals is highly prized in the literary world and adds value to the volumes where it is found. Using the example of marginalia created by John Adams (1735–1826), the second president of the USA, in three different publications, Jackson shows how Adams's extensive use of marginalia has provided future generations with a far greater understanding of his views and political outlook than would have been possible without these notes made in different volumes. An important point made by Jackson is that Adams's marginalia was not 'accidental' or intended simply as notes to himself. Books were rare and expensive during this period of history and were passed around a wide circle of potential readers. Therefore, notes made in the margin by readers such as Adams were not intended to be private – indeed there is much evidence that his extensive use of marginalia was an intentional action planned in part as a way of providing a 'public record of his life' for future generations.

The final chapter is a contribution from Sherman who is concerned primarily with readers' perceptions of marginalia and makes use of a wide range of fascinating and entertaining examples to take us through the literary history of marginalia. He draws our attention to a divide amongst readers, alluded to in the title: 'Soiled by use or enlivened by association' – between those who believe a book should never be blemished by marginalia, pen and pencil markings on the text to those who are happy to write in the margins of the volumes they read and will actively seek out and purchase copies of books that have been annotated and marked by earlier readers. Sherman explores this breach between readers using a wide range of fascinating examples of marked texts soiled by notes and marginalia, by evidence of frequent reading such as heavy thumbing of pages and perceptible food stains from readers who enjoyed books at mealtimes. He contrasts these 'messy' readers with those who have a preference for unsullied volumes. Virginia Woolf, for example, described the defacing of pristine pages as 'a sexual violation of both the text and its future readers' (Jackson, 2001: 239–40). Sherman ends his chapter by declaring his own preference for readers to continue the tradition of writing notes in the margins of books and to recognise the value of such markings to historians of the future. Thoughtfully he ends his chapter by leaving readers with a space in which to record their own marginalia!

Finally, a focus on the by-products of research and reading activities that brings together contemporary understandings of paradata, marginalia and fieldnotes, opens up an inter-paradigm and inter-disciplinary space. By-products are just as likely to consist of quantitative data, such as length of time, calculations about budgeting and so on, as they are of qualitative material, from a few short sentences to several pages. They are also just as likely to be found augmenting computer-assisted social surveys and ethnographic research as they are annotating a novel or music score. This boundary-crossing characteristic opens up the opportunity for drawing out an approach to understanding by-products that is inter-paradigmatic and inter-disciplinary. In rounding off the volume by highlighting the significance of bringing together these different disciplines and approaches, we lay the outlines of a new, relational approach to understanding and analysing paradata, marginalia and fieldnotes in our Afterword.

REFERENCES

Anderson, S. (2011) 'What I really want is someone rolling around in the text', *The New York Times Magazine*, 6 March, MM46. http://www.nytimes.com/2011/03/06/magazine/06Riff-t.html [Accessed 29 May 2016].

Ballantine, I. (1962) Contributor to: The causes of C. Wright Mills / Narrated by Elsa Knight Thompson and Saul Landau, Recorded on 7 September 1962. Los Angeles: Pacifica Radio Archive. http://pacificaradioarchives.org/recording/pz0673069?nns=C%2BWright%2BMills [Accessed 21 September 2016].

Bell, K., Fahmy, E. and Gordon, D. (2014) 'Quantitative conversations: the importance of developing rapport in standardised interviewing', *Quality and Quantity*, 50(1): 193–212.

Couper, M. (1998) 'Measuring survey quality in a CASIC environment', in Proceedings of the Section on Survey Research Methods of the American Statistical Association.

Elias, N. and Scotson, J. (1965) *The Established and the Outsiders*. London: Frank Cass.

Fajkovic, M. and Björneborn, L. (2014) 'Marginalia as message: affordances for reader-to-reader communication', *Journal of Documentation*, 70(5): 902–926.

Goodwin, J. and Hughes, J. (2011) 'Ilya Neustadt, Norbert Elias, and the development of sociology in Britain: formal and informal sources of historical data', *British Journal of Sociology*, 26(4): 677–695.

Goodwin, J. and O'Connor, H. (2006) 'Norbert Elias and the lost young worker project', *Journal of Youth Studies*, 9(2): 159–173.

Goodwin, J. and O'Connor, H. (2015) 'Pearl Jephcott: the legacy of a forgotten sociological research pioneer', *Sociology*, 49(1): 139–155.

Goodwin, J. and O'Connor, H. (2015a) *Norbert Elias's Lost Research: Revisiting the Young Worker Project*. Farnham: Ashgate.

Hollway, W. (2015) *Knowing Mothers: Researching Maternal Identity Change*. Basingstoke: Palgrave Macmillan.

Hughes, J. (2013) 'Norbert Elias and the habits of good sociology', *Human Figurations*, 2(1). http://quod.lib.umich.edu/h/humfig/11217607.0002.107/--norbert-elias-and-the-habits-of-good-sociology?rgn=main;view=fulltext [Accessed 27 February 2016].

Jackson, H.J. (2001) *Marginalia: Readers Writing in Books*. New Haven and London: Yale University Press.

Jephcott, P. (1967) *Time of One's Own*. Glasgow: Oliver and Boyd.

Kreuter, F. and Casas-Cordero, C. (2010) 'Paradata', *RatSWD Working Paper No. 136*, German Council for Social and Economic Data.

Mills, C.W. (1959) *The Sociological Imagination*. New York: Oxford University Press.

Mills, C.W. (1960) 'To Tovarich: specimen days of my life, summer 1960', in Mills, K. and Mills, P. (2000) *C. Wright Mills: Letters and Autobiographical Writings*. Berkeley, CA: University of California Press, 292–304.

Moran, J. (2011) 'Why I write in the margin', *The Guardian*, Comment is Free, 22 March. http://www.theguardian.com/commentisfree/2011/mar/22/notes-in-the-margin-social-networking [Accessed 29 May 2016].

Nicolaas, G. (2011) *Survey Paradata: A Review*. Discussion Paper. NCRM/017.

O'Connor, H. and Goodwin, J. (2010) 'Utilizing data from a lost sociological project: experiences, insights, promises', *Qualitative Research*, 10(3): 283–298.

Orgel, S. (2015) *The Reader in the Book*. Oxford: Oxford University Press.

Phoenix, A., Boddy, J., Elliott, H. and Edwards, R. (2012) 'What can we do with marginalia, notes and letters? The possibilities of narrative analysis for paradata in historical surveys', *Methods News: The Newsletter from the ESRC National Centre for Research Methods*, Winter 2012: 4.

Sherman, W. (2008) *Used Books: Marking Readers in Renaissance England*. Philadelphia: University of Pennsylvania Press.

Turner, G., Sturgis, P. and Martin, D. (2014) 'Can response latencies be used to detect survey satisficing on cognitively demanding questions?', *Journal of Survey Statistics and Methodology*. http://jssam.oxfordjournals.org/content/early/2014/12/05/jssam.smu022 [Accessed 22 September 2016].

Wagstaff, K.L. (2012) *The Evolution of Marginalia*. http://www.wkiri.com/slis/wagstaff-libr200-marginalia-1col.pdf [Accessed 8 November 2016].

2. Paradata for nonresponse investigations in social surveys

Gabriele B. Durrant and Olga Maslovskaya

INTRODUCTION

The significant increase in conducting surveys by computer-assisted modes has led to the collection of additional information about the survey process. The term 'paradata' for this type of information was first coined in a presentation by Couper (Couper, 1998). Although a uniformly accepted definition of (quantitative) paradata does not exist, paradata are generally described as a by-product of the data collection process capturing information about that process (Durrant and Kreuter, 2013; Kreuter, 2013). The specific type of paradata may depend on the survey mode, such as face-to-face, telephone or web surveys. Typical examples of paradata are call record data, capturing information about each call or visit to a sample member; interviewer observation variables, where the interviewer records additional information about each household, individual or area; recordings of the interaction between interviewer and respondent; audit or keystroke files, capturing the navigation through the questionnaire; and time stamps, reflecting the length of a question–answer sequence (Kreuter, 2013; Durrant and Kreuter, 2013). Although at first paradata was collected unintentionally, simply as a by-product, nowadays paradata may be designed and collected with a particular purpose in mind, such as nonresponse adjustment.

This chapter introduces and reviews the most important types of quantitative paradata in social survey research. It focuses on the use of paradata for nonresponse investigation with the aim of enhancing the data quality of social surveys and to reduce costs, for example by reducing unproductive call sequences. The particular interest is on interviewer observations, call record data and interviewer characteristics. Some uses for responsive and adaptive survey designs are highlighted. The chapter discusses an example where call record data and interviewer observation variables are used to predict the response outcome at the end of a call sequence to a household and also to predict how many calls are necessary until response or nonresponse is achieved.

The benefits of paradata are wide-ranging and recent years have seen a significant increase in publications demonstrating the uses of paradata. Paradata can be utilised to improve the data quality of sample surveys, such as to inform measurement error processes (Yan and Olson, 2013; Olson and Parkhurst, 2013), and to adjust for nonresponse (Kreuter et al., 2010; Biemer et al., 2013). Key benefits of paradata are the better understanding and improvement of survey data collection processes, such as for cost savings and to increase the efficiency of surveys (Laflamme et al., 2008; Moore et al., 2015; Correa et al., 2015; Kirgis and Lepkowski, 2013; Luiten, 2013; Engel et al., 2015). Specific examples, just to name a few, are to improve the allocation of interviewers to sample members (Durrant et al., 2010), to analyse variability in interviewer performance and to improve interviewer selection and training (Brunton-Smith et al., 2012; Sturgis and Brunton-Smith, 2015; West and Olson, 2010), to reduce the number of unproductive calls (Durrant et al., 2015; Moore et al., 2015) and hence to significantly reduce survey costs, to monitor nonresponse bias during data collection (Correa et al., 2015; Moore et al., 2015) and to enhance nonresponse adjustment (Kreuter et al., 2010), to evaluate the survey instrument or questionnaire, to investigate the length of time an interviewer takes to get through a question or the whole questionnaire with the aim of reducing unproductive interviewing time (Couper and Kreuter, 2013; Olson and Smyth, 2015).

Of particular interest is the use of paradata for *adaptive* and *responsive survey designs* (Groves and Heeringa, 2006). These designs make use of incoming data from the field to inform decisions about survey design changes, either in the current survey data collection period or in a future round of the same or another survey. Groves and Heeringa (2006) defined the key stages of the process followed in responsive survey designs: 1.) pre-identification of a set of survey design features that affect cost and error trade-offs; 2.) identification of indicators for these costs and errors and monitoring these during data collection; 3.) alteration of the survey design features based on the pre-identified decision rules and on the indicators in step 2. In addition to pre-planning, responsive design also includes alteration of design features following decision rules based on incoming data from the field. An example of a responsive survey design is a design which aims to control variation in response rates within subgroups of the sample. The indicators are then the subgroup response rates. The responsive design is to monitor subgroup response rates and, if any one of them falls below a particular threshold value, the subgroup receives special treatment and will be prioritised by the survey management system. In this example, there is an indicator and a decision rule that defines the alteration of the survey design, that is, it defines a new phase of data collection.

Paradata can be, however, messy and complex, and analysis may not be straightforward. Paradata may reflect multiple levels or are collected in discrete form over time, requiring more sophisticated analyses methods. For example, in a face-to-face survey call record data reflect information about each call to a household, with measurements correlated across time points. These are nested within individuals and households, which in turn may be nested within interviewers and cross-classified within areas. Time invariant information, such as interviewer observations, are usually measured at the individual- or household-level. Time-varying information may be measured at the call-level. When analysing paradata such hierarchies and complex structures should be taken into account (Wagner, 2013a, 2013b; Durrant et al., 2013b). For example, Durrant et al. (2011) and Durrant et al. (2013a) develop multilevel multinomial and multilevel logistic regression models to identify best times to establish contact and cooperation and to analyse the effects of time-varying covariates on the outcome of a call. The fact that paradata can be messy and may in itself be subject to measurement error has led to a body of literature that investigates the quality of paradata (see, for example, West and Sinibaldi, 2013; Sinibaldi et al., 2013).

Paradata may be linked to the actual survey data (either from respondents only or, in the case of a longitudinal study, to data from previous waves). With the increase in the availability and access to other data sources, in particular administrative data, paradata may be linked in addition to such external data sources, such as administrative, register or Census data, which would be available for both respondents and nonrespondents to a survey. Further, information on interviewers (either available from administrative data, such as information collected routinely by the survey agency, derived information, for example based on previous interviewer performance, or information from a separate interviewer survey), as well as area information (e.g. from administrative or Census records) can be linked. Figure 2.1 represents a typical example of such a linked data source (demonstrated in accordance with the 2001 and 2011 UK Census nonresponse link study dataset conducted by the Office for National Statistics). Again such linked data may be available at different levels. For example, survey, administrative and interviewer observation data may be measured at the individual- or household-level; characteristics of the interviewer or area are measured at the interviewer- and area-level respectively. The complex structures of the paradata may need to be taken into account when analysing such data.

The remainder of the chapter is structured as follows: First, the most important types of quantitative paradata are reviewed. Then an example of using paradata for nonresponse analysis, predicting call sequence length

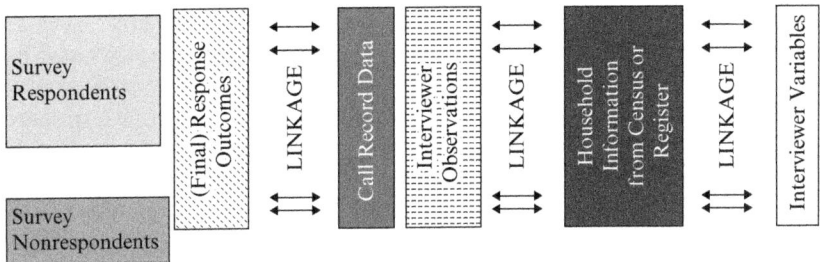

Figure 2.1   *A typical design of a dataset with respondents and*
              nonrespondents to a sample survey with linked paradata
              at the call-level, household-level, household information
              from a Census or register data and linked interviewer level
              variables (in accordance with the 2001 and 2011 UK Census
              nonresponse link study dataset)

and nonresponse outcome during data collection is discussed. The work
has practical implications for survey designs. At the end of the chapter
concluding remarks are presented.

REVIEW OF DIFFERENT TYPES OF PARADATA IN SOCIAL SURVEYS

Depending on the mode of survey, different types of paradata may be
generated. This section reviews the main forms of paradata, including call
record data, interviewer observations and doorstep interactions, interviewer characteristics, keystroke files, audit trails and audio recordings.

Call Record Data

One class of paradata is *interviewer call record data*, sometimes referred
to as *call history data* (Sangster and Meekins, 2004; Bates et al., 2008; Lee
et al., 2009; Blom et al., 2010). It is collected in interviewer-administered
surveys, including both face-to-face and telephone surveys. For both types
of surveys we will refer to interviewer calls, regardless if it is a visit to a
household or a telephone call. In such interviewer-administered surveys,
it is the interviewer who calls sample members, often several times, with
the aim of establishing contact, eligibility for the survey and subsequent
cooperation. Call record data contain, for example, information about
the day and time of the call to a sample unit and the outcome of the call.

Researchers are also able to derive additional call record variables, such as number of days between calls. Further characteristics of the call may be captured, such as voice characteristics and initial responses from the householder or observational data about the household in face-to-face surveys. Call data may be recorded automatically via a computerised system or via the interviewer. In recent years, many survey agencies have started to collect basic call history data on a routine basis. Survey researchers hope to employ such data to inform and improve responsive and adaptive survey designs (Groves and Heeringa, 2006; Laflamme et al., 2008; Kirgis and Lepkowski, 2013), that is, to monitor the survey data collection process and to inform intervention strategies. For example, the information may be used to identify more difficult cases with regards to establishing contact or cooperation, and to flag sample members that require further follow-ups or a different calling strategy. Call record data can inform survey agencies on the best time to contact a sample unit to either establish contact (Durrant et al., 2011) or cooperation (Durrant et al., 2013a). Such data may also help to evaluate interviewer performance and to inform effective calling strategies and interviewer training longer-term. Other possibilities include improvement of the survey data quality, for example, for nonresponse bias adjustment and the evaluation of measurement error in survey estimates. One advantage of paradata is that they are available for *both* respondents and nonrespondents and such data may therefore provide good candidates for nonresponse modelling to inform the reduction of nonresponse (Baruch and Holtom, 2008; Bethlehem et al., 2011). Most uses of call record data involve the modelling of such data. However, the structure of call data can be complex. For example, calls may be nested within sample members (e.g. individuals or households), interviewers and areas, and are measured across several time points, leading to dependent observations, and this nesting needs to be taken into account when modelling such data.

Interviewer Observation Variables, Doorstep Interactions and Audio Recordings

Observations about persons, households and neighbourhoods are referred to as *interviewer observation variables* and are usually recorded only once during a data collection period. (For a longitudinal survey, they may vary across waves.) For face-to-face surveys, at every call, information about the call and the characteristics of the initial conversation, the person, household or immediate neighbourhood may be recorded. The interviewer may be asked to capture additional information about each call (e.g. if the call was made face-to-face or via a closed door/window or an intercom system), as well as additional information about the characteristics of the person talked to at the doorstep (e.g. gender, likely age, physical appearances, indicators of smoking or obesity etc.), initial reactions of the person (e.g. type of questions asked or comments made), characteristics about the household (e.g. type of accommodation, presence of physical barriers, condition of the house, estimated house value, likely household member composition, presence of children), the immediate neighbourhood (e.g. presence of litter or graffiti, residential or commercial area, how the interviewer feels walking alone in the area after dark). An example of a call record form for a face-to-face survey is given in Figure 2.2. We can see that the outcome of a call may distinguish many different types (Question 3). To simplify the analysis, however, survey researchers may focus on the distinction between contact/non-contact and between cooperation, refusal and other non-participation outcomes. For the purpose of nonresponse analysis, in particular if the aim is nonresponse bias correction, such paradata should be related not just to nonresponse outcomes but also to survey target variables (Little and Vartivarian, 2005; Wood et al., 2006; Kreuter et al., 2010). For example, if researchers are interested in the health status of the householder or the living conditions of children, the survey agency may aim to record information on the presence of smokers, indicators of obesity, presence of children, condition of the house and neighbourhood, etc. Such interviewer observations may be subject to measurement error and survey researchers have started to investigate the quality of such data and their potential uses for adjustments (West, 2011; West and Sinibaldi, 2013; Casas-Cordero and Kreuter, 2013; Sinibaldi et al., 2013).

The doorstep interaction between households and interviewers is regarded as crucial in gaining response (Groves and Couper, 1998). For face-to-face surveys the doorstep interaction may be captured by the interviewer. Summary measures may be recorded such as reasons for refusal. For telephone surveys, it is possible to record the initial responses of the householder and to extract, for example, voice characteristics and to code initial responses (Maynard and Schaeffer, 1997; Sturgis and Campanelli, 1998; Conrad et al., 2013).

Specific forms of interviewer observation variables include reasons for refusal as recorded by the interviewer after contact with the sample member and an interviewer assessment of the data quality or evaluation of the likelihood of future response (Eckman et al., 2013). These can be used to inform future strategies for contacting sample members.

Using advanced computer-assisted interviewing techniques, it is also possible to record the whole or part of the interview (computer-assisted recorded interviewing), with respondents' consent. Survey methodologists

Call 01

Q1. Date of call (ddmmyyyy)

Q2. Time of call (24h: hh.mm)

Q3. Outcome of this call
Code ALL that apply

HQ refusal	1
Ineligible: not built /demolished/derelict	2
Ineligible: vacant/empty	3
Ineligible: non-residential	4
Ineligible: residential but no resident hhld	5
Ineligible: communal estab / institution	6
Unable to establish eligibility	7
Address temporarily inaccessible due to weather or other causes	8
No answer on the phone or got answerphone	9
No face-to face contact with anyone at address	10
No contact with anyone at the address but spoke to a neighbour	11
Contact made with sampled household but not with a responsible household	12
Contact made with responsible resident but not with selected respondent	13
Refusal at intro/bef int – by hhld member	14
Refusal at intro/bef int – by proxy	15
Refusal at intro/bef int – DK hhld or proxy	16
Refusal at intro/bef int – by selected resp	17
Refusal during interview	18
No interview due to language, age, infirmity, disability etc.	19
Appointment made	20
Interviewer withdrew to try again later	21
Appointment broken	22
Placement interview / checking /reminder call completed (diary surveys only)	23
Partial household interview completed	24
Hhld interview completed but non-contact with one or more elements	25
Hhld interview completed but refusal or incomplete interview by one or more elements	26
Full co-operation / interview	27
Other outcomes	28

If Q3 = 1 to 8, → Q11.
If non-contact (Q3 = 9 to 13), → Q4. Otherwise, → Q5.

Q4. Did you leave a card or message at the address / on the phone / on the answerphone?

Card/message left at address	1
Message left on the phone	2
Message left on the answerphone	3
No card/message left	4

If non-contact with anyone at address (Q3 = 9 to 11), → Q10. Otherwise, → Q5.

Q5. How did you first contact the household at this call?
Code ALL that apply

Spoke through entryphone/ intercom	1
Spoke through closed door/ window letter box/ door on a chain	2
Spoke through open door/ window	3
Spoke to informant who was outside the household unit	4
Went /invited inside the household unit and spoke to informant	5
Spoke over the telephone	6

Q6 to Q8 refer to the MAIN PERSON you made contact with.

Q6. Was the main person you talked to:

a man/boy?	1
a woman/girl?	2
Don't know, not sure	3

Q7. What is the approximate age of the main person?

Less than 16	1
16-34	2
35-59	3
60 and over	4
Don't know	5

Q8. Did the main person make any of the following comments during your introductory conversation?
Code ALL that apply

Main person did not comment	99
Positive/neutral comments:	
Received / remembered advance letter	1
Expecting someone to call	2
Make an appointment and come back	3
I'll think about it	4
Survey topic is important / or other positive comments about the survey topic	5
Enjoy doing surveys	6
Other positive /neutral comments	7
Negative comments:	
Not interested / can't be bothered	8
I'm too busy / Bad time / Just going out / About to go away	9
I don't know anything	10
We are not typical	11
Not capable / too sick/ old/ infirm	12
Waste of time	13
Waste of money	14
Government knows everything	15
Don't trust study is confidential	16
Invasion of privacy / too many personal questions	17
Don't trust surveys	18
Never do surveys / I hate forms	19
Already participated in surveys	20
Negative comments about the survey topic	21
Other negative comments	22

Q9. Did the main person ask any of the following questions during your introductory conversation?
Code ALL that apply

Main person did not ask questions	99
What is the purpose of the survey / What's it all about?	1
Who is paying for this/who is the sponsor?	2
What will happen to the information / How will the results be used?	3
Why/how was I chosen?	4
How long will the interview take?	5
Who's going to see my answers?	6
Can I be identified?	7
Is it confidential?	8
Is this compulsory?	9
Can I get more information?	10
Can I get a copy of the results?	11
What's in it for me?	12
Do I get an incentive? When / how much will I get paid?	13
Other questions	14

Q10. Diary surveys only. Non-diary surveys → Q11.
Was this call a:

call to make an appointment?	1
placement call?	2
checking call?	3
reminder call?	4
collection call?	5

Q11. When did you fill in the details about this call?

Immediately after the call	1
On the same day	2
On a different day from the call	3

Go to Accommodation Section (p.22)

2

Figure 2.2 Example of interviewer call record form for face-to-face household surveys (UK Office for National Statistics) (Information collected for person talked to, household and neighbourhood observations not shown)

may be particularly interested in the interaction between the interviewer and the respondent and to derive information that can be used to improve the instrument, for example to test the working of a survey question and to provide information for interviewer training.

Interviewer Characteristics

The interviewer plays a crucial role in gaining contact and response from sample members and for minimising measurement error and improving the data quality. Although characteristics about interviewers are not regarded as 'true' paradata by all researchers, additional information about the interviewers can significantly help to understand survey processes. Analyses of interviewer performance, in particular in interaction with sample respondents, can help to inform interviewer recruitment and training. On a routine basis often only very basic information about the interviewer may be recorded by a survey agency such as gender, age and years of experience or if a particular interviewer training has been received or not. However, there is significant interest in collecting additional information about interviewers, which is not available via administrative records. Such information may be obtained via a separate interviewer survey, capturing information about interviewers' attitudes, and behaviours, personality traits and social skills, attitudes towards privacy, data confidentiality and consent, and the interviewers' answers to the actual survey responses. Analyses of interviewer effects have highlighted the significant influence of interviewers on the survey process on both contact and cooperation (Durrant et al., 2010; West and Olson, 2010; Vassallo et al., 2015; Pickery and Loosveldt, 2002, 2004).

Audit Trails and Keystroke Files

Many other forms of paradata exist for computer-assisted interviewing and for web surveys (Callegaro et al., 2015; Nicolaas, 2011). Systems may capture all activities on a keyboard or screen, such as mouse movements. Such information can help to evaluate and improve the survey instrument, to better understand the navigation through a questionnaire and may help to identify problems with particular questions. For example, prolonged mouse movements around the answers of a survey question and high use of the help button can indicate potential problems with a question in the survey. An interviewer spending significantly less time on particular questions could indicate lower interviewer performance. However, the use and processing of such audit files is not straightforward, with the data being large, complex and messy. There is a need for tools to use and manage these vast amounts of paradata for routine monitoring and analyses.

EXAMPLE OF USING PARADATA FOR NONRESPONSE ANALYSIS: PREDICTING CALL SEQUENCE LENGTH AND NONRESPONSE OUTCOME DURING DATA COLLECTION

Researchers are increasingly interested in how best to use and analyse paradata. This section discusses a specific example on how to use paradata for nonresponse analysis during data collection for a face-to-face survey. It is hoped that a better understanding of the calling patterns and the mechanisms leading to particular call sequences will help improve data collection through reducing both costs and non-sampling errors. For statistical agencies, investing time and effort into repeated calls and follow-ups to a sample unit is very resource- and cost-intensive. It is therefore desirable to avoid long unsuccessful call sequences to improve efficiency of call scheduling. The aim then is to identify cases prone to long and unsuccessful call sequences. This chapter presents two models for call record data predicting final call outcome and final length of a call sequence early on in the data collection process, for example after the first, second or third call. Separate binary logistic models for the two outcomes are considered. The models are assessed using the widely used pseudo-R^2 statistic (for the use of further assessment criteria using classification tables and ROC curves see Durrant et al., 2015). A particular focus is the identification of explanatory variables that predict final outcome and/or length, especially those characterising long unsuccessful call sequences. A typical research question might be: How can call record predictors best be incorporated into the model(s) as summary statistics or as individual outcomes? How predictive are the models? Does their ability to predict improve once interviewer observation variables and further call records are available?

Past research mostly aimed to predict final nonresponse, often did not include paradata and relied on fully observed frame data or socio-demographic variables. However, such models have not been found to predict well the outcomes of calls (Groves and Couper, 1996, 1998; Bates et al., 2008). In recent years, researchers have explored, with some success, the potentials of including newly available paradata, such as call record data and interviewer observation variables, in models for nonresponse outcomes (Potthoff et al., 1993; Groves and Couper, 1996; Sinibaldi et al., 2013, 2014; Bates et al., 2008; Wagner, 2013a, 2013b; Kreuter et al., 2010), but typically still with low predictive power (pseudo-R^2 values between 3%

and 8%) (Olson et al., 2012; Olson and Groves, 2012; West and Groves, 2013). The research has implications for survey practice, in particular for adaptive and responsive survey designs. The method developed may be of particular benefit for longitudinal surveys, where the same or similar auxiliary variables are available for every wave. The models could then be used to predict final outcome and sequence length for future waves.

Data

Call record data and interviewer observations from the first wave of the UK Understanding Society survey are used, which is the Household Longitudinal Study in the United Kingdom. Data collection is carried out by interviewers aiming to achieve responses from individual households selected into the sample by face-to-face interviews. To achieve this, the interviewer needs to contact the household, often on several occasions. Interviewers have one month to contact households. A minimum of six calls is made at each sampled address before it is considered unproductive, but interviewers are encouraged to make further calls if possible (McFall, 2012). During the first visit to a household, interviewers collect a wide range of *interviewer observations* capturing characteristics about each household and the surrounding neighbourhood. In addition, *call record data* are available, which capture information about each call, including outcome, date and time of each call. The analysis sample includes only cases with four or more calls, since we are interested in analysing outcomes after the first three calls. The sample contains 25,358 households within 734 interviewers.

The explanatory variables used in the analysis model can be split into three main groups:

1. geographic information and design variables (e.g. urban/rural indicator, government office region, low density area for ethnic minorities and month of household issue);
2. interviewer observation variables (e.g. indicators of entry barriers, conditions of surrounding area such as litter in street, abandoned buildings, heavy traffic, type of accommodation, presence of children in a household, relative condition of the property, garden);
3. call record variables (20 variables, e.g. time of day, day of week, call outcome; also derived variables including time between calls, number of previous non-contacts, contacts, appointments and broken appointments).

Method

First, let us define the dependent variables in our models. Given our research questions and the design of the survey, we are interested in modelling short and long sequences, successful and unsuccessful call outcomes and the combination of both. Due to the survey protocol requirement of conducting a minimum of six call attempts, if contact was not established, it follows naturally to define short and long sequences at the cut-off of six calls for this study. A successful call outcome is defined as achieving at least one interview per household. The following two dependent variables are considered:

The binary dependent variable '*length of call sequence*' indicates a short call sequence (up to six calls) (coded as 1); and otherwise 0 for long call sequences (more than six calls).

The second binary dependent variable '*final outcome of call sequence*' indicates a successful call sequence, i.e. there is at least one interview (otherwise 0 for an unsuccessful call sequence with no interview).

For both binary dependent variables logistic models are employed. (The clustering of sample cases within interviewers is taken into account by using robust standard error estimation.) The models are implemented in STATA, which can estimate robust standard errors to control for the non-independence of observations.

Explanatory variables are considered step by step, depending on the type of data available after each call, including for example a.) only geographic and design variables; b.) interviewer observations, information about the timing of the first call attempt, then timing of second and third call (including time between calls); c.) information about the outcome for the first three calls one by one and as combinations, either as raw outcomes (i.e. outcome of first, second and third call, interactions between outcomes) or as summary information (i.e. number of non-contacts, contacts, appointments and interviews across the first three calls). A comprehensive sensitivity analysis was carried out using different model specifications such as different specifications of the dependent variables and the type of model, but they all resulted in very similar conclusions (see Durrant et al., 2015 for a discussion on the different model specifications considered).

Results

To compare the different models and to assess the quality of model predictions and model fits, we employ the pseudo-R^2 statistic (Nagelkerke R^2) (Field, 2009; Long and Freese, 2006; for further assessment criteria see Durrant et al., 2015). A range of models with increasing amounts of

*Table 2.1   Comparison of different models for length and (final) outcome
indicating Nagelkerke R^2 values. (Call record variables here
include date and time of the call and call outcome)*

Model	Model for Length Nagelkerke R^2	Model for Outcome Nagelkerke R^2
1 Just geographic	0.027	0.013
2 1+interviewer observations	0.062	0.053
3 2+call record for call 1 including call outcome	0.078	0.065
4 2+call record for calls 1 and 2 including call outcomes	0.121	0.098
5 2+call record for calls 1–3 without call outcomes	0.110	0.105
6 5+call outcome for call 3	0.248	0.236
7 5+4 sums of call outcomes across the calls 1–3	0.224	0.209
8 5+call outcomes for calls 1–3	0.258	0.242

explanatory variables are fitted to both of the dependent variables. Table 2.1 presents pseudo-R^2 coefficients to compare the different models. The results indicate that just controlling for geographic or interviewer observation variables does not predict the outcomes very well. Even controlling for basic call record variables, such as date and time of the outcome, does not improve the prediction by much, although it does a little. Controlling for previous call outcomes, however, in particular the outcome from the most recent call, here call three, very significantly increases the ability to predict the outcome. This is the case regardless of whether the variables are entered as individual variables or as summary measures (e.g. number of non-contacts). Table 2.1 suggests that the best models for prediction are obtained in Model 8, which contains variables from the geographic and design group, interviewer observations and call record data including raw call outcomes for the first three calls and timing of calls.

Let us now discuss the effects of different explanatory variables on both outcomes for the final models. Tables 2.2 and 2.3 present estimated regression coefficients together with odds ratios from the two binary logistic models (Model 8). The results suggest that the odds of having a short call sequence are higher for properties with two or less floors, for households which definitely do not have a car, are unlikely to have children or do not have children and if there is no unkempt garden. The odds are lower in town houses (terrace houses) and flats when compared to detached houses, also lower when properties are worse than others in the neighbourhood,

Table 2.2   Estimated coefficients (selected†) for the logistic regression models modelling length of call sequence, including geographic and design variables, interviewer observation variables and call record variables comprising timing and outcome of calls (Model 8)

Variable	Model for Length		
	β	Robust SE	OR
Interviewer observations variables			
Accommodation			
Detached house/bungalow (ref)	0.000		1.000
Semi-detached house/bungalow	−0.062	0.042	0.940
Town house (terrace house)	−0.207	0.046	0.813***
Flat	−0.296	0.061	0.744***
Rented room	0.257	0.184	1.293
Floor			
0 floors	0.809	0.236	2.247**
1 floor	0.318	0.078	1.374***
2 floors	0.196	0.075	1.216**
3 floors	0.051	0.079	1.052
4 floors and above (ref)	0.000		1.000
Car/van			
Definitely has a car/van (ref)	0.000		1.000
Likely	−0.039	0.041	0.962
Unlikely	0.153	0.078	1.165
Definitely does not have a car/van	0.666	0.095	1.947***
Cannot tell from observation	−0.137	0.041	0.872**
Child			
Definitely has a child/children aged under 10 (ref)	0.000		1.000
Likely	0.013	0.075	1.013
Unlikely	0.177	0.068	1.193**
Definitely does not have a child/children aged under 10	0.209	0.068	1.232**
Cannot tell from observation	0.058	0.062	1.060
Unkempt garden			
Yes (ref)	0.000		1.000
No	0.203	0.056	1.225***
No obvious garden	0.113	0.062	1.120
Relative conditions of the address to other residential properties			
Better (ref)	0.000		1.000
About the same	−0.047	0.054	0.954
Worse	−0.202	0.078	0.903*
Unable to obtain information	0.008	0.239	1.008

Table 2.2   (continued)

Variable	Model for Length		
	β	Robust SE	OR
Call Record Variables			
Time of day call 2			
Morning (0.00–12.00) (ref)	0.000		1.000
Afternoon (12.00–17.00)	−0.064	0.038	0.937
Evening (17.00–24.00)	−0.102	0.043	0.903*
Time of day call 3			
Morning (0.00–12.00) (ref)			
Afternoon (12.00–17.00)	−0.015	0.039	0.985
Evening (17.00–24.00)	−0.094	0.041	0.912*
Time between call 1 and call 2	0.026	0.002	1.026***
Time between call 2 and call 3	0.030	0.001	1.030***
Call 1 outcome			
No contact (ref)	0.000		1.000
Contact made	0.081	0.037	1.085*
Appointment made	0.025	0.069	1.026
Any other status	0.124	0.095	1.133
Interview done	1.022	0.240	2.780***
Call 2 outcome			
No contact (ref)	0.000		1.000
Contact made	0.095	0.038	1.099*
Appointment made	0.205	0.063	1.228**
Any other status	0.293	0.088	1.340**
Interview done	1.539	0.143	4.662***
Call 3 outcome			
No contact (ref)	0.000		1.000
Contact made	0.499	0.037	1.645***
Appointment made	2.000	0.048	7.389***
Any other status	1.227	0.065	3.410***
Interview done	2.352	0.110	10.511***

Notes: ***p<0.001; **p<0.01; *p<0.05; ref – reference category.
†   The model also includes a constant and control for geographic and design variables.

and lower when the calls are made in the evening compared to morning calls. (It should be noted that this cannot be interpreted as a causal effect since calling times are not allocated randomly but are merely determined by interviewers.) The model suggests a positive association for time between calls: the longer the time between calls, the higher the probability of a short sequence. Shorter sequences are also more likely when previous

Table 2.3   *Estimated coefficients (selected†) for the logistic regression model modelling (final) outcome, including geographic and design variables, interviewer observation variables and call record variables comprising timing and outcome of calls (Model 8)*

Variable	Model for (final) outcome		
	β	Robust SE	OR
Interviewer observations variables			
Floor			
0 floors	0.806	0.213	2.238***
1 floor	0.430	0.073	1.538***
2 floors	0.402	0.065	1.495***
3 floors	0.413	0.077	1.511***
4 floors and above (ref)	0.000		1.000
Car/van			
Definitely has a car/van (ref)	0.000		1.000
Likely	−0.189	0.039	0.827***
Unlikely	−0.452	0.075	0.636***
Definitely does not have a car/van	0.654	0.095	1.924***
Cannot tell from observation	−0.400	0.036	0.670***
Child			
Definitely has a child/children aged under 10 (ref)	0.000		1.000
Likely	−0.099	0.075	0.906
Unlikely	−0.272	0.065	0.762***
Definitely does not have a child/children aged under 10	−0.163	0.066	0.849*
Cannot tell from observation	−0.312	0.061	0.732***
Relative conditions of the address to other residential properties			
Better (ref)	0.000		1.000
About the same	−0.242	0.053	0.785***
Worse	−0.440	0.074	0.644***
Unable to obtain information	−1.248	0.260	0.287***
Call Record Variables			
Time of day call 1			
Morning (0.00–12.00) (ref)	0.000		1.000
Afternoon (12.00–17.00)	0.010	0.036	1.011
Evening (17.00–24.00)	−0.130	0.050	0.878**
Time between call 1 and call 2	−0.026	0.002	0.974***
Time between call 2 and call 3	−0.028	0.002	0.973***
Call 1 outcome			
No contact (ref)	0.000		1.000

Table 2.3   (continued)

Variable	Model for (final) outcome		
	β	Robust SE	OR
Contact made	−0.098	0.037	0.907**
Appointment made	0.242	0.065	1.274***
Any other status	−0.035	0.096	0.966
Interview done	0.372	0.207	1.450
Call 2 outcome			
No contact (ref)	0.000		1.000
Contact made	−0.062	0.037	0.940
Appointment made	0.458	0.062	1.581***
Any other status	−0.024	0.092	0.977
Interview done	0.517	0.116	1.677***
Call 3 outcome			
No contact (ref)	0.000		1.000
Contact made	−0.148	0.037	0.862***
Appointment made	2.024	0.053	7.568***
Any other status	−1.185	0.074	0.305***
Interview done	0.860	0.087	2.364***

Notes: ***p<0.001; **p<0.01; *p<0.05; ref – reference category.
†   The model also includes a constant and control for geographic and design variables.

call outcomes are a contact, an appointment, any other status or an interview when compared to non-contact. There is a marked monotone increase in the effect of the call outcome variables across the three calls, indicating that although the outcome of each call is significant, it may be the most recent call that has the highest influence, rather than, for example, the first call. As one might expect, an appointment or interview at the third call increases the odds of a short sequence by between seven to ten times compared to having a non-contact at this call attempt.

CONCLUSIONS

This chapter introduces quantitative paradata. It describes the basic types of paradata, such as call record data, interviewer observation data and paradata from different survey modes, such as keystroke files. A range of benefits and uses of paradata are highlighted. The chapter then presents an example of how to use paradata for interviewer-administered surveys.

The analysis approach employs a range of interviewer observation and call record variables to predict both final outcome and length of a call sequence early on in the data collection process. Models are developed prior to data collection and after the first, second and third call respectively to see if predictions of the models improve once more and more call record data are available. The predictions from the models inform survey managers which households to follow up on or when to stop calling. The models allow the identification of long unsuccessful call sequences early on during the data collection period.

The models proposed have the ability to predict the outcomes of interest reasonably well (length, final call outcome and the combined model) with a pseudo-R^2 of around 26% for the binary cases and 36% for the combined outcome. This is very high in a social science context and compares to values of around 3–8% for 'standard' nonresponse models in the literature (Olson et al., 2012; Olson and Groves, 2012; West and Groves, 2013). A number of variables are significant for both the model for length and the model for outcome. Interviewer observation variables (such as floor, car/van, child, relative condition of property) are found to be significant in all models. The outcomes of previous calls, in particular the most recent call, are highly significant for both final response outcome and sequence length and their inclusion greatly improves the predictive power. As one might expect, the prediction improves significantly when more and more call outcomes are available. We found evidence that it is the most recent call outcome that may have the biggest influence, rather than, for example, the first call.

REFERENCES

Baruch, Y. and Holtom, B. (2008). Survey response rate levels and trends in organizational research. *Human Relations*, 61(8): 1139–1160.

Bates, N., Dahlhamer, J. and Singer, E. (2008). Privacy concerns, too busy, or just not interested: Using doorstep concerns to predict survey nonresponse. *Journal of Official Statistics*, 24: 591–612.

Bethlehem, J., Cobben, F. and Schouten, B. (2011). *Handbook in nonresponse in household surveys*. New Jersey: Wiley and Sons.

Biemer, P.P., Chen, P. and Wang, K. (2013). Using level-of-effort paradata in nonresponse adjustments with application to field surveys. *Journal of the Royal Statistical Society, Series A*, 176: 147–168.

Blom, A., Jäckle, A. and Lynn, P. (2010). The use of contact data in understanding cross-national differences in unit nonresponse. In J.A. Harkness, M. Braun, B. Edwards, T.P. Johnson, L.E. Lyberg, P.Ph. Mohler, B.-E. Pennell and T.W. Smith (eds), *Survey methods in multinational, multiregional, and multicultural contexts*, pp. 335–354. New Jersey: Wiley and Sons.

Brunton-Smith, I., Sturgis, P. and Willams, J. (2012). Is success in obtaining contact and cooperation correlated with the magnitude of interviewer variance? *Public Opinion Quarterly*, 76(2): 265–286.

Callegaro, M., Manfreda, K.L. and Vehovar, V. (2015). *Web survey methodology*. Los Angeles: SAGE.

Casas-Cordero, C. and Kreuter, F. (2013). Assessing the measurement error properties of interviewer observations of neighbourhood characteristics. *Journal of the Royal Statistical Society, Series A*, 176(1): 227–249.

Conrad, F.G., Broome, J.S., Benki, J.R., Kreuter, F., Groves, R.M., Vannette, D. and McClain, C. (2013). Interviewer speech and the success of survey invitations. *Journal of the Royal Statistical Society, Series A*, 176(1): 191–210.

Correa, S., Durrant, G. and Smith, P. (2015). *Assessing nonresponse bias using call record data with applications to a longitudinal study*. Working Paper, University of Southampton (submitted).

Couper, M. (1998). *Measuring survey quality in a CASIC environment*. Proceedings of the Survey Research Methods Section, ASA, pp. 41–49.

Couper, M.P. and Kreuter, F. (2013). Using paradata to explore item level response times in surveys. *Journal of the Royal Statistical Society, Series A*, 176(1): 271–286.

Durrant, G.B. and Kreuter, F. (2013). Editorial: The use of paradata in social survey research. *Journal of the Royal Statistical Society, Series A*, 176(1): 1–3.

Durrant, G.B., D'Arrigo, J. and Müller, G. (2013a). Modeling call record data: Examples from cross-sectional and longitudinal surveys. In F. Kreuter (ed.), *Improving surveys with paradata: Analytic use of process information*, pp. 281–308. New Jersey: John Wiley and Sons.

Durrant, G.B., D'Arrigo, J. and Steele, F. (2011). Using field process data to predict best times of contact conditioning on household and interviewer influences. *Journal of the Royal Statistical Society, Series A*, 174(4): 1029–1049.

Durrant, G.B., D'Arrigo, J. and Steele, F. (2013b). Analysing interviewer call record data by using a multilevel discrete-time event history modelling approach. *Journal of the Royal Statistical Society, Series A*, 176(1): 251–269.

Durrant, G.B., Groves, R.M., Staetsky, L. and Steele, F. (2010). Effects of interviewer attitudes and behaviors on refusal in household surveys. *Public Opinion Quarterly*, 74(1): 1–36.

Durrant, G.B., Maslovskaya, O. and Smith, P.W.F. (2015). Modelling final outcome and length of call sequence to improve efficiency in interviewer call scheduling. *Journal of Survey Statistics and Methodology*, 3: 397–424.

Eckman, S., Sinibaldi, J. and Möntmann-Hertz, A. (2013). Can interviewers effectively rate the likelihood of cases to cooperate? *Public Opinion Quarterly*, 77(2): 561–573.

Engel, U., Jann, B., Lynn, P., Scherpenzeel, A. and Sturgis, P. (2015). *Improving survey methods, lessons from recent research*. New York: Routledge.

Field, A. (2009). *Discovering statistics using SPSS*. Los Angeles: SAGE.

Groves, R.M. and Couper, M.P. (1996). Contact-level influences on cooperation in face-to-face surveys. *Journal of Official Statistics*, 12: 63–83.

Groves, R.M. and Couper, M.P. (1998). *Nonresponse in household interview surveys*. New York: John Wiley and Sons.

Groves, R.M. and Heeringa, S.G. (2006). Responsive design for household surveys: Tools for actively controlling survey errors and costs. *Journal of the Royal Statistical Society, Series A*, 169: 439–457.

Kirgis, N.G. and Lepkowski, J.M. (2013). Design and management strategies for paradata-driven responsive design. In F. Kreuter (ed.), *Improving surveys with paradata: Analytic use of process information*, pp. 123–144. New Jersey: John Wiley and Sons.

Kreuter, F. (2013). Improving surveys with paradata: The analytic use of process information. In F. Kreuter (ed.), *Improving surveys with paradata: Analytic use of process information*, pp. 1–10. New Jersey: John Wiley and Sons.

Kreuter, F., Olson, K., Wagner, J., Yan, T., Ezzati-Rice, T.M., Casas-Cordero, C., Lemay, M., Peytchev, A., Groves, R.M. and Raghunathan, T.E. (2010). Using proxy measures and other correlates of survey outcomes to adjust for non-response: Examples from multiple surveys. *Journal of the Royal Statistical Society, Series A*, 173: 389–407.

Laflamme, F., Maydan, M. and Miller, A. (2008). *Using paradata to actively manage data collection survey process*. Proceedings of the Survey Research Methods Section, ASA, pp. 630–637.

Lee, S., Brown, E., Grant, D., Belin, T. and Brick, J. (2009). Exploring nonresponse bias in a health survey using neighborhood characteristics. *American Journal of Public Health*, 99(10): 1811–1817.

Little, R.J.A. and Vartivarian, S. (2005). Does weighting for nonresponse increase the variance of survey means? *Survey Methodology*, 31(2): 161–168.

Long, J.S. and Freese, J. (2006). *Regression models for categorical dependent variables using Stata*. Texas: STATA Press.

Luiten, A. (2013). *Improving survey fieldwork with paradata*. The Hague: Statistics Netherlands.

Maynard, D. and Schaeffer, N. (1997). Keeping the gate: Declinations of the request to participate in a telephone survey interview. *Sociological Methods and Research*, 26: 34–79.

McFall, S.L. (ed.) (2012). *Understanding society: Findings 2012*. Colchester: Institute for Social and Economic Research, University of Essex.

Moore, J., Durrant, G. and Smith, P.W.F. (2015). *Dataset representativeness during data collection in three UK social surveys: Generalizability and the effects of auxiliary covariate choice*. Working Paper, University of Southampton.

Nicolaas, G. (2011). *Survey paradata: A review*. Discussion Paper, National Centre for Research Methods, University of Southampton.

Olson, K. and Groves, R.M. (2012). An examination of within-person variation in response propensity over the data collection field period. *Journal of Official Statistics*, 28: 29–51.

Olson, K. and Parkhurst, B. (2013). Collecting paradata for measurement error evaluations. In F. Kreuter (ed.), *Improving surveys with paradata: Analytic use of process information*, pp. 37–67. New Jersey: John Wiley and Sons.

Olson, K. and Smyth, J.D. (2015). The effect of CATI questions, respondents, and interviewers on response time. *Journal of Survey Statistics and Methodology*, 3: 361–396.

Olson, K., Smyth, J.D. and Wood, H.M. (2012). Does giving people their preferred survey mode actually increase survey participation rates? An experimental examination. *Public Opinion Quarterly*, 76: 611–635.

Pickery, J. and Loosveldt, G. (2002). A multilevel multinomial analysis of interviewer effects on various components of unit nonresponse. *Quality and Quantity*, 36(4): 427–437.

Pickery, J. and Loosveldt, G. (2004). A simultaneous analysis of interviewer effects on various data quality indicators with identification of exceptional interviewers. *Journal of Official Statistics*, 20(1): 77–89.

Potthoff, R.F., Manton, K.G. and Woodbury, M.A. (1993). Correcting for non-availability bias in surveys by weighting based on number of callbacks. *Journal of the American Statistical Association, Applications and Case Studies*, 88(424): 1197–1207.

Sangster, R. and Meekins, B. (2004). *Modeling the likelihood of interviews and refusals: Using call history data to improve efficiency of effort in a national RDD survey*. Proceedings of the Section on Survey Research Methods of the ASA.

Sinibaldi, J., Durrant, G.B. and Kreuter, F. (2013). Evaluating the measurement error of interviewer observed paradata. *Public Opinion Quarterly, Special issue: Topics in Survey Measurement and Public Opinion*, 77(1): 173–193.

Sinibaldi, J., Trappmann, M. and Kreuter, F. (2014). Which is the better investment for nonresponse adjustment: Purchasing commercial auxiliary data or collecting interviewer observations? *Public Opinion Quarterly*, 78(2): 440–473.

Sturgis, P. and Brunton-Smith, I. (2015). *Detecting and understanding interviewer effects on survey data using a cross-classified mixed effects location scale model*. Working Paper, University of Southampton.

Sturgis, P. and Campanelli, P. (1998). The scope for reducing refusals in household surveys: An investigation based on transcripts of tape-recorded doorstep interactions. *Journal of the Market Research Society*, 40(2): 121–139.

Vassallo, R., Durrant, G.B., Smith, P.W.F. and Goldstein, H. (2015). Interviewer effects on non-response propensity in longitudinal surveys: A multilevel modelling approach. *Journal of the Royal Statistical Society, Series A*, 178(1): 83–99.

Wagner, J. (2013a). Using paradata-driven models to improve contact rates in telephone and face-to-face surveys. In F. Kreuter (ed.), *Improving surveys with paradata: Analytic use of process information*, pp. 145–170. New Jersey: John Wiley and Sons.

Wagner, J. (2013b). Adaptive contact strategies in telephone and face-to-face surveys. *Survey Research Methods*, 7(1): 45–55.

West, B. (2011). *Measurement error in survey paradata*. Proceedings of the Survey Research Methods Section, ASA.

West, B.T. and Groves, R.M. (2013). A propensity-adjusted interviewer performance indicator. *Public Opinion Quarterly*, 77: 352–374.

West, B.T. and Olson, K. (2010). How much of interviewer variance is really nonresponse error variance? *Public Opinion Quarterly*, 74(5): 1004–1026.

West, B.T. and Sinibaldi, J. (2013). The quality of paradata: A literature review. In F. Kreuter (ed.), *Improving surveys with paradata: Analytic use of process information*, pp. 317–340. New Jersey: John Wiley and Sons.

Wood, A.M., White, I.R. and Hotopf, M. (2006). Using number of failed contact attempts to adjust for non-ignorable non-response. *Journal of the Royal Statistical Society, Series A*, 169(3): 525–542.

Yan, T. and Olson, K. (2013). Analyzing paradata to investigate measurement error. In F. Kreuter (ed.), *Improving surveys with paradata: Analytic use of process information*, pp. 69–94. New Jersey: John Wiley and Sons.

3. Using paradata to evaluate survey quality: behaviour coding the 2012 PSE-UK survey

Eldin Fahmy[*] and Karen Bell

INTRODUCTION

Survey paradata includes information about survey processes (e.g. audit trail data, call records), data derived from interview behaviour itself and auxiliary survey metadata (Nicolaas, 2011) that, together, provide invaluable information with which to evaluate and improve survey quality. This chapter illustrates the potential of survey paradata by presenting a behaviour coding analysis of survey interview audio recordings arising from the *2012 UK Poverty and Social Exclusion* survey (2012 PSE-UK). It also compares findings derived using these methods with other techniques for developing and testing survey instruments. We argue that analysis of actual interviewer/respondent interactions in a field setting can yield genuine improvements in survey quality over and above those associated with more established survey pre-testing approaches.

Behaviour coding involves the application of systematic coding methods to survey transcripts in order to identify (overt) problems in questionnaire administration associated with interviewer and respondent behaviours. Notwithstanding the practical methodological challenges involved in analysing such data, paradata generated from behaviour during the survey interview is an under-utilised tool for rigorous development and testing of survey items. This chapter describes the implementation of a behaviour coding approach in the 2012 PSE-UK study in the context of the wider deployment of a variety of more established techniques, including interviewer debriefing, cognitive testing, and qualitative methods (focus groups). Our results suggest that in many cases actual interviewer behaviour deviates substantially from the paradigmatic question/response model typically assumed in standardised survey questionnaires. When combined with further, qualitative analysis of relevant transcripts for problematic questions, the behaviour coding approach offers a potentially powerful means of identifying, investigating and addressing survey response problems in social research studies.

Despite its potential advantages, the analysis of survey transcripts for the purposes of identifying problems associated with questionnaire design and delivery has received quite limited attention in UK academic social science in recent years. This chapter therefore begins by outlining the key features of behaviour coding methods and the claims made for this approach in improving survey quality. We then go on to describe the application of behaviour coding methods in the PSE-UK study and examine the incidence of interviewer and respondent problems based upon quantitative analysis and coding of 21 interview transcripts drawn from the PSE-UK main stage sample. The chapter illustrates in depth the nature of the question problems identified here that can facilitate selection of 'problematic' question items in future surveys. Finally, we conclude by considering the relative merits of different tools in evaluating survey response in household surveys.

USING SURVEY PARADATA IN THE PSE-UK STUDY

Evaluating the quality of survey questionnaires prior to field administration is now widely accepted social research practice and recent decades have seen growing use of questionnaire testing techniques including cognitive interviewing, behaviour coding and response latency approaches (Presser and Blair, 1994; Willis et al., 1999; Willis, 2005; Presser et al., 2004). However, the merits and limitations of different question testing approaches are poorly understood; there is little consensus on best practice in survey pre-testing and in evaluating the subsequent quality of survey response. To date, relatively few UK studies have compared methods for assessing questionnaire quality. The 2012 PSE-UK study therefore offers a useful point of entry into these debates because it provides concurrent sources of data on survey quality derived from different sources and using different methods. In addition to a traditional survey pilot and associated interviewer debriefing, the 2012 PSE-UK study employed qualitative and cognitive testing methods in order to inform decisions on survey design, content and delivery. However, these methods are mostly uninformative about the *actual* conduct and delivery of fieldwork interviews themselves, an omission that behaviour coding approaches based on interview paradata can potentially address. This chapter therefore considers the advantages of drawing on interview paradata (interview transcripts, survey process data) in informing our understanding of survey response alongside other established approaches to survey pre-testing. Before doing so, we briefly summarise PSE-UK survey design and development, and the rationale and assumptions of behaviour coding approaches.

The PSE-UK study sought to determine how many individuals and households were unable to afford minimally adequate living standards as determined by the UK public in 2012. The household survey was administered separately in Britain and Northern Ireland on behalf of the University of Bristol by NatCen and the Northern Ireland Statistics and Research Agency (NISRA), and funded by the UK Economic and Social Research Council. The PSE sample consists of respondents participating in the *2010/11 Family Resources Survey* (FRS) who gave permission to be re-contacted. Face-to-face computer-assisted interviews (CAPI) with all adults in selected households were conducted between February and September 2012. The target duration of the interview was 50 minutes for a single person household with an additional 30 minutes for each further adult. The total in-scope target sample was 7,232 and the number of productive interviews achieved was 4,205 (response rate: 58.1%).

Prior qualitative development work was undertaken on the basis of 14 focus group interviews conducted with 114 participants in locations across the UK. This qualitative development work informed the survey measurement of items relating to social and material necessities and social exclusion in the PSE Omnibus and main stage surveys (Fahmy et al., 2011a). Following these exploratory group interviews, questionnaire pre-testing using cognitive interview methods was then conducted on a selection of identified question topics. Twenty cognitive interviews were conducted in summer 2011, using a combination of think aloud and follow-up probing methods to explore specific aspects of the survey response process (Fahmy et al., 2011b). The final draft 2012 PSE-UK questionnaire was then informed by a traditional survey pilot and associated interviewer debriefing conducted in order to inform decisions on questionnaire content, length, and interview practicalities (Maher, 2011).

The growing acceptance of survey pre-testing techniques partly reflects a growing awareness of the limitations of the traditional pilot in evaluating survey response. Understanding of interview behaviour and its impact on survey response is generally limited in pilot surveys to interviewers' subjective recall of the response process (which may reflect a variety of exogenous factors), in combination with analysis of item non-response (which is uninformative about the potential for covert response problems). Whilst qualitative and cognitive interviewing approaches address some of these issues, they are of little value in analysing questionnaire delivery in the field. Qualitative development methods can be helpful in exploring question content but provide little guidance on the design and delivery of survey instruments themselves. More formalised survey pre-testing approaches tend to emphasise the cognitive aspects of survey response (e.g. Schwarz, 2007) and shed little light on the effects of interviewer behaviour and interviewer/respondent interactions for subsequent survey response. Paradata generated from interview behaviour (our main focus here) offer one means, however, for survey methodologists to analyse 'real-world' interviewer/respondent interactions in order to evaluate research instruments and procedures, and subsequent data quality.

Building on the pioneering work of Charles Cannell and colleagues at the University of Michigan, behaviour coding approaches involve the application of a systematic coding framework to survey interview transcripts in order to identify problems in the administration of questionnaires (e.g. Cannell et al., 1975; Cannell and Robinson, 1971; Cannell et al., 1991). Within the behaviour coding paradigm, 'problem free' interactions are assumed to be those where interviewers read survey questions verbatim and respondents provided a code-able answer. On this assumption, it is then possible to develop and apply a rigorous coding framework to interviewer/respondent interactions to identify potential response problems (see e.g. Ongena and Dijkstra, 2006).

Although in its early implementation behaviour coding was associated mainly with the evaluation of interviewer behaviour rather than survey questionnaire pre-testing per se, in recent years the approach has been more widely applied in the development of survey methodology. Nevertheless, it makes assumptions that may be questionable in real-world research practice. First, it is assumed that analysis of *overt* interview behaviour as reflected in interview transcripts provides a reliable means of identifying question problems. Covert problems may be missed, for example, those arising from unspoken differences in respondents' cognition of key terms, or interpretation of relevant time frames and response categories. Partly in response to growing interest in the cognitive aspects of survey methodology (Schwarz, 2007; Sudman et al., 1996), cognitive interviewing techniques based on respondents' verbal reports soliciting the use of think aloud and probing methods have become increasingly popular (e.g. Campanelli, 1997; Collins, 2003; Drennan, 2003; Willis, 2005). However, how these methods measure up against behaviour coding techniques is less well established.

Second, it is assumed within behaviour coding that deviations from the paradigmatic, standardised survey interaction are a source of measurement error to be minimised. However, survey interviews are also rule-bound social encounters, and survey respondents and interviewers draw upon tacit knowledge and conversational norms in the survey interaction (Walton et al., 2012; Maynard and Schaeffer, 2002). Although standardised interviewing procedures limit negotiation of meaning, this is a natural feature of meaningful communication including in the survey context (Bradburn et al., 2004; Bell et al., 2014). Although the researcher's interview script sets boundaries to the conversation the interviewer/respondent interaction inevitably implies some local conversational control, which cannot be standardised.

Finally, no general consensus exists regarding what is coded and how within behaviour coding. Coding schemes differ widely (e.g. Ongena and Dijkstra, 2006), and the implications of different approaches for the evaluation of survey questionnaires is not well understood. Although behaviour coding schemes generally focus on adherence to standardised interviewing practices, the approach can also be used to assess the accuracy of question and response interpretation and survey administration. At a more practical level, behaviour coding raises significant resource and operational challenges. The logistic requirements of large-scale audio capture and storage, and the time-intensive nature of behaviour coding analysis itself, are one reason why this method has not been widely applied in UK social surveys. We reflect on these issues by describing the key features of the application of behaviour coding methodology in the 2012 PSE-UK survey. We then go on to outline initial findings from our behaviour coding analysis and compare these with the insights offered by cognitive methods. In doing so, we also explore the points of convergence and divergence in results derived using behaviour coding and cognitive interview methods.

DATA AND METHODS

A total of 23 survey interviews were audio-recorded and transcribed verbatim and, following disclosure control by the survey organisation, the transcripts were subject to subsequent behaviour coding. Although a relatively small sample, existing work in this area suggests that useful information can be derived from much smaller samples than has often been assumed in behaviour coding practice (e.g. Willis et al., 1999). The interviews to be audio-recorded were selected by the survey organisation from *experienced* interviewers with respondents giving their consent for the interview to be audio-recorded. The sample is not therefore randomly selected and interviewers and respondents were both aware that subsequent analysis of the interview transcripts would be conducted. In all cases, the full interview was transcribed verbatim.

Table 3.1 (below) compares the demographic profile of survey interviewers and respondents for PSE-UK sample respondents providing full interview data. PSE-UK survey interviews were often conducted by interviewers who were considerably older than the survey respondents.

Table 3.1 Productive PSE-UK full interviews: interviewer and respondent characteristics (%)

		Respondents %	Respondents %	Interviewers %
		raw	weighted	
Age	18–34	12.7	19.3	1.4
	35–44	17.7	19.0	3.6
	45–54	20.1	19.7	22.7
	55–64	18.5	16.4	43.2
	65–74	17.5	12.7	25.6
	75+	13.4	12.8	3.6
Ethnicity	White	89.6	92.2	94.5
	Non-white	10.4	7.8	5.5
Gender	Male	44.8	48.5	49.4
	Female	55.2	51.5	50.6
N		5,152	5,210	4,205

More than two-fifths (43%) of productive PSE-UK full interviews were conducted by interviewers aged 55–64. Given the selection bias introduced by focusing on experienced interviewers only, we might expect some slight variance between respondent and interviewer profiles here. In fact, however, the achieved PSE sample undercounts younger adults, and when this is corrected for by re-weighting (Column 3) the difference between interviewer and respondent profiles is especially stark. Respondents aged under 45 account for nearly two-fifths (38%) of the re-weighted PSE-UK sample but just 5% of interviews were conducted by interviewers aged less than 45. In contrast, gender and ethnic differences are much less substantial.

The coding scheme subsequently applied to these data is summarised in Table 3.2 (below). The 23 interview transcripts were coded by a single researcher. As Willis (2005) notes, a key limitation of behaviour coding approaches in the evaluation of survey instruments are concerns over the reliability of the coding process itself, for example, with regard to differences between coders in what constitute 'major' or 'slight' changes in question wording by interviewers. Using multiple coders allows for assessment of the degree of inter-rater consistency using established statistical measures but this is a resource-intensive approach. Some degree of subjectivity is thus inherent to the coding process described here.

Behaviour coding can be conducted at a variety of different levels where the unit of coding represents respectively: the full interview; question–

Table 3.2   2012 PSE-UK behaviour coding framework and frequencies (%)

INTERVIEWER CODES		%
Exact Wording	Interviewer read question exactly as worded	52
Slight Change	Interviewer read question with slight change that did not affect question meaning	38
Major Change	Interviewer made changes to the question that either changed, or possibly could have changed, the meaning of the question	7
Skipped Question	Interviewer entirely omitted an applicable question	3
Non-Directive Probe	Follow-up question/information is not leading (i.e. not suggesting a particular way of answering)	3
Directive Probe	Follow-up question/information is leading (i.e. suggesting a particular way of answering)	3
Inaudible Interviewer	Interviewer was not audible on the recording	<1
Adequate Clarification	Explanation in line with accurate interpretation	4
Showcard inadequately read	Not read in line with accurate interpretation	<1
Inadequate Clarification	Explanation not in line with accurate interpretation	1
Interprets response inadequately	Mishears, misunderstands etc.	<1

RESPONDENT CODES		%
Adequate Answer	Respondent provided response that meets the objective of question and can easily be coded	80
Inadequate Answer	Respondent provided a response that does not meet the objectives of the question and cannot easily be coded	5
Qualified Answer	Respondent provides a conditional response (e.g. 'If you mean X, then the answer is Y')	1
Uncertain Answer	Respondent uncertain about response provided AND/OR changes first answer	3
Request to Repeat	Respondent requests that a part of, or the entire, question be repeated	1
Request for Clarification	Respondent requested that a concept or entire question be stated more clearly (or expresses uncertainty about meaning)	6
Requested Read Showcard	Respondent requests that showcard be read out at some stage of the interview	2

Table 3.2   (continued)

RESPONDENT CODES		%
Don't Know	Respondent stated they did not have the information or that it was not applicable	1
Refusal	Respondent refused to provide a response	<1
Interruption	Respondent interrupts the first reading of the question	1
Inaudible Respondent	Respondent was not audible on the recording	<1
Misinterprets Question	Respondent responds in a way that is not in line with its meaning, and has misunderstood	<1
Any interviewer or respondent problems		59

answer (QA) sequences; specific exchanges between interviewer and respondent within QA sequences; and individual utterance by interview participants (Ongena and Dijkstra, 2006: 422; see also Sala et al., 2008). Analysis of QA sequences is perhaps the most widely adopted implementation of behaviour coding and this approach is adopted in the analyses presented here. Assessing QA sequences for the purposes of behaviour coding involves evaluating the extent to which specific interactions or exchanges conform to the paradigmatic 'signal/response' model and, where appropriate, identifying problematic interactions.

However, the classification of problematic responses and subsequent analysis is not straightforward. The unit of measurement is the respondent interview (n=23) and the unit of analysis is the question administration. In total the analysis presented below is based upon 111 question items drawn from the CAPI interviews with the Household Respondent Person (HRP) only (i.e. excluding the self-completion questionnaire and interviews with additional household members). The total number of possible observations within the resultant dataset is therefore 23*111=2,553, but as a result of the complex routing of question items in surveys of this type the selected respondents provided code-able responses to only between 62 and 84 of the 111 question items (mean=73.4; SD=6.3). In the analyses that follow we focus on those question items yielding complete or nearly complete sample coverage, that is, question items asked in at least 20 of the 23 transcripts. The achieved number of valid observations is therefore 1,689.

FINDINGS

How Widespread are Survey Response Problems in the 2012 PSE-UK Study?

Table 3.2 (above) shows the distribution of response problems identified on the basis of a behaviour coding of the respondent interview transcripts. Overall, problems associated with the interviewers' delivery of the question items were more common than interviewees' response problems. Despite the guidance provided by the research contractor to fieldworkers, in only slightly more than half of these cases (52.3%) did the interviewer read the question exactly as scripted. In fact in only a minority (47.5%) of instances did interviewer behaviour conform to the paradigmatic stimulus/response model with the interviewer reading questions exactly as worded without additional (audible) unprompted behaviours (directive or un-directive probes, additional clarification, etc.).

Changes in question item wording were by far the most common interviewer problems. Although as Table 3.2 shows, these were mostly coded as 'minor' changes in question wording occurring in 37.7% of all interviewer/respondent interactions, as we will go on to show later the potential impacts on survey response may nevertheless be substantial depending on the question format, intended meaning, task complexity, etc. Nevertheless, aside from changes in question wording other interviewer problems were comparatively rare (though significant differences may exist across question topics). In comparison, respondent problems were much less frequent with four-fifths (79.6%) of interviewer/respondent interactions resulting in an adequate (code-able) response. The most common response problems were associated with requests for clarification (5.9%), and responses inadequate for coding (5.2%) and uncertain (3.1%) answers.

Is There an Association Between Interviewer and Respondent Problems?

We might expect that respondent problems in the PSE-UK study might be more common where problems with question delivery are evident. There is some evidence of a clear relationship between interviewer behaviour and the likelihood of subsequent response problems. The proportion of observations characterised by respondent problems is twice as high where interviewer problems also existed (26%) compared with those where no interviewer problems were detected (13%) and this association is highly significant (Chi Sq 44.3, p<.001). Nevertheless, given the ubiquity of interviewer problems within these data the overall association between interviewer and respondent problems is modest (Cramer's V=.165).

To What Extent can Question Problems be Explained by Interviewer and Respondent Characteristics?

Given the evident problems associated with question delivery, it is useful to examine the extent to which question problems are associated with the demographic characteristics of survey respondents and interviewers such as age and gender. Our analyses identified few statistically significant differences in the frequency of interview problems according to interviewer and respondent characteristics, though this is perhaps unsurprising given the small sample size (N=23). Nevertheless, there are some suggestions that interviewer characteristics may affect question delivery. The mean number of interviewer problems is higher for male interviewers (T=2.1, p<.1) and for interviewers aged 75+ (F=4.1, p<.05). However, interviews conducted by this latter group comprise a small proportion of productive full PSE-UK interviews (3.6%) (see Table 3.1). In comparison, respondent problems do not appear to be clearly associated with interviewer or respondent characteristics.

How Does the Incidence of Question Problems Vary by Question Type?

A key objective of behaviour coding is to examine the distribution of question problems for specific question items in order to improve their formatting, wording and delivery. Table 3.3 (below) examines variations in the mean number of question problems for interviewers (Int) and respondents (Resp) separately, as well as the mean number of combined problems (Any). Since we are interested here in making comparisons both between question items, and between interviewer and respondent problems, it is useful to compare standardised scores for all three measures.[1] Table 3.3 shows that measures such as WeekAm (estimated income needed to avoid poverty), LcSvPr (adequacy of local services), and DayHrs (time use) are especially problematic. These question items have high standardised scores indicating that the mean number of total problems is substantially higher than the mean for the question set as a whole – in the case of WeekAm, +3.2 standard deviations above the mean. At the foot of the table are listed items where the mean number of total problems is substantially lower than the mean for the question set as a whole. Items such as AccmSt (satisfaction with accommodation), Illness (physical or mental health conditions), Repair (state of repair of home), and Small (ever made to feel small because of low income) are all items where fewer question problems were detected.

Overall, as measured by the coefficient of variation there is clearly more variability in interviewer behaviour (Cov=.56) than is the case for

Table 3.3   Mean number of question problems by question item: interviewer, respondent and all problems (z scores)

Var	Description	a. Int	b. Resp	c. Any	
WeekAm	Income needed to avoid poverty	1.6	4.0	3.2	Most interview
LcSvPr	Adequacy of local services	2.6	1.5	2.7	problems
DayHrs	Time use	1.6	0.5	1.4	
HCstCh	Housing costs change (since FRS survey)	0.2	2.5	1.4	⬆
FREQF	Frequency of seeing/speaking to friends	0.7	1.5	1.3	
GenPor	Subjective poverty	1.0	1.0	1.3	
ImpFac	Factors important in preventing R from doing activities	1.6	0.2	1.3	
SocAct	Memberships of organisations	1.4	0.0	1.0	
------	------	---	---	---	
AreaSt	Area satisfied	−1.2	−0.3	−1.1	
Problem	Area problems	−0.9	−0.8	−1.1	
Cleaner	Regularly employs cleaner or gardener	−1.0	−0.8	−1.2	
SoLRate	Rating of standard of living	−1.6	0.0	−1.2	
AccmSt	Satisfaction with accommodation	−1.9	0.2	−1.3	⬇
Commit	How well keeping up with bills and credit	−1.2	−0.8	−1.3	
Expenses	Can household afford to pay unexpected necessary expense	−1.0	−1.1	−1.3	
Illness	Physical or mental health conditions	−0.9	−1.3	−1.3	Fewest
Repair	State of repair of home	−1.2	−0.8	−1.3	interview
Small	Ever made to feel small because of low income	−1.0	−1.1	−1.3	problems
Raw means		.56	.22	.79	
Coefficient of variation		2.25	1.31	2.36	

respondent behaviour (Cov=.22). However, as the above analyses suggest, the correlation between mean scores for interviewer and respondent problems is modest (r=.24, p<.1). For example, with regard to political efficacy (Effic) it seems that whilst interviewers appeared to have difficulty in asking the question as intended (with mean interviewer scores of +1.2SD), in general there were few problems detected with respondents' answers (with mean respondent scores of −0.5SD). Conversely, when we compare interviewer and respondent scores for measures of social contact (Txtfr, LSNS4) it is clear that whilst interviewers generally had relatively few problems in asking these questions the mean number of respondent problems was substantially higher than for the question set as a whole. These differences are summarised graphically

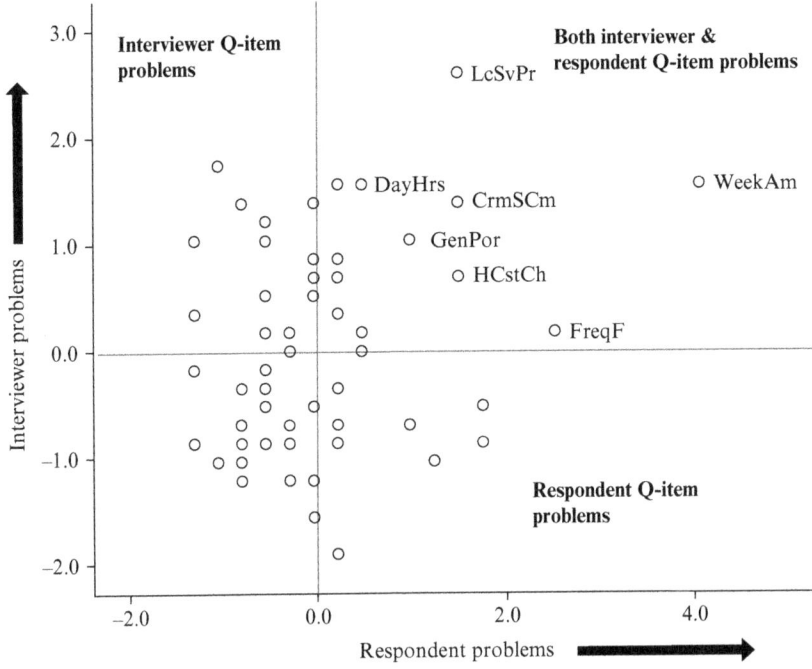

Figure 3.1   Scatterplot of interviewer and respondent problems by question item: standardised mean scores

in Figure 3.1 (above) which plots standardised mean scores for the number of interviewer (y-axis) and respondent (x-axis) problems.

ANALYSING RESPONSE PROBLEMS IN THE PSE-UK SURVEY

Whilst behaviour coding and subsequent quantification of interviewer and respondent problems is a useful means of identifying problematic question items, it is not informative regarding the nature and meaning of these problems. However, linking these results to a qualitative analysis of the interview transcripts for these problematic questions can provide additional insights into their causes and how they may be remedied. In this section we therefore examine the nature of these response effects on the basis of analysis of field interview transcripts for selected question items. Given the problems identified with the following question items we focus here on these variables: FreqF (frequency of seeing/speaking to friends), WeekAm (income needed to avoid poverty), HCstCh (housing costs change since FRS survey), and LcSvPr (adequacy of local services). Further details on question wording and routing for these items is given in the Appendix to this chapter.

The availability of external sources of evidence concerning at least some of these questions within the 2012 PSE-UK study allows us also to compare and triangulate these results with other established approaches to the testing and evaluation of survey questionnaire content. These include evidence from interviewer debriefing following the survey pilot, focus group development work and subsequent cognitive testing of the draft survey questionnaire. The kinds of problems identified with these questions included the following issues which we expand upon below: task complexity; problems associated with question delivery; difficulties in implementing survey protocols; and problems associated with respondent cognition, recall, estimation and response.

Task Complexity

In some cases the complexity of the survey task placed unreasonable demands upon respondent and interviewer. This was evident with regard to the following question: 'how many pounds a week, after tax, do you think are necessary to keep a household, such as the one you live in, out of poverty?' (WeekAm).

The pilot survey had revealed concerns regarding this item with inter-viewers reporting that respondents had difficulty in estimating how many pounds per week their household needed to avoid poverty. Clearly, this survey task makes substantial demands in terms of recall of relevant infor-mation and in complex estimation and judgement regarding 'necessities'. Moreover, some respondents were unclear how to interpret 'a household such as theirs'. As we have commented elsewhere (Fahmy et al., 2015), these judgements may require information on household circumstances and resources that are unavailable to respondents. Respondents are likely to have radically different interpretations of poverty itself so that the comparability of such estimates is in any case uncertain. Many of these problems are also evident in the survey interviews themselves, as illustrated in the following interaction:

> Int: How many pounds a week, after tax, do you think are necessary to keep a household, such as the one you live in, out of poverty?
> Resp: read the question again.
> Int: Yeah, sure. How many pounds a week, after tax, do you think are necessary to keep a household, such as the one you live in, out of poverty? There's no right or wrong, it's an opinion one, but it's quite a hard one [laughs].
> Resp: I wouldn't know where to start with that.

Int: So you've got, well I guess, you'd need food, and then anything to do with housing, then you've got heat and light, clothing . . .
Resp: okay, well . . .
Int: You know, council tax, house insurance.
Resp: Per week or per month did you say?
Int: Either.
Resp: I'd have to say, housing such as this, £1500 a month.

In fact, the first response of many respondents was to comment on how difficult the question was to answer. Some indicative comments are detailed below:

#3105: Very difficult!
#0204: Well, it's hard . . .
#0105: I don't know, it's very difficult is that.
#9405: I honestly don't know. I've never had to work it out. Those days have gone.
#6701: I wouldn't know where to start with that.
#7205: Let me just use my calculator . . . I'm just working out what I get a month and what I need.

Problems of Question Delivery

Despite the guidance provided by the research contractor to fieldworkers, in only slightly more than half of these cases (52%) did the interviewer read the question exactly as scripted. Whilst survey methodologists devote substantial efforts to question testing, comparatively little attention has been devoted to the conduct of interviews, and specifically to interviewer behaviour. In the 2012 PSE-UK behaviour coding analysis more interviewer problems were associated with the items on access to services (LcSvPr) than with any other question items.

This does not necessarily imply a lack of competence on the part of interviewers, but may indicate unrealistic expectations on the part of researchers regarding the feasibility of the survey task, and/or a lack of clarity on the task itself. These concerns were voiced by interviewers at the pilot stage. Interviewers were concerned about the number of similar questions in this block, which became tedious and repetitive for respondents. Similarly, response categories were felt to be overly complex, encouraging respondents and interviewers to skip scripted follow-ups prompting evaluation of the quality of services. Difficulties in implementing survey protocols (e.g. card sort exercises) and a lack of clarity on the survey task (i.e. what was required of participants and interviewers) were also evident.

It may be therefore that in the context of a 50-minute interview, this section made unrealistic expectations of interviewers and respondents. In addition to problems of question delivery (and omission), both behaviour coding analysis of interview transcripts and interviewer feedback on the survey pilot identified additional cognition problems, for example, associated with the interpretation of 'local area' and 'public' services.

Respondent Problems

In comparison with problems associated with task complexity, or problems in the delivery of question items in the survey setting, problems associated with respondent cognition, recall, judgement and response were less common. As Figure 3.1 shows, the distribution of response problems suggests serious concerns related to a relatively small number of question items including WeekAm (discussed above) and many of the 'feed-forward' questions included in the survey. Since the survey was based upon a follow-up, sub-sample of 2010 FRS respondents, it was desirable in principle to update responses collected during FRS fieldwork in the PSE-UK study, for example, to estimate changes in household incomes, spending, etc. between the two surveys.

However, both interviewer feedback and behaviour coding of responses suggested that feed-forward data on housing costs and individual incomes did not work well. The following interactions are typical here. As these examples illustrate, and in common with the difficulties in reliably estimating the income needed to avoid poverty, the complexity of these calculations and especially the expectations the question makes in terms of respondent recall are clearly unreasonable. Given the issues raised by the following examples regarding the accuracy of responses here, these feed-forward data may be little more than guesswork in many cases, and (despite subsequent modifications) unsurprisingly these items were characterised by high levels of item non-response:

Int: How much of your total housing costs changed since you were last interviewed? How much would you say you're paying more per week or year, whatever?
Resp 1: Yeah, oh, I can't say. I can't give the figures.
Int: about. . .
Resp 2: well, I'd say about an extra £20 a week.
Int: yeah.
Resp 1: No, I wouldn't give the figures, I can't [laughs].
Int: No, no problem.
Resp 2: Well, I don't mind having a guess at.

Int: By approximately how much have your total housing costs changed since you were last interviewed?

Resp: Phew! Without looking at all the bills, I'll just have to take a guess at this. I would say probably about three, level three, about 1000 to one five.
Int: £20 to £29 a week?
Resp: Yeah, I was looking at annual there. . . We don't look at things monthly; we look at them annual. . .I would say about three, it could be even higher but that is a difficult question to answer without, you know. . .

DISCUSSION AND CONCLUSION

Survey paradata derived from transcripts of interviewer/respondent interactions offer an invaluable insight for survey methodologists into the real-world delivery of survey questionnaires. When combined with rigorous methods of coding interview behaviour, these data provide one means of identifying question problems using a relatively systematic measurement framework. In this chapter, we have examined and applied one coding framework for doing so and illustrated some of the problems identified using this approach on the basis of a qualitative analysis of the interview transcripts themselves. These findings suggest that more attention needs to be given to how survey questionnaires are actually delivered in the field in order to better identify and address deviations from paradigmatic question/response sequences. Information about survey processes (e.g. audit trail data, call records), data derived from interview behaviour itself, and auxiliary survey metadata are all informative on this issue especially when combined.

Our findings suggest that interviewer behaviours involving a deviation from the scripted interviewer/respondent interaction may be an underestimated source of bias in the delivery of survey questionnaires in comparison with the cognitive aspects of survey response. This suggests a need to refocus not only upon the factors shaping respondent cognition and response but also upon the interview setting as a social interaction subject to conversational norms. Improving the quality of survey response therefore requires greater recognition of the role of interview setting and interaction. In general, the results described here also suggest a high degree of consistency with interviewer feedback on the survey pilot, and (where available) with the results of cognitive testing. However, unlike interviewer debriefing, analysis of actual interviewer/respondent interactions allow for a much more objective assessment of the survey response process since findings derived using this approach are independent of the interviewer. Thus, whilst behaviour coding in its early development focused on the evaluation of interviewer performance (e.g. Cannell et al., 1975), in more recent years its potential in evaluating questionnaire delivery has been increasingly emphasised (e.g. van der Zouwen and Dijkstra, 1995).

However, non-reactive methods drawing upon survey paradata are less informative about potential covert problems associated with question wording, delivery and response, for example, where respondents' implicit understandings of question items differ substantially from the research team's intended meaning or interpretation. This should remind us that there is no single method which is superior in an absolute sense, but rather that by drawing upon the complementary strengths of different question testing approaches we can generate a more comprehensive and sensitive picture of the factors shaping survey response. The challenge currently facing survey methodologists therefore concerns how best to draw on the complementary strengths of different question testing methods in order to improve survey quality. To date, the main focus in questionnaire development has been upon the evaluation of question items, rather than upon the evaluation of survey questionnaires as a whole to take account of issues such as item ordering effects, respondent fatigue, difficulties in implementing survey protocols, etc. Combining information about survey processes (e.g. audit trail data, call records), with data derived from interview behaviour itself and auxiliary survey metadata, offer one means of beginning to address these wider questions. They also illustrate the potential of combining qualitative analysis of interview transcripts with quantitative behaviour coding approaches in order not simply to identify question problems but also to provide an insight into their nature and causes. Given the extent of question problems highlighted here in the everyday practice of experienced survey interviewers further attention is clearly needed in order to more effectively monitor and evaluate real-world interview survey practice.

NOTES

* *Corresponding author.* Contact: School for Policy Studies, Univ. of Bristol, 8 Priory Rd., Bristol UK BS8 1TZ. T:+44(0)1179546703; E: eldin.fahmy@bris.ac.uk.

1. Standardised scores describe the (signed) number of standard deviations of a given data point from its group mean, giving us a measure of the dispersion of scores which is comparable between different measures.

REFERENCES

Bell K, Fahmy E, Gordon D (2014) Quantitative conversations: the importance of developing rapport in standardised interviewing. *Quality and Quantity*, doi: 10.1007/s11135-014-0144-2.

Bradburn N, Sudman S, Wansink B (2004) *Asking questions. The definitive guide to questionnaire design – for market research, political polls, and social and health questionnaires.* Jossey-Bass, San Francisco.

Campanelli P (1997) Testing survey questions: new directions in cognitive interviewing. *Bulletin De Methodologie Sociologique*, 5–17.

Cannell CF, Robinson S (1971) Analysis of individual questions. In J Lansing, S Withey, A Wolf (Eds) *Working papers on survey research in poverty areas* (Ch. 11). Ann Arbor, MI: Institute for Social Research.

Cannell CF, Lawson SA, Hausser DL (1975) *A technique for evaluating interviewer performance.* Ann Arbor, MI: Survey Research Centre, University of Michigan.

Cannell CF, Oksenberg L, Kalton G (1991) New techniques for pretesting survey questions. *Journal of Official Statistics*, 7: 349–365.

Collins D (2003) Pretesting survey instruments: an overview of cognitive methods. *Quality of Life Research*, 12: 229–238.

Drennan J (2003) Cognitive interviewing: verbal data in the design and pretesting of questionnaires. *Journal of Advanced Nursing*, 42: 57–63.

Fahmy E, Pemberton S, Sutton E (2011a) Cognitive testing of the 2011 UK Poverty and Social Exclusion Survey. *2012 PSE-UK Working Paper 17.* URL: http://www.poverty.ac.uk/system/files/attachments/WP%20Methods%20No.17%20-%20Cognitive%20Testing%20Report%20(Fahmy,%20Pemberton,%20Sutton).pdf [accessed 3.10.16].

Fahmy E, Pemberton S, Sutton E (2011b) Public perceptions of poverty, social exclusion and living standards: final report on focus group findings. *2012 PSE-UK Working Paper 12.* URL: http://poverty.ac.uk/sites/default/files/attachments/WP_Analysis_No3_Focus-groups_Fahmy-Pemberton-Sutton.pdf [accessed 3.10.16].

Fahmy E, Pemberton S, Sutton E (2015) Are we all agreed? Consensual methods and the 'necessities of life' in the UK today. *Journal of Social Policy*, doi: 10.1017/s0047279415000033.

Maher J (2011) *Poverty and social exclusion survey: pilot findings.* NatCen. Unpublished research report. URL: http://www.poverty.ac.uk/pse-research/pse-uk/methods-development [accessed 1.11.15].

Maynard DW, Schaeffer NC (2002) Toward a sociology of social scientific knowledge: Survey research and ethnomethodology's asymmetric alternates. *Social Studies of Science*, 30(3): 323–370.

Nicolaas G (2011) *Survey paradata: a review.* National Centre for Research Methods Review Paper 17. URL: http://eprints.ncrm.ac.uk/1719/1/Nicolaas_review_paper_jan11.pdf [accessed 1.11.15].

Ongena YP, Dijkstra W (2006) Methods of behavior coding of survey interviews. *Journal of Official Statistics*, 22(3): 419–451.

Presser S, Blair J (1994) Survey pretesting: do different methods produce different results? *Sociological Methodology*, 24: 73–104.

Presser S, Rothgeb J, Couper M, Lessler J, Martin E, Singer E (2004) *Methods for testing and evaluating survey questionnaires.* Wiley, New Jersey.

Sala E, Uhrig S, Lynn P (2008) The development and implementation of a coding scheme to analyse interview dynamics in the British Household Panel Survey. *ISER Working Paper 2008–19.* University of Essex.

Schwarz N (2007) Cognitive aspects of survey methodology. *Applied Cognitive Psychology*, 21: 277–287.

Sudman S, Bradburn N, Schwarz N (1996) *Thinking about answers: the application of cognitive processes to survey methodology.* Jossey-Bass, San Francisco.

van der Zouwen J, Dijkstra W (1995) Trivial and non-trivial question–answer sequences: types, determinants and effects on data quality. *Proceedings of the International Conference on Survey Measurement and Process Quality*. Virginia, American Statistical Association.

Walton L, Stange M, Powell RJ, Belli RF (2012) Exploring interviewer and respondent interactions: an innovative behaviour coding approach. *Paper Presented at the 2012 Midwest Association of Public Opinion Research*.

Willis GB (2005) *Cognitive interviewing: a tool for improving questionnaire design*. Sage, Thousand Oaks, CA.

Willis GB, Schechter S, Whitaker K (1999) A comparison of cognitive interviewing, expert review, and behavior coding: what do they tell us? In *Proceedings of the American Statistical Association*, Alexandria, VA. pp. 28–37.

APPENDIX

Selected 2012 PSE-UK Questionnaire Items

[FREQF] How often do you see or speak to friends? (SHOWCARD L1)

0. Less than once a month
1. Once a month
2. A few times a month
3. Once a week
4. A few times a week
5. Every day

If [FREQF] = 1–5, ASK IF FREQF IS 'MONTHLY OR MORE'
(1 THRU 5). IF FREQF IS 'LESS THAN MONTHLY' (0) THEN
LSNS1=0

[WeekAm] How many pounds a week, after tax, do you think are necessary to keep a household such as the one you live in, out of poverty?

Ask HHResp (i.e. HRP or HRP's partner) if [WeekAm] is not refusal or don't know
Ask only if Housing Costs have Changed

[HCstCh] By approximately how much have your total housing costs changed, since you were last interviewed? (SHOWCARD F1)

Ask HHResp (i.e. HRP or HRP's partner)

[LcSvPr] The next questions are about services which may exist in your local area and which affect your standard of living

I am now going to ask you about services which may exist in your local area. Using this SHOWCARD, can you tell me whether you (or a member of your household) have used these services in the last 12 months. For the services you use, please tell me whether you think they are adequate or inadequate. For the services you do not use, please tell me whether you do not use them because 'you don't want to' or because 'they are unavailable or inadequate' or because 'you can't afford to' use them.

(SHOWCARD E1)

[UsPbSv] Do you, or a member of your household, use . . .

	Use – adequate	Use – inadequate	Don't use – unavailable or inadequate	Don't use – don't want / not relevant	Don't use – can't afford
[UseLib] Libraries					
. . .	. . .	. . .	. . .	. . .	. . .

4. 'Another long and involved story': narrative themes in the marginalia of the *Poverty in the UK* survey

Ann Phoenix, Janet Boddy, Rosalind Edwards and Heather Elliott

INTRODUCTION: PARADATA, FIELDNOTES AND MARGINALIA

This chapter contributes to the understanding of paradata as method and substantive data, by examining the marginal comments written on the paper questionnaires completed in Peter Townsend's influential 1967–68 *Poverty in the UK* survey (PinUK). This classic study was conducted in a period before surveys used computer technology and paradata had become an accepted survey tool. We analysed the types of marginalia recorded by the interviewers and research team and investigated whether the marginalia was sufficiently storied to enable narrative analysis. Here, we present the background to the study and a brief overview of findings. The chapter then explores examples of the different identity positions that the interviewers construct for the research participants and themselves in writing to the senior researchers who were responsible for running the study. The final section considers the relevance of narrative analysis of paradata to contemporary quantitative and qualitative social science.

The handwritten jottings on the *Poverty in the UK* questionnaires were designed to improve the quality of data and recruitment of participants, a focus that arguably places the study reported here between quantitative paradata, marginalia as studied in the humanities and the fieldnotes analysed in qualitative social science. But our analysis attends to an issue that is frequently ignored in discussions of marginalia and paradata: how, and why, researchers construct their codes, notes and observations.

THE STUDY

The research was conducted in a collaboration between the ESRC National Centre for Research Methods (NCRM) and the Novella (Narratives of Varied Everyday Lives and Linked Approaches) NCRM research node. It sought new insights into the methodological utility of analysing paradata by bringing together the focus on paradata from quantitative analysis with epistemological interest in qualitative research and how researchers are implicated in their analyses. We analysed the marginalia recorded by field interviewers on paper booklet questionnaires completed for PinUK. This survey played a pivotal role in redefining poverty and its measurement, and influenced contemporary social science understandings.[1] The PinUK sample consisted of 3,566 households, comprising 9,584 household members recruited from 59 parliamentary constituencies and four particularly deprived 'special areas'. Our project (*Possibilities of Paradata*: POP) had five overall objectives, of which two are particularly relevant here. First, to explore the possibilities of conducting narrative analysis on micro-level marginalia from a subset of the archived PinUK survey material and second, to extend the understanding of secondary narrative analysis with data not collected for this purpose.

Since paradata were not the focus of Townsend's PinUK study, an initial task of the POP study was to map the paradata in the booklets. POP was a small-scale study and narrative analysis is time- and labour-intensive, so it was not possible to analyse all the booklets that contained paradata. Sixty-nine booklets were selected, including examples of each of four types of geographical areas represented amongst those in the original study ('special', seaside, affluent, minority ethnic migration).

The paper PinUK survey booklets were stored on shelves at the UK Data Service, University of Essex, along with the Peter Townsend archive collection. They were ordered in bundles tied with string according to geographical area and so our entry-point into the data was through place, rather than, for example, household type or interviewer or date when the interviews were conducted. In this way, our initial familiarisation and sampling processes were to a certain extent dictated by the materiality of the data (Moor and Uprichard, 2014), and by the way Townsend and his research team had organised the bundles decades previously. Beyond that order, we had to begin somewhere when confronted with an array and extent of fascinating material. An initial thematic analysis was conducted by the whole research team, with most booklets thematically analysed by two researchers. Six booklets were then theoretically sampled for narrative analysis (by area, interviewer and type of household). Two of these were collaboratively analysed and the other four were analysed in pairs before being discussed by the whole team. The analytic process was facilitated by the fact that all the coding decisions and revisions, together with the para-data, were handwritten on the interview booklets, which also contained the name of the field interviewer. Since the Peter Townsend (1979) volume, *Poverty in the United Kingdom: A Survey of Household Resources and Standards of Living*, acknowledges many of the interviewers, coders and central research team, we were also able to work out which role a particular person had played in the project. In addition, our research team had access to papers connected to the study archived in the Townsend collections at the London School of Economics and University of Essex, as well as those stored at the University of Bristol. We also had the benefit of the memories of 12 of the original interviewers, coders and researchers on the project who were traced and video interviewed for a follow-on study.

The project took a social constructionist perspective, viewing par-ticipants and researchers as meaning making within particular socio-historical contexts and so as co-constructing the paradata. The narrative method employed involved close reading of all the booklet paradata, with attention to the genre of 'story' constructed by the interviewer and how the interviewer positioned his- or herself narratively, as well as shifts in voice and tone. The dynamics of the narratives were also examined to see how they were built up and repeated, attending to inconsistencies and non sequiturs. The PinUK survey was conducted with pen and paper, and this allowed analysis of graphic data, such as placement on a page, emphatic notations such as underlining, and punctuation, as well as linguistic mate-rial and calculations (e.g. of incomes and expenditure).

Just under half of interviewers in the surveys we sampled wrote both numerical and textual paradata on the booklets, and coders and check-ers from the central research team frequently added their own paradata, so there were sometimes multiple sources of paradata on booklets. Space was left for notes and narrative accounts at the end of the questionnaire, but some interviewers wrote their main narratives at the beginning of the questionnaire booklet, or interspersed their comments throughout.

The thematic analyses showed that the PinUK paradata could be typified in six ways:

1. *Amplifications* of the codes, noting figures and computations of income, benefits, expenses and background clarification, and/or direct quotes.
2. *Justifications* of coding decisions or lack of coding.
3. *Explanations* related to the substantive focus and coding.
4. *Evaluations of informants' characters or their claims.* The evalu-ation of character discussed individual personality or household

characteristics, emotions and material resources. The evaluation of claims discussed the veracity of the information given by informants.

5. *Debriefing.* This mostly consisted of comments on the research focus to the core research team. Some appeared to be 'offloading' explanations to the self. Some were exchanges between interviewers and the core team.

6. *Standpoint.* Interviewers commented on the wider political context, the general or local social situation, or presented an active voice that went beyond contemporary expectations for the fieldworker role.

Much of the paradata in the booklets constituted amplification, justification and explanation, and provided insights into the issues with which contemporary quantitative paradata analysts are concerned. The study helped to illuminate the historical specificities of the period in which the interviews were conducted and the ways in which the interviewers' concerns shaped how they pursued and interpreted the survey responses.

The analyses also demonstrated that it is possible to conduct narrative analysis on paradata from the PinUK study. The narrative analysis provided important insights into the interview process and informants' stories, adding valuable nuances to the thematic analysis in showing that the same theme could be addressed through different genres and by positioning researchers and researched in differing ways. For example, one interviewer wrote paradata that could be analysed as a 'flash fiction' narrative (Boddy, 2010), vividly presenting a series of short stories of the informant's life. Another presented a story of the struggles and manners of the apparently wealthy, opening the paradata narrative with the header 'Upper Level Living', followed by the summative phrase, 'Charming people, but [unclear] so full of difficulties and complexities'; the narrative's ironic tone and layered meanings were reminiscent of the 'genteel poverty' genre of Jane Austen novels (see Tomalin, 1997). In another, the codes and paradata together presented a narrative of a household that could be read as a Shakespearian tragedy in that it contained themes reminiscent of *King Lear*, building a picture of decline and loss of power in old age, ill-advised intergenerational transfer of property and mental ill health.

The narrative analyses also showed how interviewers position themselves, in relation to informants and to Townsend's research team. Since the narrative analyses were of interviews conducted by different interviewers, we cannot comment on the extent to which interviewers had particular and consistent narrative styles across interviews. However, by looking across interviewers it is possible to see how different narratives are constructed in the paradata.

Some interviewers positioned themselves as dispassionate observers; one

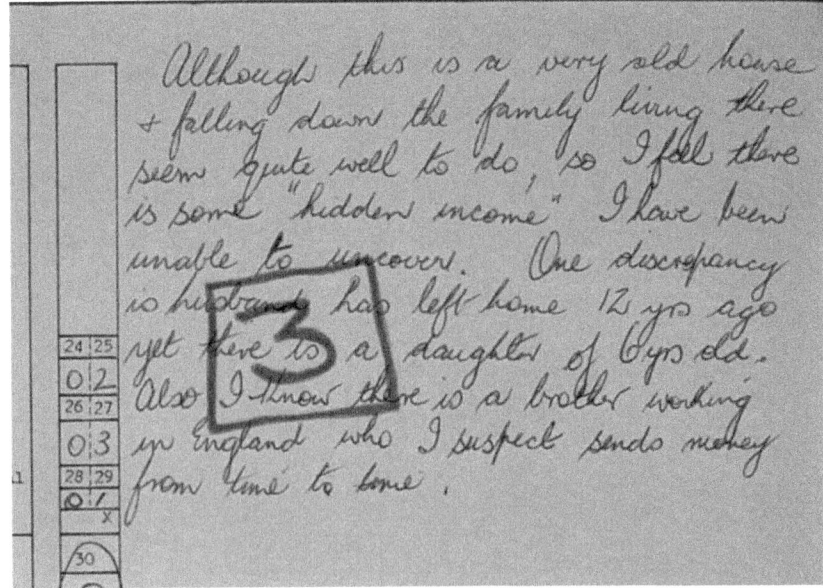

Note: Although this is a very old house and falling down, the family living there seem quite well to do, so I feel there is some 'hidden income' I have been unable to uncover. One discrepancy is husband has left home 12 yrs ago yet there is a daughter of 6 yrs old. Also I know there is a brother working in England who I suspect sends money from time to time.

Figure 4.1   Interviewer notes 1

set of paradata consisted of brief notes, with an absence of names and relationships, depersonalising both the 'informant' and the interviewer. Others presented counter-narratives that challenged social prejudices of the time or told stories in factual, social campaigning styles that evoked our sympathy as readers. The role of 'detective' interviewer is a genre form apparent in several interviewers' accounts. One such case (booklet 319X52), analysed in depth for a working paper (Elliott et al., 2014; see Figure 4.1), has relatively little paradata recorded, but what there is presents a consistent, strong narrative of mystery around the family's finances. This is set out from the first paradata: the words 'hidden income', 'unable to uncover' and 'suspect' suggest that the family is being duplicitous about their income. The interviewer establishes a puzzle on the basis of assumed discrepancies between the 'well to do family' in their 'old and falling down' surroundings and the contrast made between the age of the six-year-old daughter and the husband's departure from the family home 12 years previously.

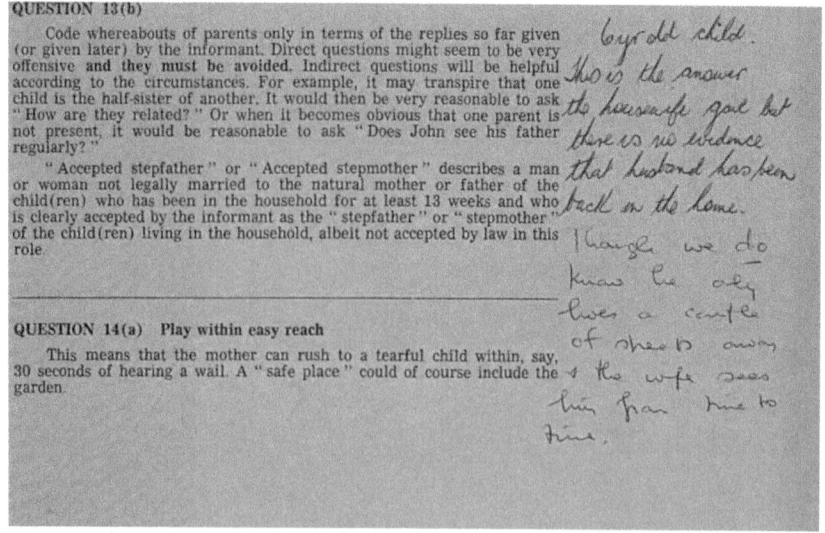

QUESTION 13(b)

Code whereabouts of parents only in terms of the replies so far given (or given later) by the informant. Direct questions might seem to be very offensive and they must be avoided. Indirect questions will be helpful according to the circumstances. For example, it may transpire that one child is the half-sister of another. It would then be very reasonable to ask "How are they related?" Or when it becomes obvious that one parent is not present, it would be reasonable to ask "Does John see his father regularly?"

"Accepted stepfather" or "Accepted stepmother" describes a man or woman not legally married to the natural mother or father of the child(ren) who has been in the household for at least 13 weeks and who is clearly accepted by the informant as the "stepfather" or "stepmother" of the child(ren) living in the household, albeit not accepted by law in this role.

QUESTION 14(a)   Play within easy reach

This means that the mother can rush to a tearful child within, say, 30 seconds of hearing a wail. A "safe place" could of course include the garden.

Note: 6 yr old child. This is the answer the housewife gave but there is no evidence that husband has been back in the home. [handwriting style 1]
Though we do know he only lives a couple of streets away and the wife sees him from time to time. [handwriting style 2]

Figure 4.2   Interviewer notes 2 and additional comment

The detective work is extended in the final paradata presented (Figure 4.2), with additional marginalia in new handwriting – presumably one of the checkers in the office. The interviewer's formulation – 'this is the answer the housewife gave' – distances the interviewee's answer, casting doubt. But, the coder disagrees, accepting the original 'answer the housewife' gave: that the child is from her (current) marriage. The coder, whose comments will not have been seen by the interviewer, provides the rationale for this judgement in his or her own paradata: namely that the husband lives nearby.

Overall, the paradata narratives highlight the labour of interviewing, of interviewer efforts and expertise. We see stories of hard work, and of the embodied efforts of interviewing. For example, the paradata for booklet 2101061 begins on the Introduction page of the survey booklet, 'This was my HEADACHE HOUSEHOLD!', vividly evoking a challenging interview:

> In a small room she SHOUTS – the effect is extraordinary – the children whine about each other and the dog barks – frequently –

Some informants' accounts were treated as jigsaw puzzles, piecing together information to make coding decisions in complex cases and defending the interviewer against the possibility that the central team would disagree with their coding. In one case, the interviewer presents four voices in the paradata, three for 'informants' and one for herself, separated into different colours of ink and kinds of writing. Others tell stories of persistence with reluctant interviewees, and sceptical detective work, attempting to uncover whether informants' socioeconomic circumstances were as they portrayed them and making inferences about interviewees' moral culpability.

The remainder of this chapter focuses on two cases that exemplify contrasting narrative constructions – positioning themselves as interviewers and their interviewees (referred to as 'informants') in particular ways, through genre and characterisation, but in both cases evidently writing for the more senior members of the research team at the university. Both show how the interviewer feels about the interview and the participant, their moral stance in relation to the participants' circumstances and how they position themselves as professional research interviewers who are accountable to the central research team.

POSITIONING SELF AND PARTICIPANT: A NARRATIVE OF DISTANCED EQUITY, SOCIAL JUSTICE AND INFORMED PROFESSIONALISM

This interview (booklet 6360409) was with a family where the father was Iraqi and the mother English. The parents, both unemployed, lived with their two preschool-age children in a terraced house recorded as being in a poor condition, with an outdoor toilet and no bathroom. The family had recently moved across country.

The paradata recorded on this survey booklet amount to over 11 pages of text and, in our thematic analysis, we coded much of it as 'amplification'. This was clearly a careful and thorough interviewer, working to ensure that the central team were able to make judgements about the accuracy of her coding. Much of her writing thus fits with the form of paradata required by contemporary quantitative researchers, to assess whether questions or codes need amendment or interviewers need further training or debriefing.

The PinUK study aimed to interview all household members, with women usually being the primary informants. The mother and father in this family were, therefore, both interviewed. However, most of the marginalia presented relates to the father's interview (referred to as the '2nd' [respondent]), partly because he appears to have spoken at greater length, but also because his narratives raised questions for the interviewer or made her feel that they required contextualisation. Her marginalia takes care to represent his story accurately, by reporting his words where possible. The result is a series of 'small stories' (Bamberg, 2011) that present testimony from the interviewee, but often include analytic commentary from the interviewer. A good example of this concerns the narrative presented in response to a question about a change of job, which constitutes a carefully nuanced counter-narrative, countering taken-for-granted racist ideas that were commonly expressed in the 1960s, and a distanced, partial display of sympathy tempered by scepticism.

> 2nd was concerned about the practice of 'greasing' which he claimed had oper-ated in the last two jobs he had and which he thought was responsible for him losing his job the last time. Briefly his story was that bribes (watch, shirts, cig lighters etc.) had been offered by Pakistanis to the foreman (English and white) in exchange for jobs which they got. Once in the jobs they (there were 2) con-tinued to give 'presents' to the foreman while also accepting money from other Pakistanis and West Indians to procure jobs for them. 2nd claimed that this money (often £50 from each job seeker) was shared out between the foreman and the Pakistanis already in jobs. The foreman then made life as unpleasant as he could for those workers not giving him 'presents' and either waited until they were so miserable at [unclear] avoided, shouted at etc. that they left of their own accord or found an excuse to sack them. 2nd claimed that the sort of reason given for dismissals were 'rule-book' things like smoking in the toilets, which everyone infringed but only the few were sacked for. In his last job, 2nd and 3 English/white workers were the only ones left out of 15 men, who were not bribing the foreman. One English worker then left of his own accord, while 2nd and the other 2 were sacked for taking 5 minutes over the allowed tea-break. Within four hours of his dismissal 2nd claims his job was taken by a Pakistani. He was understandably bitter about this series of events which happened in Bradford (Yorks) and said that his case was not unique. It unmistakeably influ-enced his opinion of Pakistanis, whom he despised and was upset because being coloured himself he was lumped in with those who were 'getting every decent man a bad reputation'. I asked him whether job seeking for friends and relatives wasn't characteristic of Arabs too and said it was: the difference was he said that an Arab would do it as a matter of duty and try to use influence. He admitted that some Pakistanis might be doing this too, but was convinced that for the majority it was a money making racket 'based on bribery and without any sense of what is right for one's family and oneself'. It was sad to realise during this interview that even within a minority group (non-white) what was really a social situation (the situation at work) was now being viewed in terms of race by the participants and had been generalised out to include other aspects of behaviour. He even ended up saying 'And what's more they are terrible with women!' which in view of some similar comments often heard about Arabs, struck me as rather ironic!

The paradata above is neatly written, with few abbreviations. It seems clearly designed to provide a background for understanding the participant's employment and benefit history, which the interviewer has taken pains to establish, but appears more detailed than is strictly necessary. The interviewer works hard to be fair to the participant and his account, informing the coders and understanding the story for herself in terms of what seem to be progressively liberal worldviews, particularly for mid-1960s UK. The small story presented was not strictly germane to the aims of the PinUK study. That she both followed it up with the participant, and then set it out and elaborated on it carefully and in some detail, makes it important to understand the work that this written narrative is doing.

The interviewer steers a course between showing sympathy for her male participant ('he was understandably bitter') and taking care not to stereotype and essentialise any ethnic group or to reproduce racist discourses. She keeps two narratives going – her own and the informant's – and is careful to distinguish which is which. 'Briefly his story was' introduces the informant's narrative: 'his story' indicates that it is not necessarily a version which everyone would accept but it ushers in a telling that is meticulous and detailed, despite its brevity (recording, for example, the specific value of bribes and nature of the gifts); the interviewer makes no comment on this. She clearly notes when her report of the interview moves from the interviewee's story on to the interaction between interviewer and interviewee: 'I asked him'. We thought that this was likely to have been a difficult issue to follow through, given the strength of the interviewee's opinion, how expansive he was and the need to get through the questionnaire. 'Admitted' has the sense of a response to incisive questioning or possibly refers to the interviewee's demeanour in answering or her feeling that it is illegitimate to draw a contrast between what was right for one's family and what he called the 'greasing' process.

The section starting 'It was sad' moves into the researcher's interpretation, resisting individualising, cultural and racist explanations and turning to social and generalised explanations. The social problem (the situation at work) is carefully spelled out, avoiding any problematising of migration or multiculture. The 'it was sad' rather than 'I was sad' underlines this turn to the general, particularly since this particular interviewer did bring her emotions into her paradata in other interviews. The implication of her account is that suffering should result in a kind of sanitised and heroic narrative and some solidarity. That the interviewer positions herself as distant from the interviewee's position is exemplified in the following sentence: 'He even ended up saying "And what's more they are terrible with women!" which in view of some similar comments often heard about Arabs, struck me as rather ironic!'

However, once again she claims this statement as her personal opinion, rather than making generalisations; 'struck me' rather than 'was'. There are clearly two stories set out together here. Her social commentary is sympathetic to a member of a minority ethnic group she knows to be subject to racism but not uncritical or unchallenging in terms of the racism he displays. Her sense of social justice and anti-essentialism in regard to racism did not make her shift away from a professional stance to be sympathetic to this family and, overall, she took a distanced, and sceptical stance to both the husband (the 2nd) and the main informant, his wife, for whom there is less paradata. Indeed, the next long piece of paradata also relates to the husband, alongside a question about tax relief:

> Another long and involved story! 2nd was receiving tax relief for the support of his mother and children abroad but this has been suspended. Partly due to the new vigilance of tax board about money sent out of the country to relatives and partly* (see below) due to change of job (difficulties about tax code number etc.). 2nd has been asked to furnish proof that the money actually goes to his mother. This is difficult, since in fact being a female and widowed she cannot [unclear] out to the bank to collect it (purdah et al) so 2nd's cousin acts as messenger which is highly suspect to the tax people. At present, 2nd has been waiting for 13 weeks for a letter sent from this cousin to Inland Revenue to be translated from Arabic to English and accepted as proof. Meanwhile has been paying tax.
> * 2nd was married in Aden and has 2 children there. His wife died in 1950 he came to England and re-married; the children are looked after by his mother. He pays what he can when he can to support them.

On the survey booklet the two items of paradata were connected not by an asterisk (as in the transcript above), but by a bent arrow, which was heavily drawn and a little smudged (see Figure 4.3). A mix of emotions are contained in the interviewer's comment, 'another long and involved story!' – frustration, possibly exhaustion and also apologetic justification to the central research team. The interviewer reports this story clearly but not particularly sympathetically, and with less detail than in the previous account – of note, given that the cumulative story of the interview is that the family were experiencing hardship. There is a sense of her having to piece together a somewhat puzzling story about tax, benefits and income. The shorthand phrase, 'purdah et al' is more distancing than the careful setting out of the long story about 'greasing', but again the level of detail is precise, and clearly conveyed. The interviewer wrote fluently both in terms of telling the story and graphically, in how the story was set out on the page, with few crossings out or signs of hesitation in the writing.

These paradata constitute a counter-narrative in that the interviewer was concerned to counter what she implicitly seemed to constitute as dominant, master discourses about minoritised ethnic groups (in the first extract above), although it is not clear that she is countering dominant

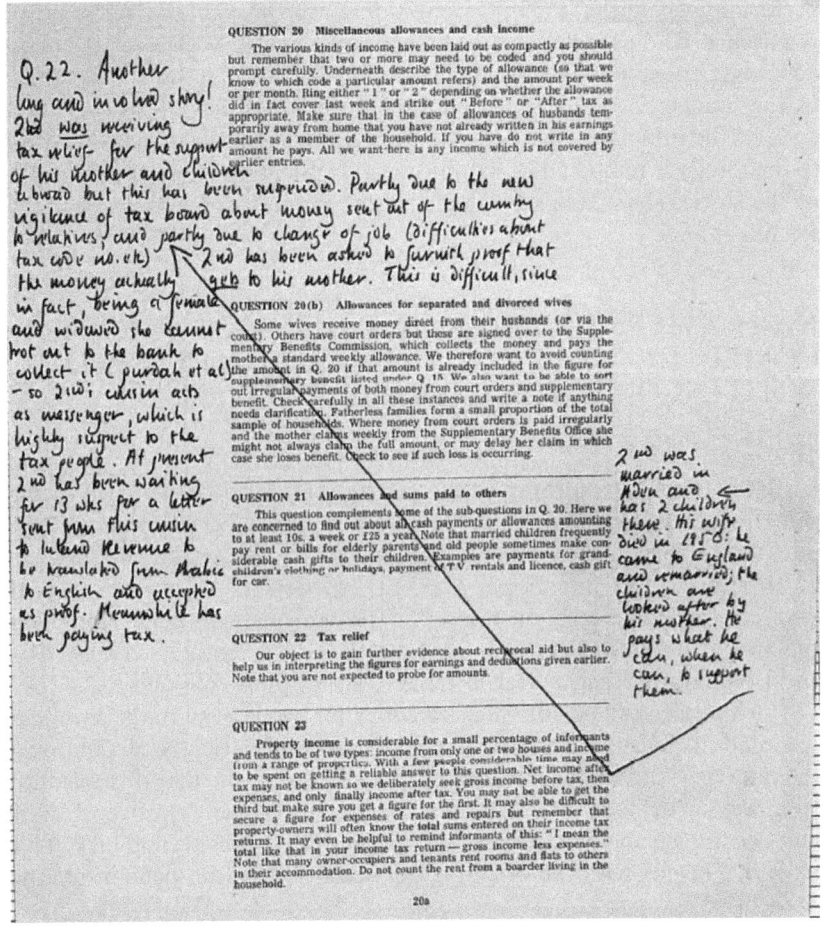

Figure 4.3   Interviewer notes 3

discourses about Arabs. In the second extract presented above, the interviewer is equally careful to present the interviewee's narrative without comment, but presents herself as less sympathetic, less concerned to counter ethnicised stereotypes, and as somewhat wearied by the length of the stories the '2nd' was telling her. This move from counter-narrative to positioning herself as a somewhat impatient sceptic fits with Bamberg and Andrews' (2004) argument that counter-narratives are multi-layered, fluid, relational and positional categories that in 'narratives-in-interaction' often use both counter- and master-narratives in the construction of identities (Bamberg, 2004). The paradata functions performatively in that the interviewer 'does' self-presentation as a careful researcher who is concerned with equity and social justice and who defends against possible negative readings of, for example, Pakistanis by the (imagined) research team in the university office on the one hand and, on the other presents herself as a careful researcher whose openness to the family is tempered by an objective, sceptical stance to at least some of the stories she is told so that she neither invokes nor evokes sympathy for this family.

NARRATIVES OF INTERVIEWER DILIGENCE AND COMPETENT SELF-POSITIONING CONTRASTED WITH INCOMPETENT, UNWILLING PARTICIPANT

This interview booklet (number 6351309) pertains to a single woman in her late 50s who, according to the coding, had lived on her own in the same fourth floor flat for between five and 15 years. She worked long part-time hours in a café kitchen and as a cleaner, and had some form of disability. The interviewer was an experienced interviewer tasked with converting refusals on the survey to agreement to participate, and procuring interviews in difficult circumstances. The paradata consisted of short paragraphs that, together, came to about three A4 pages.

The interviewer's positioning as a converter was central to the paradata recorded in that much of it tells the story of the difficulty of obtaining the interview and of the interviewer's persistence in the face of resistance from the participant. The paradata construct a heroic narrative of difficulty overcome and success achieved as a result of struggle and luck. This narrative begins with the orienting paradata on the first page inside the booklet.

> This woman was disabled and very nervous. I caught her coming to the door to a neighbour and interviewed [her] in the hall. She got very tired of the questions and one/two were genuinely beyond her. I think like the other interviewer I would have had great difficulty in getting her to answer the door if I had not been lucky.

The notions of 'caught her' and 'interviewed in the hall' sets up expectations that this will be an adversarial relationship and, from a twenty-first century vantage point, raises ethical issues about participant consent. This is borne out by later paradata which show that it was more acceptable in the 1960s to insist robustly on conducting an interview, since the interviewer makes clear to the central team exactly how reluctant was the informant, at one point describing how the interviewee was, 'practically pushing me out of door!'. The paradata also present the participant as somewhat simple and a difficult interviewee:

> I finally got her to say that rent, light and heating came to about £4 per week. She does not have the central heating switched on much. I think this woman who was not intelligent was getting very tired and bewildered and she couldn't cope with this question. I had to let it go. She was quite definite about having no resources apart from wages.

It is noteworthy that despite this positioning, the paradata still reveal the informant to be courageously agentic and self-sufficient in difficult circumstances and with stretched resources. *Her* story is that her disability (to do with her hip) does not disable her and that she 'does without what can't afford'. She does not appear to want to reveal the privations she faces and does not invite pity in her account. This is apparent from the paradata, even though it is not the narrative the interviewer tells. Instead, the interviewer repeatedly depersonalises and distances the participant by referring to her repeatedly as 'this woman' and highlighting her lack of intelligence. Her independence is described as 'fiercely' so.

This unsympathetic portrayal contrasts with the interviewer's construction of herself as highly skilled and tenacious, successfully obtaining an interview in the most unlikely of circumstances. She presents this tenacity when she writes, 'I finally got her to say', and her description of the 'tired and bewildered' informant further suggests that any information that she did not get was unobtainable because of the informant's deficiencies, not her shortcomings as an interviewer. These characterisations recur throughout the interview, documented through messages to the coders and research team about the process of conducting the interview. For example, showing her skill as an interviewer, as well as her labour, she writes:

> I had to talk generally to this woman between questions to keep her going. I suspect she spends very little on food as in addition to meals at the café where she works she brings home things like sandwiches, pies which would otherwise be wasted. I couldn't however tactfully I tried get an estimate of the saving to her by this kind of thing.

The words 'I suspect. . .' further position the interviewer as a detective, investigating this participant's finances. Overall, this is an uncomfortable narrative for a contemporary reader, producing a sense that the interviewer disliked the participant and viewed her as recalcitrant, but despite this, invested considerable skill and effort in securing this case for Townsend and his team.

CONCLUSIONS

An examination of the qualitative paradata written in the margins of the PinUK survey booklets show how the interviewers struggle to make meanings in different ways, making sense of the lives of their participants and of the project. In particular, they made meanings about what is expected of them from the more senior researchers, including their employer's expectations and of their own feelings about the interview process, the interviewees and their positioning within the research project. This process of meaning making was not decontextualised. Jackson (2001, 82) suggests that 'Those who choose to make the effort to register their responses must foresee some advantage for someone', so that a fruitful question is 'For whose benefit is it done?' As employees working for a university research team, the interviewers had to negotiate their relationships with the central team and present themselves as competent, professional interviewers.

Attenborough (2011) found that students wrote marginalia that did not reveal personal investment or 'stake' in what they are studying. This 'stake inoculation' (Potter, 1996) was frequently also evident in the qualitative paradata in our study. Interviewers frequently presented themselves as diligent, fair and not taking particular sides. Yet, it is well established that identities and worldviews are visible in narrative accounts (Andrews et al., 2013) and the analysis of the paradata in this study shows that paradata can also constitute narrative accounts. This is in keeping with Jackson's (2001) argument that 'Marginalia can be used to construct and to monitor identity'...'We hope to see signs of mental life in the annotator' (2001, 91, 210). The paradata were thus what Bamberg (2011) calls 'narratives-in-interaction', communicating more than information for coding or on the interviewees' lives. The 'small stories' told by the paradata construct the interviewers as particular kinds of professionals, evident in, for example, the genre the interviewer adopted and, cumulatively, across the interview booklets, the particular narratives they constructed.

In revealing the tensions and labour of the interviewer's work, and between responsibilities to the researcher and the researched, this historic paradata highlights ethical issues in Townsend's study that remain very relevant to contemporary researchers – including our own research, which constructs the interviewer as subject in ways they could not have imagined. The idea of 'converting' refusals – as in the second case we describe – sits uncomfortably with contemporary understandings of freely given consent in social research. But Townsend's use of 'converters' could also be seen as ethically motivated, as he was concerned to ensure that the survey included households and experiences of poverty that had not been well represented in prior research. As Maguire (2005, 6) commented, 'at the ethical core of researching [. . .] are issues of equity, inclusion and exclusion and who gets to speak after all and whose voices are heard, recognised, or silenced'.

These paradata constitute marginalia in being produced to engage with the texts and codes as well as the research team (Sherman, 2009). As such, they complement quantitative paradata and resonate with analyses of marginalia in the humanities. They allow the possibility of enhancing the accuracy of coding by giving a fuller, more holistic picture than codes alone can provide. In doing so, they sometimes allowed the coders to make different judgements about codes from the interviewers. For the narrative analyst, qualitative paradata of the kind presented here show how participants' stories are constructed through the research process, revealing more about the co-construction of interviewers, participants and analysts than can be made visible by analysing codes and themes.

NOTE

1. See http://www.poverty.ac.uk/definitions-poverty/deprivation-and-poverty [accessed 10.11.16].

REFERENCES

Andrews, M., Squire, C. and Tamboukou, M. (eds) (2013, 2nd edn) *Doing Narrative Research*. London: Sage.

Attenborough, F. (2011) '"I don't f***ing care!" Marginalia and the (textual) negotiation of an academic identity by university students', *Discourse and Communication*, 5(2), 99–121.

Bamberg, M. (2004) 'Considering counter narratives', in M. Bamberg and M. Andrews (eds), *Considering Counter Narratives: Narrating, Resisting, Making Sense* (pp. 351–371). Amsterdam: John Benjamins.

Bamberg, M. (2011) '"Who am I?" Narration and its contribution to self and identity', *Theory and Psychology*, 21(1), 3–24.

Bamberg, M. and Andrews, M. (eds) (2004) *Considering Counter Narratives: Narrating, Resisting, Making Sense*. Amsterdam: John Benjamins.

Boddy, K. (2010) *The American Short Story Since 1950*. Edinburgh: Edinburgh Press.

Elliott, H., Edwards, R., Phoenix, A. and Boddy, J. (2014) *Narrative Analysis of Paradata from the* Poverty in the UK *Survey: A Worked Example*, NCRM Working Paper: http://eprints.ncrm.ac.uk/3720/ [Accessed 23.9.16].

Jackson, H.J. (2001) *Marginalia: Readers Writing in Books*. New Haven: Yale University Press.

Maguire, M.H. (2005) '"What if you talked to me? I could be interesting!" Ethical research considerations in engaging with bilingual/multilingual child participants in human inquiry' [39 paragraphs]. *Forum Qualitative Sozialforschung/Forum: Qualitative Social Research*, 6(1), Art. 4, http://nbn-resolving.de/urn:nbn:de:0114-fqs050144 [Accessed 23.9.16].

Moor, L. and Uprichard, E. (2014) 'The materiality of method: The case of the Mass Observation Archive', *Sociological Research Online*, 19(3), 10. DOI: 10.5153/sro.3379.

Potter, J. (1996) *Representing Reality: Discourse, Rhetoric and Social Construction*. London: Sage.

Sherman, W. (2009) *Used Books: Marking Readers in Renaissance England*. Philadelphia, PA: University of Pennsylvania Press.

Tomalin, C. (1997) *Jane Austen: A Life*. London: Penguin.

Townsend, P. (1979) *Poverty in the United Kingdom: A Survey of Household Resources and Standards of Living*. London: Penguin/Allen Lane.

5. 'The house seemed to be falling in round their ears': contesting and amplifying observations of housing through qualitative survey paradata

Daniel Kilburn

This chapter explores how qualitative paradata can provide methodological and substantive insights into informants' housing situations based on an analysis of marginalia recorded by interviewers undertaking the 1967–68 Survey of Household Resources and Standards of Living in the United Kingdom, which formed the basis for Peter Townsend's (1979) *Poverty in the United Kingdom* (PinUK) study. An analysis of these paradata illuminate the process through which aspects of informants' housing situations were coded in the course of survey interviews conducted for the PinUK fieldwork. The paradata are drawn from handwritten notes or marginalia, ranging from a couple of words to several pages, which were recorded by field researchers in blank spaces of the survey booklets. These paradata show how the coding of some housing situations was subject to contestation, as revealed in areas of discord or disagreement between interviewers and informants, while in other instances interviewers amplified the codes they recorded by elaborating upon the housing conditions that were observed or recounted in the course of the survey interview.

The housing situations experienced by people in any given time and place must be understood in the context of the material and social relations associated with the production, exchange, and consumption of housing (Ball, 1986). At the time of Townsend's PinUK study, housing provision was dominated by the construction of state-funded council housing and the demolition of nineteenth-century terraces and tenements, as part of an unprecedented modernisation of the UK's housing stock (Dunleavy, 1981). Local councils were charged with allocating sought-after public housing to those on waiting lists, while those relying on the private sector for affordable housing often endured poor conditions in rented properties or lodgings. Townsend's (1979) own analysis of the PinUK data suggest that many respondents experienced housing that was overcrowded, dilapidated or lacking amenities such as indoor sanitation and heating. The act of 'dwelling' therefore comprises the ability to access and utilise a property for adequate shelter and comfort, together with the collective and individual emotions, aspirations and experiences associated with being in (or being excluded from) housing (King, 2008).

This complexity of housing as an object of study makes for a challenging empirical terrain, within which large-scale social surveys have historically constituted the dominant mode for gathering (quantitative) data on housing (Kemeny, 1984). Paradata provide us with unique insights into the process by which survey responses are collected and coded into data, through observations and reflections recorded by survey interviewers themselves (Phoenix et al., 2013). Qualitative paradata may be of particular value for research into housing, given that informants' homes often constitute the context in which interviewer-completed surveys are conducted. The marginalia recorded by the PinUK interviewers offer a range of observations and reflections on the housing situations encountered during fieldwork. Analyses of these paradata suggest that 'housing effects' arose in the course of the survey interview, which framed – and in some cases influenced – how responses were given by informants and received by interviewers. These effects can be seen in the form of contestations between the perceptions of housing situations formed by interviewers and those held by informants, and in instances where the housing conditions that were encountered or recounted during the interview were amplified within the marginalia.

By considering the contestation and amplification of survey responses as housing effects, mediated by individual, relational, and structural aspects of 'dwelling', we can elucidate some of the methodological challenges of coding data on people's housing situations. In doing so, these paradata may also provide substantive insights into housing conditions experienced by low-income households in 1960s Britain. This chapter proceeds by first considering the case for developing analyses of paradata within the context of research methods for housing studies, before presenting a worked example of an analysis of housing effects within the PinUK survey.

RESEARCH METHODS FOR HOUSING STUDIES: A CASE FOR PARADATA?

The sourcing and analysis of paradata from social research is a comparatively new methodological field (Nicolaas, 2011). As a result, to date there has been little direct engagement with paradata relating to housing, although a number of studies have included the physical housing characteristic derived from quantitative 'macro' paradata in analyses of survey response rates (Abraham et al., 2006; Durrant et al., 2013; Foster, 1997; Groves and Couper, 1998; Sinibaldi et al., 2013). The paradata derived from the PinUK survey differ significantly in terms of including 'micro' qualitative paradata. The textual detail of these paradata, coupled with their significance as a historical record of housing conditions, constitute a so far unexplored methodological and substantive resource for housing research. Studies of housing have historically formed part of efforts to systematically document living conditions, especially amongst the urban poor, that characterised the emergence of empirical social science towards the end of the nineteenth century. Early accounts of housing conditions in Britain originated from beyond the academic confines of 'housing studies' per se (such as Engels' 1950[1892] accounts of working class housing conditions, or the Mass Observations studies of the 1940s). In the post-war period, the expanding role of the state in providing mass housing precipitated the emergence of housing studies as an interdisciplinary field in its own right. A 'dominant' methodology also emerged, 'influenced by a Fabian tradition of empiricism' that privileged positivist approaches for diagnosis and prescription of housing issues (Jacobs and Manzi, 1996, 543). In this period, the questionnaire was 'without doubt the single most important instrument for sifting and collecting data in housing studies' (Kemeny, 1984, 151). Under this methodological 'veneer of pragmatism', questions of method were rarely discussed (Ball, 1988, 8).

Qualitative methods occupied a marginal position in the early history of housing studies (Jacobs and Manzi, 1996). This departure from a positivist paradigm for housing research has been widely discussed in terms of methodology and epistemology (Lawson, 2002; Jacobs and Manzi, 2000; Somerville and Bengtsson, 2002; Kemeny, 2004), However, somewhat less systematic attention has been paid to the development and operationalisation of the actual research methods used to gather and code data on housing. Methods for historical research into housing have been particularly under-explored, beyond a 'taken for granted' acceptance of the value of historical material for providing background or context for analyses of housing (Jacobs, 2001, 127). Applying a historical lens to the act of researching housing, especially in the form of quantitative social surveys that remain a dominant mode for generating large-scale empirical data on housing, offers a means by which we might explore the intersection between the substantive qualities of housing and the research methods that are used to study it.

A fundamental rationale for the analysis of paradata (whether qualitative or quantitative) therefore lies in its potential to render the research process visible. This stems from a broader argument that scientific knowledge is *produced* in ways that are contingent upon the methodological instruments used and thus is both fallible and open to critique (Pratt, 1995). Qualitative paradata derived from interviewers' observations may work in this regard to show how, and in what context, responses are formulated and communicated by informants. Through analysing these paradata, we have the potential to explore how social scientific data – in the form of responses to survey questions – might emerge from situated discourses that are 'contingent, contested and subject to considerable diversity of interpretation' (Jacobs et al., 2004, 3). As Pratt (1995, 70) concludes:

> By making the research technique more open, in fact making it part of the research, 'discoveries' from the information gleaned from both intensive and extensive survey modes can then be fed back into the theoretical understanding.

As the vast majority of large-scale social surveys take place within people's homes, exploring how information on housing emerges from these data-gathering processes may help us to arrive at a more situated and relational understanding of informants' housing experiences, taking into account the contexts in which fieldwork is carried out. We may think of these as *housing effects* on the survey interview that are recorded in interviewers' observations, details shared by informants or fragments of narrative from the interview itself.

Analyses of paradata constitute an emerging domain in which housing researchers may lay claim to the social scientific methods used to generate data on housing phenomena. While recent scholarship has considered the theory-making potential of housing studies (King, 2009), equivalent attention has yet to be paid to any similar methodological role. In this respect, there is scope for housing researchers not only to capitalise upon, but also to participate in, developments in paradata. This chapter now turns to present a worked example of the housing effects that arise in the form of contestation and amplification of housing-related codes from a historical corpus of qualitative paradata from a large-scale social survey.

HOUSING PARADATA FROM THE PINUK SURVEY

This section examines two key themes concerning housing effects that arose in the qualitative paradata recorded in a sample of 69 PinUK survey booklets that had been digitised for analysis.[1] The first theme involves the contestation of coding surrounding informants' housing situations. The second involves the amplification of coded information to give a more detailed impression of the housing conditions experienced by informants.

The analysis presented here draws on marginalia written by interviewers in the survey booklets themselves. These qualitative paradata 'provided crucial information about the basis for the field interviewers' decisions about codes' (Elliott et al., 2015, 4). A close, qualitative, analysis of these data yield methodological insights into the coding of housing characteristics, together with substantive insights into housing conditions themselves.

The PinUK Survey

Townsend's (1979) PinUK study involved an interviewer-completed questionnaire administered to a random sample of 2,052 properties, plus a further 1,541 in special areas of high deprivation, within a clustered sample of 62 parliamentary constituencies across the UK. The survey itself comprised a large printed booklet with over 150 questions, many with multiple parts, organised into nine sections. Townsend (1979, 102) describes the considerable lengths taken to maximise the accuracy and response rates in administering the survey, that were undertaken by 'some of the most highly skilled and experienced interviewers in survey work in the country'. The process itself took 12 months, with interviewers sometimes calling on multiple occasions to complete the survey, which often took several hours. In this process, Townsend (1979, cited in Elliott et al., 2015, 4) instructed interviewers to 'do all that is humanly possible to record vital information' in addition to the coded survey responses. The first section of the survey addressed 'housing and living facilities'. Respondents were asked to provide factual information about their property, such as:

> The number and type of rooms, and whether heating and electricity was available;
> Access to facilities such as a cooker, indoor toilet, sink/wash basin, shower or bath, and a garden/yard;
> The presence of items such as central heating, carpet, furniture and electrical appliances.

Respondents were also asked to provide subjective information on their housing situation, in the form of categorical responses to whether:

> The property and its outdoor space were of an appropriate size;
> The air in the neighbourhood was clean;
> The property suffered from structural defects and whether these posed a danger to the inhabitants' health.

In addition, respondents were asked if they felt themselves to have a 'serious housing problem', either in the present property or at any point in their adult residential history. Additional questions in the booklet also make reference to the provision of housing (tenure, details of rent or mortgage payments, and receipt of housing from the local authority). The paradata analysed here were generated from the process of posing and coding these various questions.

The survey booklets provided ample space for interviewers to write marginalia, together with a dedicated area at the end of the booklet for 'additional notes' (Elliott et al., 2015). These marginalia took the form of written notes, an example of which – relating to the situation of a young couple in poor-quality rented housing – is shown in Figure 5.1. Interviewers also included calculations, corrections, and various other notations in the

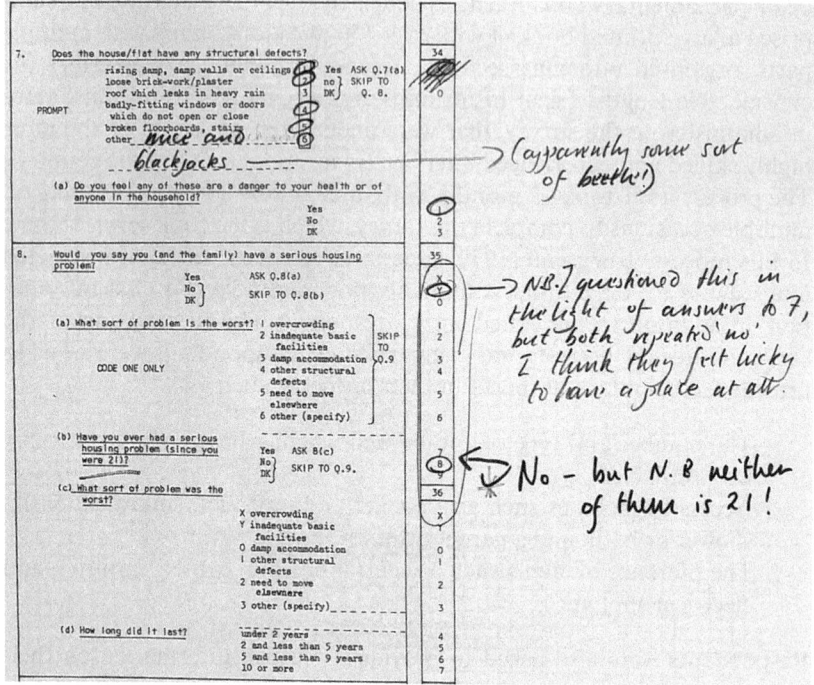

Source: Copyright Peter Townsend, 1968, accessed under public licence (CC BY-NC-SA 4.0) from the UK Data Service Qualibank archive (http://discover.ukdataservice.ac.uk/ QualiBank)

Figure 5.1   Interviewer-recorded coding and marginalia in PinUK survey booklet 6351869, in response to questions 7 ('Does the house/ flat have any structural defects?') and 8 (Would you say you have a serious housing problem?')

survey booklets, and in some cases longer memo-style notes were penned on blank pages or sheets of notepaper. Together, these constitute a sizeable corpus of qualitative paradata within the booklets that is now held at the UK Data Service archives at the University of Essex. Macro paradata on the survey process itself, such as the number of visits made and the length of the interview, were also recorded by interviewers on the call-record sheet that accompanied the survey booklet. As qualitative paradata were found in nearly half (46%) of PinUK booklets, a sample of 69 were drawn and digitised for detailed analysis (Elliott et al., 2015). These paradata provide a rich textual and graphical record of the interview process, formed through interviewers' candid observations as well as incidental traces (such as a child's fingerprint, as described by Elliott et al.) that reflect the 'dynamics of fieldwork in busy households' (Elliott et al., 2015, 8). This combined record of housing as the context and situation for the interview, the paradata generated on the housing-specific questions in the survey, and the detail provided by the survey responses themselves, constitutes a unique source of insight into research *in* and *on* housing.

Contestation

The process through which responses to the survey items were coded is rendered visible through the paradata recorded by interviewers. This includes evidence of re-coding (through crossings-out and amendments), verification (through researchers' initials and other markings), and querying (through written marginalia and separate notes). Each booklet also reveals the input of several researchers during the process of finalising the coding (through the use of different coloured inks, initials, names, or various other hieroglyphics), with some appearing to contain a 'sign off' from Townsend himself (a large capital 'P'). These paradata reveal how the process of coding people's housing situation was sometimes subject to contestation by informants, both directly and indirectly. In some cases, interviewers struggled to arrive at coding decisions based on what they had heard or observed during the course of an interview. These housing effects encountered during the interview process reflect the considerable degree of complexity and ambiguity associated with the contexts, conditions and perceptions of housing experienced in the course of the fieldwork. Coding these housing situations therefore presented challenges that had to be mediated in the course of the research. The PinUK paradata offers a rare elucidation of the contested and conflictual process through which housing-related codes were ascribed.

The main area of contestation concerned the physical condition of the housing, which formed a key theme of the housing-related sections of the survey. In particular, one question constituted a particular focus for contention – whether or not the informant(s) perceived themselves to have a 'serious housing problem' (the question itself is reproduced in Figure 5.1). In the course of the interview, this question followed those concerning the availability of facilities/amenities, the extent of overcrowding and issues regarding the physical condition of the property. The paradata here reveal how, even when seemingly major issues were reported in response to some (or even all) of these questions, some informants did not acknowledge that these constituted a 'serious housing problem'. For instance, in one case a woman in her eighties described to the interviewer how the two-bedroom terraced house in which she had raised nine children suffered from damp (booklet 6351759). The interviewer's marginalia note how the woman saw the damp as 'bad for health'. However, she did not perceive that she had a serious housing problem, asserting instead that the damp 'is not as bad as a lot in Salford'. Here, the paradata recorded by the interviewer work to rationalise the informant's perception based on the relational component of her housing experiences that were contextualised through, and compared to, her surroundings.

A set of paradata from one interview provides a particularly lucid illustration of contention over the coding of 'serious housing problems' (booklet 3630469). This interview was conducted with a young couple in their late teens, living with their infant son in a two-bedroom terraced house. Both respondents were unemployed and seeking work, with their only income from unemployment and supplementary benefits. The coded responses on the survey form indicate that this young family faced a range of housing issues. The house, which was rented from the male respondent's former employer, had no indoor toilet, shower or bath, no central heating (with only one room being heated by a fire or stove), and was 'condemned' for demolition. The informants reported that the house suffered from structural defects including damp, loose brickwork/plaster, badly fitting windows or doors, broken floorboards and mice and beetle infestations.

However, this young couple rejected the notion that they had a serious housing problem. The marginalia reproduced in Figure 5.1 reveal how the interviewer queried this response:

> NB. I questioned this in light of answers to 7 [a categorical question on the presence of structural defects], but both repeated 'no'. I think they felt lucky to have a place at all.

In this case, the perception of a serious housing problem appeared to have been directly contested in a dialogue between the interviewer and the informant(s). Here, the interviewer provides her own explanation for the young couple's response, inferring that they felt 'lucky to have a place at all'. Again, this suggests how informants' perceptions of housing situations take a relational view of questions posed by the survey, based on their particular circumstances, while the interviewers, following coding guidelines, are seeking responses that fit more absolutist and closed categories.

A number of respondents also rejected the contention that they were experiencing serious housing problems in the form of overcrowding. This revealed a different set of relational housing effects surrounding household composition, family configurations, life-stages and support structures, as well as past experiences. In one such case (booklet 4193192), a married couple in their twenties and their infant son were living with parents in a three-bedroom terraced house. Here, despite appearing to have a sufficient number of bedrooms to accommodate each couple and the child, the paradata indicate that the interviewer felt this situation could be perceived as overcrowding:

> Informant [the mother] obviously enjoyed having daughter and family living with her. Some might consider them overcrowded, but she did not.

In this instance, the interviewer clearly felt inclined to record the informant's 'enjoyment' of co-habiting with her daughter's family, in relation to a situation 'some' might perceive as overcrowded. The following paradata entry (booklet 5262061) again relates to the coding of a serious housing problem involving overcrowding:

> Informant's answer to this is NO, but in fact she and her family had serious problems for about ten years. Informant and her four children were bombed out of their house during the War and rehoused by council in a flat with only one bedroom. They lived in flat for ten years – until family consisted of six children and two parents, although for part of this time at least, two of the children were living with a grandparent.

This detailed elaboration of the household's residential history appears as a means of contesting the informant's response. The 'facts' of the large and growing family, housed in an inadequately sized flat, are perhaps recorded here with a view towards future re-coding in the office (although there was no evidence that this occurred). Although the reason for the informant rejecting the contention that this situation constituted a 'serious problem' is not elaborated in the paradata, this example illustrates how 'first-order' concepts that are used to construct widely acknowledged norms in relation to housing – such as the accommodation of nuclear families within a contiguous 'household' – are used to frame the presence of 'problems' such as overcrowding (Kemeny, 1984, 152).

These paradata are revealing of a dissonance between the perceptions of the researchers and those of informants regarding their housing situation. Residents' experiences are shown here to be subject to what Lawson (2006, 28) terms the 'contingent conditions' surrounding experiences of housing. These contingencies may reflect individual, contextual or structural factors that, together, may shape relational perceptions of housing and, in doing so, form areas of discord between the questions and codes ascribed in the survey instrument and informants' responses. In some instances, contestation over the coding of housing situations arose from the subjective position of the informant and that of the interviewer themselves (based on what the latter had witnessed or been told during the interview), with the paradata ascribing what the interviewers felt to be a more accurate, factual or true reflection of the situation at hand. In one particularly revealing example (booklet 6292293), the marginalia record how an elderly woman responded to having 'no difficulty' in undertaking 'heavy housework', although the interviewer observed 'it <u>must</u> be 20 years since anyone did any type of housework in <u>this house</u>'.

These contrasts between the relational positions held by interviewers and by their informants that arise from the process of coding survey responses raises deeper questions over who has the right to generate housing *knowledge* (or social scientific knowledge more broadly). This is especially pertinent given the historical context of housing as a site for the monitoring and surveillance of residents' conduct (Damer, 2000). In this context, the use of paradata to elucidate the contested nature of the research process supports the methodological argument that studies of housing must 'acknowledge both the importance of "subjectivity" and how the act of research entails [. . .] pre-conceived idealisations' with regard to housing concepts or problems (Jacobs and Manzi, 2000, 36).

Amplification

Within their emerging typology of qualitative paradata, Phoenix et al. (2013, 4) identify another category of paradata in the form of the 'amplification of codes to capture the complexity of the data'. These paradata constitute efforts made by survey interviewers to record additional information regarding the coding decision they reached, typically in the form of marginalia or notes included elsewhere in the survey booklet. Codes may be amplified based on interviewer observations, accounts provided by informants or a combination of the two. In some cases, the amplification appears to have been made for the benefit of the survey process (for instance, to justify the code assigned). In other cases, the amplification paradata conveyed a sense that the interviewers felt compelled to offer some substantive elaboration or elucidation of the housing situations or conditions they encountered (beyond what was strictly necessary for coding decisions).

The physical condition of informants' properties constituted the greatest focus for amplification within the corpus of PinUK paradata. A stark illustration is provided by one particular interview (booklet 6292293) with a woman of 81 who lived alone in the same privately rented house in which she had been born, having been widowed at 35. The property had two bedrooms, two living/dining rooms, and a small kitchen. It was equipped with a toilet and washbasin, but did not have a bath/shower, cooker or central heating. The informant reported that the house suffered from damp, loose brickwork/plaster, a leaking roof, badly fitting doors/windows, and broken floorboards and that the air in the neighbourhood was always dirty, smoky or foul-smelling. The woman's sole income was a state pension.

A series of marginalia notes recorded in the course of this interview clearly convey the interviewer's sentiment that the coding alone could not capture the full picture of the woman's housing situation:

> The description of 'detached house' does not really give any kind of picture of this property, although perhaps the rent of [seven shillings and eight-pence[2]] does!! It stands alone in this street, backing onto a yard owned by Timber Merchants and is in a fearful state of disrepair.

Despite coding the presence of the property's physical defects in the survey booklet, the interviewer also stresses how this housing situation was 'very difficult to code to give the correct impression'. Instead, the interviewer describes the property's situation and refers to the rent as a means of contextualising and amplifying the coded responses. These marginalia are augmented by a number of briefer notes, such as on how the informant 'sleeps in parlour – very cold and damp upstairs'. However, the interviewer also recorded how:

> This old lady has lived here 81 years (all her life) and her parents about 25 years. Despite its appalling condition she does not want to move.

Here, the amplification extends beyond the physical condition and material circumstances of the housing, to elucidate something of the relational component of the informant's living situation. This amplification thus works to rationalise the coding entries while also elaborating upon aspects arising from the interview that could not be captured or conveyed by the survey instrument.

Interviewers' amplifications were not confined to material housing conditions. Some also addressed the provision of housing itself, especially in terms of large-scale 'slum clearance' demolitions and the removal of tenants to new council housing that was being built around the time of the PinUK study (Dunleavy, 1981). These amplifications emphasised the vulnerability to change of some respondents' council tenancies that would not be captured by the codes for the duration, or the duration of past and present housing tenures, for instance (booklet 5262323):

> [Informant] lived in privately owned flat. It was taken over by council and she was council tenant there for 15 years before demolition of area began. She was then moved to council <u>built</u> flat and has lived there for about 9 years.

Another paradata entry (booklet 6351239) describes a tenant who had recently been rehoused in a modern council flat, having waited 21 years on the 'housing list'. The interviewer recorded how, during this time, the inform-ant was living in a property in which he 'felt like an animal'. As Ball (1986, 147) argues 'it is important to place analysis in the context of the social rela-tions associated with the delivery and reproduction of housing as a useful physical entity'. These amplifications on housing provision show the poten-tial of paradata to contextualise housing within social relations and to extend analyses beyond the sort of 'subject-fixated' approach that, as Kemeny (1991, 13) warns, risks abstracting housing out of broader social relations.

A closer examination of marginalia recorded in the PinUK survey booklets reveals the processes by which informants' responses were ampli-fied within the paradata. Figure 5.2 shows two sets of marginalia recorded during the course of one interview with a family facing multiple housing problems (booklet 6351869). In what appears to be the first set of margina-lia recorded, within the right-hand margin of the survey booklet, the inter-view makes a series of very brief notes. It is reasonable to deduce that these were recorded in haste during the interview conversation itself. A second set of marginalia are then recorded in the left-hand margin, in which the interviewer appears to have developed upon the points they noted down opposite, perhaps after the conclusion of the interview itself. The accom-panying transcript reproduced as Figure 5.2 provides a clearer picture of how these marginalia were recorded as abridged notes, before being formu-lated into fuller prose. In addition to providing a worked example of the original presentation and subsequent transcription of these marginalia, Figure 5.2 offers a rare glimpse into the processes through which ampli-fications were crystallised into qualitative paradata in the course of the interview. In this case, it appears that the interviewer went to some lengths to formulate a clear amplification of the coding recorded in order to com-municate the 'deplorable housing conditions' experienced by this family to those who may subsequently review and analyse the survey booklet.

These amplifications of housing-related codes in the PinUK paradata provide an insight into the methodological challenges involved in condens-ing housing situations into coded survey responses. Paradata that constitute

Page 1a:

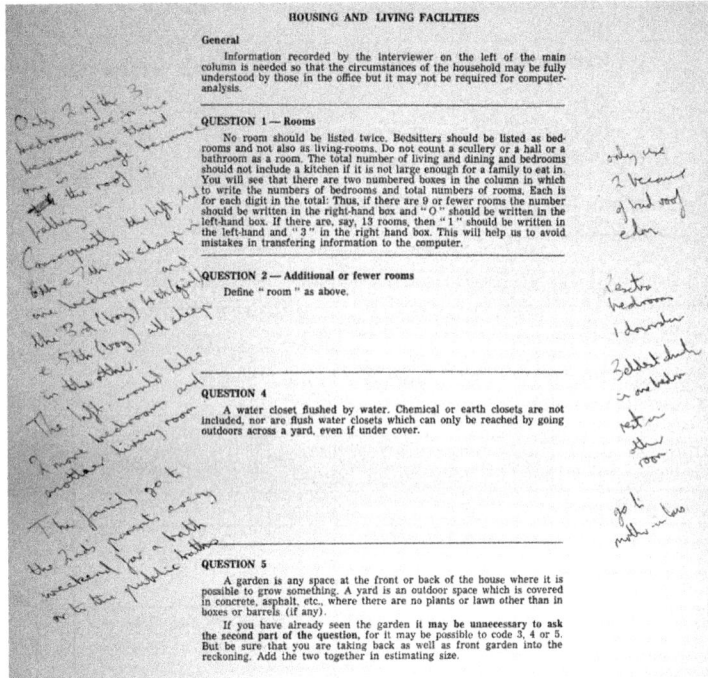

Page 2a:

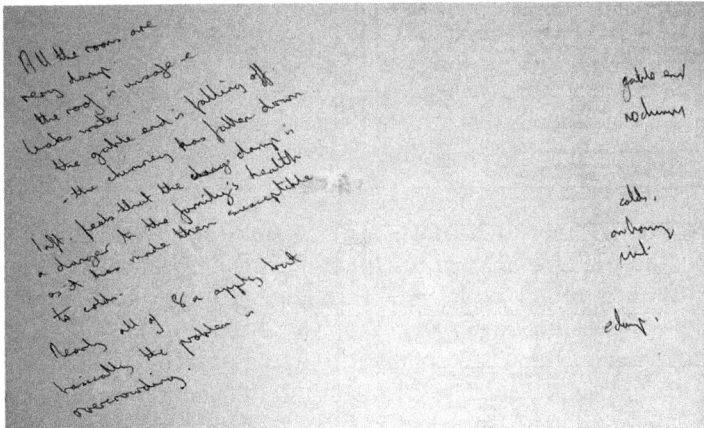

*Figure 5.2   Amplification in the marginalia of booklet 6351869, scanned
original (above) and transcript (below)*

Figure 5.2   (cont.)

Transcript of Page 1a:

Detailed marginalia (left)	**Abridged marginalia (right)**
Only 2 of the 3 bedrooms are in use because the third one is unsafe because the roof is falling in.	only use 2 because of bad roof [unclear, may be '& damp']
Consequently, inft [informant], 2nd [her husband], 6th [daughter, 5–9] & 7th [son, 5–9] all sleep in one bedroom and the 3rd (boy) [son, 15–19], 4th (girl) [daughter, 15–19] and 5th (boy) [son, 10–14] all sleep in the other.	rest of bedrooms 1 downstairs 3 eldest child in one bedroom
The inft.[informant] would like 2 more bedrooms and another living room	rest in other room
The family go to the 2nds [husband's] parents every weekend for a bath or to the public baths	go to mother-in-law

Transcript of Page 2a:

Detailed marginalia (left)	**Abridged marginalia (right)**
All the rooms are very damp.	
The roof is unsafe and leaks water.	gable end no chimney
The gable end is falling off – the chimney has fallen down.	
Inft. [informant] feels that the damp is a danger to the family's health as it has made them susceptible to colds.	cold. on housing list
Nearly all of 8a [codes for structural defects in response to the question 'what sort of problem is the worst'] apply but basically the problem is overcrowding.	& damp

---

amplification, rather than contestation, of informants' survey responses work to illustrate the housing conditions encountered by interviewers and to justify their coding decisions. The nature of these paradata reinforce concerns over the inadequacies of applying fixed, preceded categories to housing situations that are complex and contingent in reality (Kemeny, 1984, 1988; Allen, 2009). They also attest to the importance of relational, emotional, or affective aspects of shaping residents' experiences of dwelling in housing (King, 2008). At the same time, contingencies surrounding broader structures of housing provision are also acknowledged in interviewers' amplifications (Ball, 1988), which in turn reflect how respondents were positioned with the social relations associated with the production, allocation and consumption of housing at the time. For instance, these paradata illustrate the realities of years (or in some cases decades) spent in difficult housing conditions while on council housing waiting lists, even at the zenith of mass social housing provision in the 1960s.

CONCLUSION

This analysis has illustrated the potential of qualitative paradata to offer new methodological insights into the process of gathering and coding survey data on housing, and into the conduct of large-scale social survey research more broadly. Qualitative paradata drawn from marginalia recorded by the PinUK researchers reveal two housing effects that arose during the course of the survey interviews. First, contestations over coding arose when interviewers' perceptions of informants' housing situations did not correspond to the responses given by the informants themselves. In line with the methodological rigour and transparency involved in Townsend's research design, there is no indication that codes were changed as a result of these contestations. Instead, the paradata indicate relational tensions between the perceptions held by informants and those being formulated by interviewers, that in turn illustrate the potential de-correspondence between 'objective' social scientific observations and the contingent nature of individual attitudes or experiences (Allen, 2009; Flint, 2011). Second, the amplification of coded survey responses arose when the interviewers felt the need to elaborate upon the housing conditions that they encountered, or that their informants recounted, during the course of the interview. These amplifications illustrate the potential inadequacies of coded survey response as a means of capturing the complex inter-relationship between the material components of housing, underlying structures of housing provision, and relational experiences of dwelling.

Qualitative paradata can reveal the socially constructed nature of survey data by elucidating how coded responses emerge from the social interaction of the interview. These data provide new evidence of the effect of housing as a context for survey interviewing and as an object of study, the categorisation of which may belie the relational nature of residents' housing experiences or perceptions. Some aspects of the effect of housing upon the survey interview stemmed from researchers' own observations, while others stemmed from the responses communicated by informants. Together, the contestation and amplification of survey responses arising from these effects highlight the limitations inherent to the taxonomic nature of survey research in housing studies (Kemeny, 1984). The wealth of potential data available also provides both a strong rationale and a source of opportunity for continuing the project of identifying, disseminating and analysing qualitative paradata on housing. These data hold considerable potential to ground methodological and epistemological concerns through empirical analyses of the process by which survey responses are formulated from a social interaction between the interviewer and informant, which often takes place in the context of people's homes. These insights may help to provide rich and contextualised substantive observations, as well as advancing methodological reflections on the production of social scientific knowledge. This suggests a fruitful terrain for the future use of paradata in research, both within and beyond the domain of housing studies.

NOTES

1. These were sourced and digitised for the UK National Centre for Research Methods' *Possibilities for a Narrative Analysis of Paradata* project.
2. This reference to pre-decimal currencies is also indicative of how historically situated knowledge ascribed in these paradata would have been taken for granted by researchers at the time.

REFERENCES:

Abraham, K. G., A. Maitland, and S. M. Bianchi. 2006. 'Nonresponse in the American Time Use Survey: Who Is Missing from the Data and How Much Does It Matter?' *Public Opinion Quarterly* 70 (5): 676–703. doi: 10.1093/poq/nfl037.

Allen, C. 2009. 'The Fallacy of "Housing Studies": Philosophical Problems of Knowledge and Understanding in Housing Research'. *Housing, Theory and Society* 26 (1): 53–79.

Ball, M. 1986. 'Housing Analysis: Time for a Theoretical Refocus?' *Housing Studies* 1 (3): 147–66.

Ball, M. 1988. 'Housing Provision and Comparative Housing Research'. In *Housing and Social Change in Europe and the USA*, edited by M. Ball, M. Harloe and M. Martens, 7–40. London and New York: Routledge.

Damer, S. 2000. '"Engineers of the Human Machine": The Social Practice of Council Housing Management in Glasgow, 1895–1939'. *Urban Studies* 37 (11): 1895–939.

Dunleavy, P. 1981. *The Politics of Mass Housing in Britain, 1945–1975: A Study of Corporate Power and Professional Influence in the Welfare State*. Oxford: Clarendon.

Durrant, G. B., J. D'Arrigo, and F. Steele. 2013. 'Analysing Interviewer Call Record Data by Using a Multilevel Discrete Time Event History Modelling Approach'. *Journal of the Royal Statistical Society: Series A (Statistics in Society)* 176 (1): 251–69. doi: 10.1111/j.1467-985X.2012.01073.x.

Elliott, H., R. Edwards, A. Phoenix, and J. Boddy. 2015. *Narrative Analysis of Paradata from the* Poverty in the UK *Survey: A Worked Example*. NCRM Working Paper: National Centre for Research Methods.

Engels, F. 1950[1892]. *The Condition of the Working Class in England in 1844*. London: G. Allen and Unwin.

Flint, J. 2011. 'Housing Studies, Social Class and Being Towards Dwelling'. *Housing, Theory and Society* 28 (1): 75–91. doi: 10.1080/14036096.2010.511884.

Foster, K. 1997. 'The Effect of Call Patterns on Non-response Bias in Household Surveys'. *Survey Methodology Bulletin* 41: 37–47.

Groves, R. M., and M. P. Couper. 1998. *Nonresponse in Household Interview Surveys*. New York: Wiley.

Jacobs, K. 2001. 'Historical Perspectives and Methodologies: Their Relevance for Housing Studies?' *Housing, Theory and Society* 18 (3–4): 127–35. doi: 10.1080/14036090152770492.

Jacobs, K., and T. Manzi. 1996. 'Discourse and Policy Change: The Significance of Language for Housing Research'. *Housing Studies* 11 (4): 543–60. doi: 10.1080/02673039608720874.

Jacobs, K., and T. Manzi. 2000. 'Evaluating the Social Constructionist Paradigm in Housing Research'. *Housing, Theory and Society* 17 (1): 35–42.

Jacobs, K., J. Kemeny, and T. Manzi. 2004. *Social Constructionism in Housing Research*. Aldershot: Ashgate.

Kemeny, J. 1984. 'The Social Construction of Housing Facts'. *Scandinavian Housing and Planning Research* 1 (3): 149–64. doi: 10.1080/02815738408730045.

Kemeny, J. 1988. 'Defining Housing Reality: Ideological Hegemony and Power in Housing Research'. *Housing Studies* 3 (4): 205–18.

Kemeny, J. 1991. *Housing and Social Theory*. London: Routledge.

Kemeny, J. 2004. 'Extending Constructionist Social Problems to the Study of Housing Problems'. In *Social Constructionism in Housing Research*, edited by K. Jacobs, J. Kemeny and T. Manzi, 49–70. Aldershot; Burlington: Ashgate Ltd.

King, P. 2008. *In Dwelling: Implacability, Exclusion and Acceptance*. Aldershot; Burlington: Ashgate Ltd.

King, P. 2009. 'Using Theory or Making Theory: Can there be Theories of Housing?' *Housing, Theory and Society* 26 (1): 41–52.

Lawson, J. M. 2002. 'Thin Rationality, Weak Social Constructionism and Critical Realism: The Way Forward in Housing Theory?' *Housing, Theory and Society* 19 (3): 142–4.

Lawson, J. M. 2006. *Critical Realism and Housing Research, Critical Realism: Interventions*. London: Routledge.

Nicolaas, G. 2011. *Survey Paradata: A Review*. NCRM working paper. National Centre for Research Methods.

Phoenix, A., J. Boddy, H. Elliott, and R. Edwards. 2013. *MethodsNews Winter 2012*. Newsletter from the ESRC National Centre for Research Methods.

Pratt, A. 1995. 'Putting Critical Realism to Work: The Practical Implications for Geographical Research'. *Progress in Human Geography* 19 (1): 61–74.

Sinibaldi, J., G. B. Durrant, and F. Kreuter. 2013. 'Evaluating the Measurement Error of Interviewer Observed Paradata'. *Public Opinion Quarterly* 77 (S1): 173–93. doi: 10.1093/poq/nfs062.

Somerville, P., and B. Bengtsson. 2002. 'Constructionism, Realism and Housing Theory'. *Housing, Theory and Society* 19 (3–4): 121–36. doi: 10.1080/14036090232112789.

Townsend, P. 1979. *Poverty in the United Kingdom*. London: Allen Lane and Penguin Books.

6. The secondary analysis of fieldnotes, marginalia and paradata from past studies of young people

Henrietta O'Connor and John Goodwin

INTRODUCTION: OUR STARTING POINTS

The value of textual additions to documents in the form of marginalia and annotations has long been recognised by arts and humanities scholars yet in social science the significance of such by-products, which are also created in social research, has gone largely unnoticed. In our own restudies of past empirical research we have come to rely very heavily on the materials created around, and at the margins of, the substantive areas of enquiry. Indeed, we have relied on such materials to help us to reconstruct the histories of these past projects and the intricate web of relations between those involved in the research design, the fieldwork and so forth (see, for example, Goodwin and O'Connor, 2006a, 2009). However, while we have outlined the benefits of (re)using such substantive data and the need for researchers to return to existing studies, accessing and using supporting materials where they exist (see O'Connor and Goodwin, 2010, 2012, 2013; Goodwin and O'Connor, 2006), we also need to acknowledge that for us the initial fascination of the restudies was *not* the substantive data contained in the past interview schedules per se but, instead, the materials that existed around the actual research. We were directly drawn to the fieldnotes, the correspondence and letters, the grant applications, the researcher notebooks, the photographs and the wealth of other ephemera these past researchers created. When we were confronted with these data, we became like the proverbial 'children in a sweetshop' – not knowing where to begin, we dived straight in to analysing these materials precisely because they held the most fascination and held our attention.

These were the materials produced by the actual researchers themselves and the mere act of handling them, as the original research teams had once done, proved irresistible. However, in our haste to engage directly with these materials we did not spend a significant amount of time thinking about how we needed to define what we were doing or design a typology and categorise our approach. Our starting point was not with technical definitions of the data or method and we did not create a hierarchy of data privileging one form or type of data or material over another. Instead, we focused on what these materials could tell us, what they had to offer as 'data' in terms of insights to aid our understanding. So, we would define fieldnotes, marginalia and paradata quite broadly in how we have used these items in our own research practice. For us it was/ remains all those materials collected as part of supporting, or in addition to, the research process; annotations, augmentations revealed through the analysis of original documents, by-products, non-standard data, ephemera, letters, pictures and notes. In short, we viewed everything that had been collected as a potential source of data suitable for secondary analysis.

In this chapter, we will use examples from our research, especially three historical studies of youth employment from the 1960s and 1980s and our research on Pearl Jephcott, to illustrate the importance of these 'by-products' of social research for the social science researcher. We begin by briefly outlining the restudies from which the fieldnotes, marginalia and paradata derive.

THE RESEARCH CONTEXT: YOUTH EMPLOYMENT RESTUDIES 1960–1985

For the last 15 or so years we have been engaged in various restudies relating to work on youth, work, employment and community undertaken by past sociologists, mainly in Leicester, between the early 1960s and the mid-1980s. This research journey, and our interest in reusing and repurposing data from past projects, began with the rediscovery in an attic office of hundreds of interview booklets that were from a project led by Norbert Elias at the University of Leicester in the 1960s – *Adjustment of Young Workers to Work Situations and Adult Roles* project. The interview schedules were focused on the adjustment that young people made when they moved from school to work. However, the interview schedules offered more than this as they captured the reality of everyday life for this group of young people in 1960s Leicester.

In 1999, we undertook a project to do two things: one, analyse the data contained within the 1960s schedules and two, trace the original respondents and re-interview them 40 years later,[1] thereby creating a longitudinal study from a once cross-sectional section of young people. The success of this research led us to repurpose the interview schedules from two further legacy studies of youth transitions from education to work conducted in the 1980s – *Young Adults in the Labour Market* (1986) and *The Changing Structure of Youth Labour Markets* (1987) – for the project '*The making of the "precariat": unemployment, insecurity and work-poor young adults in harsh economic conditions*'. All of the original interview schedules from these two projects had been stored in an external storage room at the University of Leicester. As well as this, we have explored research and researchers that have been allied to these projects such as the two key figures in the development of British sociology during the 1950s and 1960s, namely Ilya Neustadt, Head of the Department of Sociology at Leicester, and Norbert Elias, the renowned sociologist (see Goodwin and Hughes, 2011) and the innovative sociological researcher Pearl Jephcott whose work we came across by chance during our archival research (see Goodwin and O'Connor, 2015; Goodwin, 2015).

FIELDNOTES, MARGINALIA AND PARADATA

Fieldnotes from the 1960s

The Young Worker Project was an ambitious and large-scale research project funded by a significant external research grant and, as such, was a well-organised project: the team kept meticulous notes in the form of letters, meeting minutes and project plans. Access to these specific by-products of the research process has enabled us to reconstruct the evolution of the project and to understand how and why the team made certain decisions. These documents reveal, for example, that Elias, as project lead, had significant input into the design of the interview schedule. One of the additions he requested was a closing section in which fieldworkers were asked to note their reflections on the interview process and to capture insights that may have been missed in the formal part of the interview. In this fascinating endnote to the interviews, entitled 'Interview Notes', the researchers were asked to answer specific questions relating to the experience of the interview (the respondent's demeanour, the interview atmosphere, the home environment, willingness to be re-interviewed and overall general impressions). These were handwritten by the fieldworkers at the end of each interview and were often lengthy, detailed descriptions, very evocative of the period. It is this section to which we first turned our attention as it is here, in what is little more than a footnote to the formal interviews, that the most telling details of the lives of this group of 1960s teenagers are revealed. Although these notes did not constitute a formal part of the interview encounter, and effectively became 'by-products' of

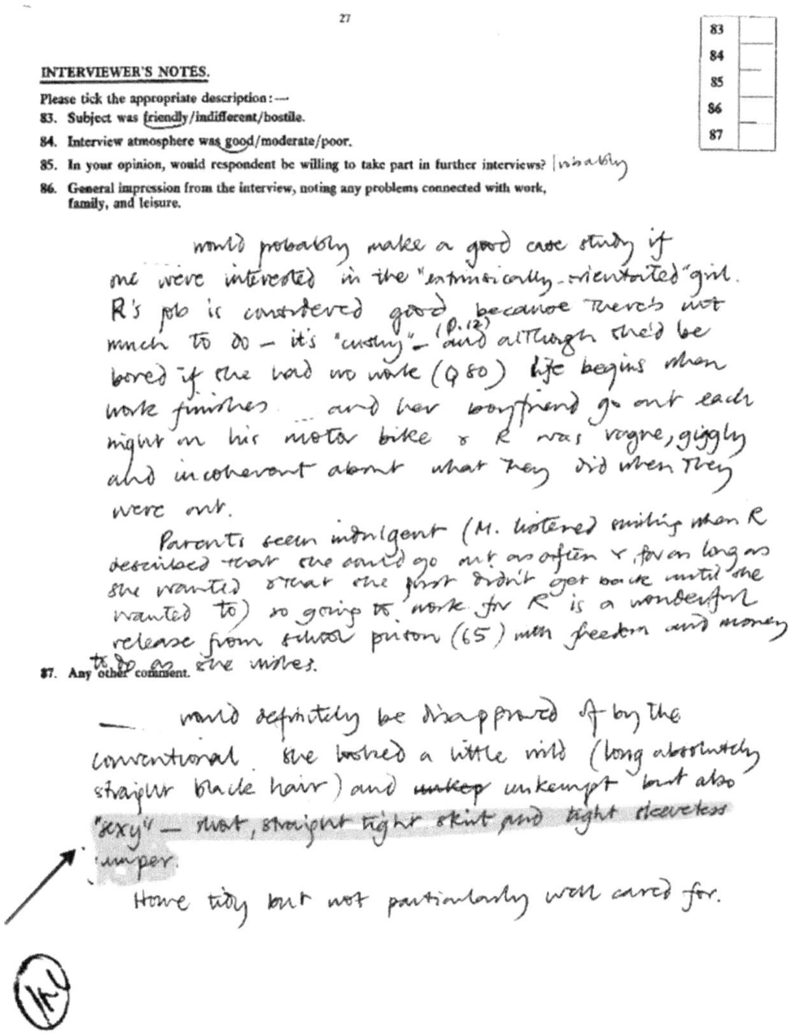

Figure 6.1   Interview notes example 1 – young worker project 1962–1964

the research process, it is the data generated here that proved to be invaluable in understanding the complexities of each life history.

In Figure 6.1 we have provided an example of the type of details noted by the fieldworkers in this additional section of the schedule. In this example the interviewer has signalled to the intended reader (the research team and the principal investigator) that the respondent would 'make a good case study' (something Elias had asked interviewers to make a note of). She (we know the identity of this interviewer through her handwriting) goes on to explain the reasons for this viewpoint, providing links to responses to specific interview questions. This is followed by a description of the respondent's demeanour, an observation about the parents, who 'seem indulgent' and the girl's attitude to work. The last section of the notes is taken up with a vivid description of her appearance and the domestic environment. The comments, while not particularly derogatory in this case, are written in a slightly judgemental tone, for example: 'house tidy but not particularly well cared for' and 'would definitely be disapproved of by the conventional'. The focus of the description on the respondent's appearance is remarkably redolent of the 1960s – 'she looked a little wild (long absolutely straight black hair) and unkempt but also "sexy" – short, straight tight skirt and tight sleeveless jumper' (annotations on the original schedule have been added by us to highlight specific comments). However, in many cases the candid accounts of interviewers' observations raise ethical issues for present-day researchers operating under very different codes of researcher conduct (see Gillies and Edwards (2012) for a more detailed discussion of research conventions and ethics).

Elias's interest in exploring the 'shock hypothesis' (Elias, 1962) and the experience of the transition of young people into employment is reflected in the guidance provided to the fieldworkers to record, in particular, any 'problems connected with work, family and leisure'. His intention here was for the team to note any evidence of what he considered to be 'sociological problems' related to the transition from childhood to adulthood and the changing relationships with others (such as parents and work colleagues). However, the researchers who were working in the field understood this focus on 'problems' to refer more to social problems per se. Therefore, the researchers tended to provide much more detailed notes on the perceived social problems of the respondents and their families rather than the adjustment of young people to the adult world. This tendency, as Savage (2005) has noted, harks back to a time when fieldworkers viewed their role as close to that of social workers and often made moral judgements on the households and families they encountered. The post-war period had seen growing policy concerns with 'problem families' (Innes and McKie, 2006) and the focus of the interviewers was very much in keeping with the contemporaneous social research practices that reflected these concerns. Indeed, in one case the fieldworker notes that the respondent's family was 'known to social services', and a friend of the interviewer, who was a social worker, had explained the problems of the family in some detail before the interview took place. Sharing such information would now clearly be considered a serious breach of client confidentiality.

Other researchers who have revisited classic studies have unearthed comments of a similar nature and Phoenix et al. (Chapter 4, this volume) provide rich examples of this type of commentary. It is easy, however, for secondary analysts to become perhaps overly judgemental of the behaviours of past researchers and to judge their actions by contemporary standards and conventions. Evans and Thane (2006), for example, revisited the interviewer notes collected during the fieldwork for Marsden's (1969) study of lone mothers and argue that Marsden, as the interviewer, perceived his role as something of a moral 'crusader' and that the respondents themselves viewed him with suspicion, suspecting that he was somehow associated with the 'authorities' and may have intended to report undesirable behaviours. However, Gillies and Edwards (2012) make the valid point that at the time the research was carried out the observations made by Marsden were intended to be objective rather than moralistic and to uncover poverty and highlight the challenges that this group of mothers faced during this period.

Suspicion of the research team, as reported by Marsden (1969) is not uncommon in accounts of fieldwork and we also came across notes suggesting interviewers were sometimes treated with hostility. In one example the notes describe a subject as acting 'indifferent or hostile' towards the interview, and the resulting interview atmosphere as poor, however:

> It turned out that, in this case, the respondent, I gathered, the boy is in trouble with the police and was very anxious to get away from me to go with his friends to Charles Street Police Station.

There was, then, some suspicion of the research team, but in this case it was due to the respondent's underlying anxiety about an appointment with the police for a reason unknown to the team.

Another aspect of the respondents' lives that attracted a great deal of attention from the interviewers was the home environment. Whereas in the case highlighted in Figure 6.1 the focus was the respondent herself, other accounts gave more prominence to the domestic environment and family life. Graphic descriptions of living conditions in 1960s 'slum dwellings', many of which had already been condemned, were a common feature of the notes and resonate with photographs that are frequently used to depict the domestic conditions of the period (see, for example, the work of photographer Shirley Baker[2]):

> The boy, to use his own phrase, was rather miserable-faced but friendly. He lived in one of the decrepit slum dwellings. The front room was filthy, dirty, smelt, and the wallpaper was peeling off. There was no carpet, very little furniture,

apart from a large TV set. The children were filthy dirty but the mother was very pleasant.

The influence of family on school-to-work transitions was a key concern of the research team and in order to capture data on this a detailed question on household composition was asked. Although this captured traditional family formations, and the wording would seem to have been designed to encourage the interviewers to explore different household relationships, it appears from the data itself that the more complex arrangements were often not noted during the interview. Instead detailed observations on the composition of the families were included in the notes. Hence, in a number of cases we find that the interviewer has added details in the margins of the interview booklet or in their final reflections that the interview schedule did not capture. For example:

> The boy seemed to imply that he had two fathers and it seems probably that one of them has left home and the other moved in, a rather sad case of a boy with a poor home surrounding who had experienced being out of work himself and had seen his father unemployed.

Where such comments were made in the margins these were cross-checked with the data collected in the formal part of the interview. In a number of cases this additional information gave a much greater insight to the existence of non-traditional family formations amongst the sample. In one example the interview data records the eldest female in the household as the respondent's mother, however, a closer examination of the ages of each inhabitant of the household reveals that this woman was only ten years older than the respondent. It is from the interviewer notes, rather than the interview, that we discover the true nature of the relationships within this household and find that the woman listed as the mother is not related to the respondent but is a woman who has moved in with the respondent's father. This important detail was not recorded during the interview, suggesting either that the interviewer assumed the relationship at that point or, when, writing up the notes after the interview, made a note about the possible nature of the relationships. Alternatively, this information may not have been disclosed until the end of the formal interview.

The lack of detail surrounding what were evidently complex and often diverse family formations reflects both the social and sociological concerns of the time, for example that the individual performing the social role of a parent was considered to be the mother or father and the biological relationship was not prioritised. It is therefore not surprising that where there was any doubt in the interviewer's mind about the relationships in each family this was rarely noted in the interview itself but included as an observation in the notes. Indeed, it was not until the publication of Burgoyne and Clark's (1984) study of step-families, some 20 years later, that sociologists and policymakers began to explore non-traditional family formation in more detail. Until then, atypical families such as step-families appeared 'to represent a reconstituted form of the so-called natural nuclear family' (Allan et al., 2011, 27) and this is reflected in the data collected.

Often however, although the interviewer evidently understood that particular respondents lived in complex families it was rare for this to be explored during the interview. The interviewer would make assumptions and guess at relationships within the household and make notes recording this but not ask direct questions of those present. This leads us to wonder whether such areas of questioning were considered taboo in the 1960s, or whether the interviewers felt that probing for further information on the household fell outside the remit of the interview purpose. Nonetheless we do invariably find comments relating to non-traditional families, particularly absent parents, for example:

> The mother had clearly died but no one wanted to talk about it.

The explanation of the absence of the respondent's mother and the lack of communication about this from the respondent is based solely on the interviewer's supposition and it was rare for us to find anything more than a note in the margin about such circumstances. The mother's death is not formally recorded in the interview and the respondent does not appear to have offered any explanation as to her absence. Revisiting the data we have no way of knowing the precise reason for the mother's absence or the apparent lack of discussion of this. We could equally suppose that the mother had simply moved out of the family home, perhaps in difficult circumstances or that she was simply not included in the answer to the main question on family structure. Having access to the interviewer notes gives us more information than we would have had without this kind of very rich contextual data. This has enabled us to then question some of the assumptions that would otherwise have arisen from the data. So, for example, a careful interrogation of the interviewer notes has enabled us to explore in more depth the existence of not only fatherless families but also motherless families, which were more prevalent than a simple, purely quantitative analysis would have uncovered. It also begins to provide an insight to 1960s research practices and contrasts these with present-day survey data and interviewing techniques. A good example of this is the family structure question. The question itself and the way that the interviewer tackled this question – even when clearly faced with complex family structures – reflects what were perhaps assumptions of the time that respondents would live in normative family set-ups or that questioning living arrangements was not permissible. Current research practice would inevitably reflect the far more complex living arrangements in which many young people find themselves (e.g. step-families, blended families and so on) whereas this data suggests that the extent of diversity was almost certainly not fully recorded in the past.

Another complicated family set-up only came to light when the team of secondary analysts re-interviewed respondents 40 years after the original interviews took place. We have discussed this case at length elsewhere (O'Connor and Goodwin, 2013) but it is worth recounting here. The description of the respondent's home environment and his mother's apparent detachment is amongst the most dismal and heart-wrenching that we encountered in our reanalysis:

> This was quite the most squalid home I have been in for years. The whole place was dingy and filthy. I sat in the living room to do the interview, I rather suspect it was the only habitable room downstairs. Respondent's mother sat watching whatever happened to appear on ITV during the time I was there and the only heating was from a paraffin stove.

Some 40 years later, on re-interviewing the respondent, we discovered that the woman recorded as his mother was his father's first wife who had returned to live with them when the respondent's mother – who had never married the respondent's father – had died.

MARGINALIA AND PARADATA: DATA FROM THE 1980S

The research practices of the 1960s, then, seemed to have been rooted firmly in the anthropological, ethnographic practice of the period. The marginalia, gleaned from the 1960s research that proved so valuable in our reanalysis, consisted of detailed 'thick' descriptions of respondents' 'real lives', adding rich detail to the interview data. We came to rely heavily on the fieldnotes that we were fortunate enough to have access to as these notes provided the context for so much of the 'official data'. Yet we recognised that the marginalia and fieldnotes reflected the sociological practice of the period and were not written in the 'self-critical, self-conscious and self-reflective' (Fine, 1993, 268) style that has become standard practice in the intervening period. Nonetheless, we cannot assume that research practices moved on with any particular speed in this regard as, turning to the 1980s data, similar examples are evident.

The 1980s research team were not formally given the space to reflect on the experience of the interview or to make extensive fieldnotes, neither were they encouraged to expand on the domestic lives of respondents as the 1960s team had been. This, however, did not prevent individuals from making notes in the margins of the schedules and it is from these notes, as with the 1960s data, where the most fascinating insights frequently emerged when we came to reanalyse the data.

Perhaps the most extreme example of this concerns a female respondent who, at the time of the interview, was heavily pregnant. The interviewer completed the respondent's event history diary as required without recording the pregnancy in the early notes. Just under a third (29%) of the women interviewed had dependent children therefore pregnancy and/or motherhood were not uncommon in the sample and this would have been unlikely to have warranted a note from the interviewer. The event history diary reveals that although she had been employed since leaving school there was some confusion over her employment history. Her employment details come to an abrupt stop and it is here that we learn of the pregnancy by means of a note in the margin recording that the respondent was 'heavily pregnant'. Accompanying the event history diary we also discovered a handwritten note torn from a notebook and attached to the respondent's interview schedule, which explains the situation in more detail:

> The respondent was very pregnant, recently widowed, and hostile, so, (1) I didn't pursue the details of job one, whether it was a full-time job in a hairdresser's or just a fill-in, part-time job (2) [Didn't] ask her for her deceased husband's occupation as it seemed in poor taste.

It is easy to understand that it may have been difficult to pursue such a sensitive subject (the recent loss of her husband and her pregnancy) with the interviewee who was in a vulnerable state. Indeed, this short note raises again a whole raft of ethical issues and, in retrospect, the interviewer appears to have acted appropriately and ethically here, by present day research standards. However, without the marginalia this case may well have been frustrating to the secondary analyst who, without these hastily scribbled notes, would have had no information on the respondent's apparent abrupt exit from the labour market. What this also highlights is that although pregnancy and motherhood were not unusual amongst the sample, very little account was taken of the circumstances of the women impacted by this. Pregnancy, motherhood and the impact of these on the employment trajectories of the young women were aspects of the young people's lives that were not explored further.

As the previous example suggests, the data from our 1980s restudies was also rich in marginalia but, in contrast to the 1960s data, the data collection in this case was carried out 'door to door' and the interview schedules were far more quantitative in design. Whereas the 1960s team arranged the interviews in advance and expected to be invited into the respondent's home and to spend considerable time there, often recording the interview on a reel-to-reel tape recorder and writing them up later, the 1980s fieldworkers literally knocked on doors to find their respondents and carried out doorstep interviews. This led to far greater problems in reanalysis, as the handwritten notes appeared to have been written in haste, often only in pencil and using particular types of shorthand with which the new team were not familiar. Without a formal codebook to work from, the use of scribbled 'codes' such as 'CH' (council house) and 'OLF' (out of the labour force) took us some time to decipher and interpret. Other codes and abbreviations were often unfamiliar to the team of secondary analysts, for example, those that denoted youth employment schemes long since forgotten such as 'WEEP' (Work Experience on Employer's Premises) and 'WEP' (Work Experience Programme). These abbreviations also took time to decode although it is worth noting here that young people participating in these multiple schemes in the 1980s found the acronyms confusing and were often not sure on which of the many schemes they were enrolled.

Whereas we came to 'know' some of the 1960s respondents very well through the detailed written accounts of their teenage lives, and came to rely quite heavily on the interview notes as the means of understanding each individual trajectory, we did not have the same rich data for the 1980s respondents. Nonetheless, as we have seen, there were numerous examples of interviewers adding additional detail that would otherwise have been lacking. A good example of this is apparent in the 'activity sheets' that documented the details of individual employment histories, many of which included detailed accounts of what had led to changes in circumstances. Figure 6.2 (arrow inserted to highlight relevant text) below illustrates this very well.

This shows the case of a male respondent who had participated in a number of government schemes. Without the benefit of the accompanying notes this case appears to be a list of failed attempts to complete relatively short YTS schemes. The notes, however, provide far more insight and provide a snapshot of the reality of life on a youth training scheme in the 1980s which, had we relied simply on the quantitative data, would have been missed.

Supporting Letters and Correspondence

As suggested above, we have adopted quite a broad definition of para-data, marginalia and fieldnotes and we are keen to emphasise that the

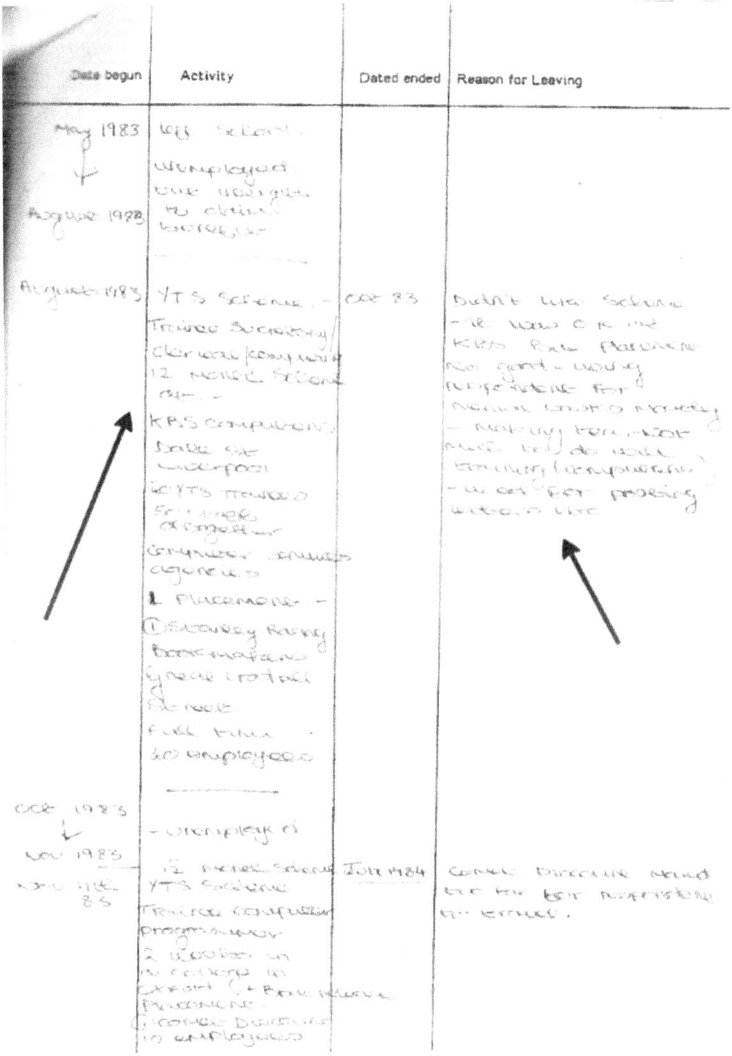

Figure 6.2 Activity sheet – the changing structure of youth labour markets (1986)

value of such data is not just to be found in, for example, old interview schedules themselves. Instead it is everything that existed around the research projects and any by-product that was created as part of, or which is germane to, the research. For example, if we consider again the 1960s Young Worker Project, there exists an extensive archive of correspondence, collated by the Norbert Elias Foundation and deposited at the German literary archive in Marbach, Germany. The letters relating to the research are correspondence between Ilya Neustadt, Head of Sociology in the 1960s at Leicester, and members of the original research team. The letters are referents of social change, of relationships (both revealed and alluded to), of social and academic networks, of ideas, tensions, fights and disputes. This correspondence also contains significant marginalia which, taken together with key epistolary forms, mean that such letters are essential as 'objects' of analysis in their own right. For example, in the following letter (see Figure 6.3 – names and other identifiers deleted to ensure anonymity), which Ilya Neustadt dictated to his secretary, he is writing to Norbert Elias who was in Ghana at this point. We can see that, alongside the formal information and content of the letter, he goes through and annotates aspects of the correspondence to highlight parts for emphasis, extending certain points or adding emphasis or extra detail. Looking at the correspondence as a whole it is clear that this is a consistent aspect of Neustadt's letter-writing style and appears in many of his letters. However, these marginalia are revealing in a number of ways. First, as suggested, the letters were often dictated and so there may be issues around 'voice' and 'representation'. We read multiple voices in the letters, that of Neustadt's formal 'Departmental voice', we read the voice of his secretary, Mrs Butler, and finally we read Neustadt's informal voice, the voice of the annotations included just before posting and added once the letter had been formally typed up. It could be that the annotations contained materials that Neustadt did not want his secretary to be party to or have knowledge of. They are often more personal and reflect Neustadt's own views as well as the more formal line contained within the main contents of the letter. Second, some of the comments, such as the annotations that we can read in this example, also serve as corrective to the contents of the letters. In this letter Neustadt is very critical of the research team in the main text of the letter (in his Departmental voice) but then in his more informal voice adds that they are working hard and that, perhaps, he is 'unfair' towards one of the team.

The letters provided essential contextual material and, as considered elsewhere (see Goodwin and O'Connor, 2006; Goodwin and Hughes, 2011), without the correspondence it would have been near impossible to reconstruct what had happened on the original project. Without the letters we would not have been able to understand the very basics of the research design, the management of the research or why, ultimately, the study collapsed and the research team resigned.

While many may discard such materials, for us this material was crucial in the insights it reveals. Pictures and notebooks are also often discarded,

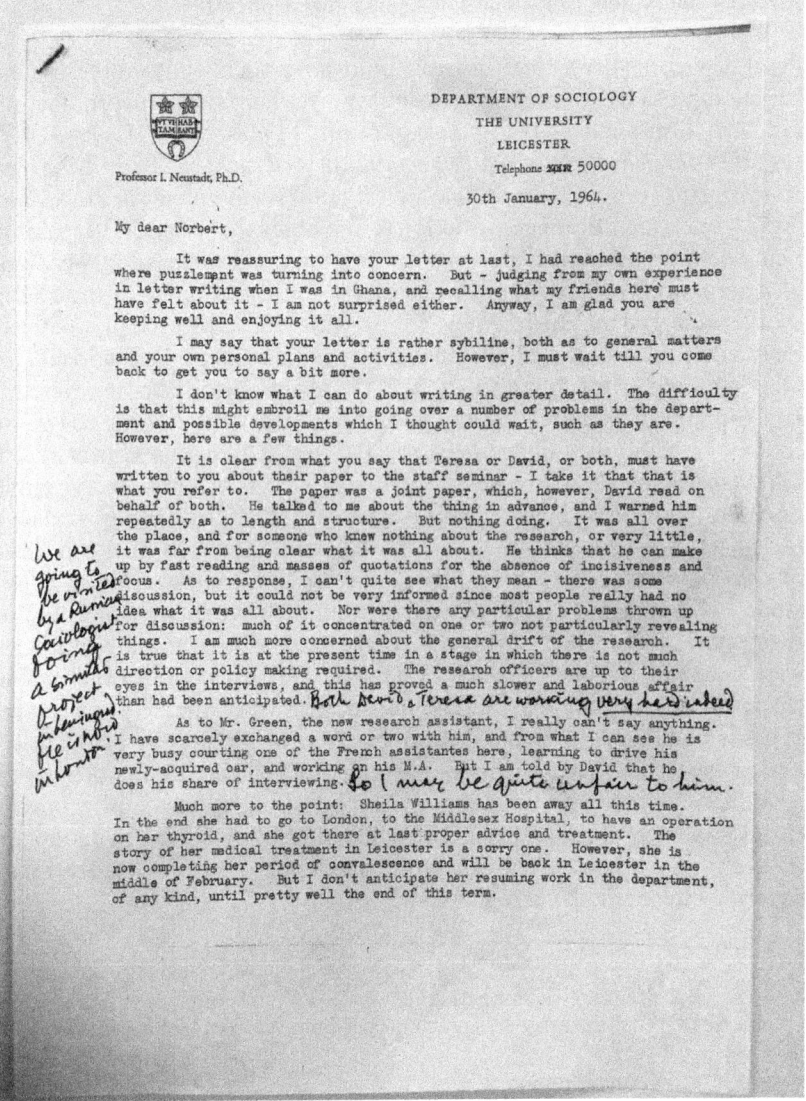

Figure 6.3   Letter from Ilya Neustadt to Norbert Elias, 30 January 1964

after the substantive parts of the research have been completed yet these can also reveal so much.

Pictures and Notebooks – The Works of Pearl Jephcott

Pearl Jephcott (1900–1980) was an innovative sociologist who has now largely (and sadly) disappeared from view. Yet her body of work, including *Girls Growing Up* (1942), *Rising Twenty* (1948), *Some Young People* (1954), *Married Women Working* (1962), *A Troubled Area: Notes on Notting Hill* (1964), *Time of One's Own* (1967) and *Homes in High Flats* (1971), was a significant contribution to sociology that is ground-breaking, richly detailed and which also retains a contemporary relevance. We stumbled across Pearl's work purely by chance in the earlier phase of the Young Worker research and then followed it up with a broad search of what was retained in the archives of the universities for whom she had worked (see Goodwin and O'Connor, 2013, 2015; Goodwin, 2015). We discovered a large archive of materials at the University of Glasgow relating to two of the books mentioned above (see files DC127/23/22 at the University of Glasgow Archives). At the heart of *Time of One's Own* was a very simple research question – 'how do young Scots use their free time nowadays?' (Jephcott, 1967: 1). However, despite the simple research question *Time of One's Own* is an early exemplar of the use of visual methods in youth studies with images being deployed to examine what young people did in their spare time in three areas – a ten-year-old housing estate in northwest Glasgow (Drumchapel), an established urban district of Glasgow (Dennistoun) and an 'expanding' industrial town in the Scottish central belt (Armadale). Although a great book in its own right one of the fascinating aspects of *Time of One's Own* is the very distinctive use of images. There are 24 images in the book and Jephcott begins in a fairly conventional way, incorporating black and white photographs as representations of each of the research areas. However, Jephcott also offered a more experimental method where she asked:

> young professional artists to make sketches of how the adolescents in the three areas were spending their hours after work. This technique was used on the assumption that the artist sees much deeper than the man [sic] in the street.
>
> (Jephcott, 1967, 9)

In these files were these original amazing artist's impressions of young people at work, and alongside the original pictures contained in the book there were 13 additional images that were collected as part of the research but not used in the final publication. We were amazed by the wealth, and quality, of these additional images held by the University of Glasgow Archive, not least because it is so unusual to have such complete records of these early social studies. For us, such images were as interesting as those included in the text and the original study itself as they clearly fell into our orientation towards paradata, marginalia and fieldnotes. These pictures are ephemera; they are objects associated with the project but not central to it. They were created and then archived so they are available for a re-reading, a reanalysis or secondary analysis given their immense analytical potential.

Figure 6.4 is an image entitled 'Place of Employment' from the Jephcott archives held in Glasgow. It is a very striking black and white line drawing depicting a young male at a drilling machine in his place of work. The image is incredibly evocative of the late 1960s with the young male wearing what appear to be jeans and a jumper to work as opposed to overalls. No sign of safety equipment or a guard around the drill. The image is richly

Figure 6.4   Pearl Jephcott image 'Place of Employment' – Time of One's Own *(1967)*

detailed from the hammer and screwdriver on the workbench to the dials, sockets and power switches next to the drill itself. The image provides a glimpse of a workplace and youth employment from the recent past. While it is not entirely clear that the artist-created images offered more analytical insights than a photograph would, as per Jephcott's aspirations, it is clear that the artist-created images are more arresting or 'attention grabbing' than perhaps a standard photograph. This suggests the images are interesting analytical objects in and of their own right. The stark black and white lines do draw and hold the viewer's gaze while the composition and content is decided upon by the artist. This also suggests some purpose in the composition with a deliberate intention to draw the details included in the image to the attention of the viewer.

Using artist-created images does provide evidence of Jephcott's innovative methodological style but in relation to images she goes much further. Indeed, it is also clear that the use of images was central to Pearl Jephcott's broader sociological craft as she was not only the commissioner of artist-created visual images but she also created and used her own images and the images of others extensively in her research notebooks (Goodwin, 2015). During his biographical research on Jephcott, Goodwin (2015) documents where her relatives were located and how these relatives had retained some of Jephcott's research notebooks. On examination, and as with her published written work, these notebooks were richly detailed and replete with images, pictures, photographs, line drawings and paintings. It is clear that Jephcott continually documented and recorded visually what she observed as well as making textual notes. An example from her notebooks is presented in Figure 6.5. This is taken from an East European Notebook collated in the summer of 1971 and depicts a splash-play area in the grounds of a nursery school. One of Jephcott's key sociological concerns, one of the areas of enquiry that defined her work as 'Jephcottian' (Goodwin and O'Connor, 2015a; Goodwin, 2015), was an aim to understand and improve children's play areas. A concern with children's play areas appears in her earlier works and is revisited in her very last work (see Jephcott, 1975).

This note meticulously details what Jephcott observed during that visit, from the layout of the splash-play area to the surrounds of the area, as well as offering an explanatory note that the splash-play areas were not a paddling pool – the emphasis here indicating some clear significance. The black and white photograph situates the observations and is also richly detailed; the uniform-patterned clothes of the children and the starched uniforms of the adults all in dappled sunlight in front of a conservatory of some description. Yet this is just one page in hundreds of pages spread across multiple notebooks. These notebooks are detailed ethnographic

Figure 6.5   *The Pearl Jephcott Notebooks – Eastern European Notebook 1971*

fieldnotes, carefully crafted during the research process. Richly detailed and accurately observed they offer a wealth of opportunity and possibilities for the secondary analyst.

CONCLUSION

The social sciences are full of 'nice' and really 'neat' typologies of data, data use and data collection techniques. Methodologists have created a mini industry in advising us how we 'should' design research, collect data, analyse materials and present findings. As we have argued above (and it may also be a form of sociological heresy to acknowledge this) in all of our 'starting points' to the various projects we have never really been concerned with how these data are defined, but more with the analytical possibilities that paradata, marginalia and fieldnotes present. Instead, our most likely starting point is to locate the most interesting materials and dive straight into them – and we would advise others to do the same. These assorted forms of paradata, marginalia and fieldnotes, as suggested above, were too irresistible to ignore and, in many respects have proved far more interesting than the actual 'formal' substantive data collected as part of these various projects. To that end, when we were supposed to be writing about the adjustment of young workers to work situations, when we were supposed to be writing about precarious work in the 1980s, the irony is that we were actually far more engaged with those materials from around the edges, more attracted to the by-products of the research process. When we did write about the substantive topics, journal reviewers invariably came back and asked for *more* detail on the original methodology and *more* insights into the various forms of data that we were using. As such, our interests in these paradata, marginalia and fieldnotes are not unique and this suggests, to us at least, that more should be made of these materials in future analyses as there is clearly an appetite for such approaches.

NOTES

1. This research was funded by the ESRC (R000223653:).
2. http://thephotographersgallery.org.uk/shirley-baker-women-children-and-loitering-men-2 [accessed 6 March 2016].

REFERENCES

Allan, G., Crow, G. and Hawker, S. (2011) *Stepfamilies*. New York: Palgrave Macmillan.
Burgoyne, J. and Clark, D. (1984) *Making a Go of It*. London: Routledge and Kegan Paul.
Elias, N. (1962) Second Memorandum, Unpublished manuscript, Deutsches Literaturarchiv, Marbach.

Evans, T. and Thane, P. (2006) Secondary Analysis of Dennis Marsden *Mothers Alone*. *Methodological Innovations Online* 1 (2), 78–82. http://www.esds.ac.uk/ qualidata/support/mio.asp [Accessed 10 March 2016].

Fine, G.A. (1993) Ten Lies of Ethnography: Moral Dilemma of Field Research. *Journal of Contemporary Ethnography* 22 (3), 267–294.

Gillies, V. and Edwards, R. (2012) Working with Archived Classic Family and Community Studies: Illuminating Past and Present Conventions Around Acceptable Research Practice. *International Journal of Social Research Methodology* 15 (4), 321–330.

Goodwin, J. (2015) *Searching for Pearls: Reflections on Researching the Life and Work of Pearl Jephcott*. Scottish Centre for Crime and Justice Research, University of Glasgow, 11 November 2015.

Goodwin, J. and Hughes, J. (2011) Ilya Neustadt, Norbert Elias, and the Development of Sociology in Britain: Formal and Informal Sources of Historical Data. *British Journal of Sociology* 26 (4), 677–695.

Goodwin, J. and O'Connor, H. (2006) Contextualising the Research Process: Using Interviewer Notes in the Secondary Analysis of Qualitative Data. *The Qualitative Report* 11 (2), 374–392.

Goodwin, J. and O'Connor, H. (2006a) Norbert Elias and the Lost Young Worker Project. *Journal of Youth Studies* 9 (2), 159–173.

Goodwin, J. and O'Connor, H. (2009) Through the Interviewer's Lens: Representations of 1960s Households and Families and in a Lost Sociological Study. *Sociological Research Online* 14 (4).

Goodwin, J. and O'Connor, H. (2013) Embodying Leisure: The Use of Images in Jephcott's *Time of One's Own*. *LERN Occasional Papers No. 2*. University of Leicester.

Goodwin, J. and O'Connor, H. (2015) Pearl Jephcott: The Legacy of a Forgotten Sociological Research Pioneer. *Sociology* 49 (1), 139–155.

Goodwin, J. and O'Connor, H. (2015a) *Pearl Jephcott: Biographical Starting Points*. Pearl Jephcott Symposium: Youth, Community, Methodology and More: A Symposium Celebrating the Life and Work of Pearl Jephcott. University of Leicester, 9 July 2015.

Innes, S. and McKie, L. (2006) 'Doing What is Right': Researching Intimacy, Work and Family Life in Glasgow, 1945–1960. *Sociological Research Online* 11 (2), http://www.socresonline.org.uk/11/2/innes.html [Accessed 10 March 2016].

Jephcott, P. (1967) *Time of One's Own: Leisure and Young People*. Edinburgh: Oliver and Boyd.

Jephcott, P. (1975) *Young Families in High Flats: A Short Study Based on Sustained Contact with Parents and Children in Three Areas of Birmingham*. Birmingham: Birmingham City Council Housing Department.

Marsden, D. (1969) *Mothers Alone: Poverty and the Fatherless Family*. London: Allen Lane.

O'Connor, H. and Goodwin, J. (2010) Utilizing Data from a Lost Sociological Project: Experiences, Insights, Promises. *Qualitative Research* 10 (3), 283–298.

O'Connor, H. and Goodwin, J. (2012) Revisiting Norbert Elias's Sociology of Community: Learning from the Leicester Restudies. *The Sociological Review* 60 (3), 476–497.

O'Connor, H. and Goodwin, J. (2013) The Ethical Dilemmas of Restudies in Researching Youth. *YOUNG: Nordic Journal of Youth Research* 21 (3), 289–307.

Savage, M. (2005) Revisiting Classic Qualitative Studies [43 paragraphs]. *Forum Qualitative Sozialforschung / Forum: Qualitative Social Research* 6 (1), Art. 31 http://www.qualitative-research.net/index.php/fqs/article/view/502/1080 [Accessed 8 November 2016].

7. John Adams's marginalia: then and now

H.J. Jackson

In Paris, most likely in the early months of 1785, Benjamin Franklin borrowed a new pamphlet by Richard Price from John Adams, a future President of the United States, and had Adams's manuscript notes transcribed from it into his own copy. In Toronto at the end of 2008, I was able to examine dozens of Adams's annotated books page by page, conceivably at the same time as enthusiasts in Washington, Durban, St. Petersburg, and Buenos Aires. Instead of having to make copies laboriously by hand I could print out as many pages as I wanted, notes and all. The technological gap is mind-boggling and I shall have something to say about it shortly, but first I wish to address another greater but less obvious gulf in attitudes and understanding between then and now.

In Western society today there is a strong prejudice against writing in books. Libraries forbid it. Connoisseurs deplore it. Readers who are caught doing it are liable to find themselves rebuked by total strangers. Second-hand book dealers refuse books that have been heavily marked up, and even charity book sales will reject volumes "defaced" with handwriting as unsalable. We discourage our children and students from making notes on the page as they read, and if we occasionally do it ourselves we feel guilty about it and try to conceal our bad habit from others. There are good reasons for the general disapproval of marginalia in the modern world. The examples we encounter, typically in library books, tend to be hasty, messy, anonymous, and cryptic—pretty much meaningless to everyone but the person who put them there. We rightly consider this sort of behaviour as private and selfish. But it was not always so, it is not always so today, and I'd like to think that it will not always be so in the future. Even now, we make an exception for notes written by famous people, which have association value and hence inspire awe in the exhibition hall, besides attracting large sums in the salerooms. It's unlikely that the most diehard bibliophile would say or even *think* that the world would be a better place if John Adams had left his books alone.

The two opposite, reflex reactions of disgust and reverence that I have been describing are curiously alike in certain ways. Often passionately felt, they are nonetheless equally unproductive. For a more temperate assessment—to see what the example of John Adams might do for our understanding of the past and our own practice in the future—we have to take the trouble to read the notes and make the imaginative effort of engaging with them. It helps to have contemporary examples to set beside them: individualized as they are, Adams's notes are not incomparable. In this chapter I shall introduce a sampling of notes and briefly survey Adams's history as a writer of marginalia in order to answer two questions: what contribution do marginalia make to the profile of Adams as a reader, and how do *we* read *him*? Three books that I shall focus on particularly are Richard Price's *Observations on the Importance of the American Revolution* (1784), the pamphlet that Franklin borrowed from Adams in Paris; Mary Wollstonecraft's *Historical and Moral View of the Origin and Progress of the French Revolution* (1794) which is the most heavily annotated of all Adams's books, with about 12,000 words commenting on 500 passages (Haraszti, 1962: 186, 187); and Richard Hurd's *Moral and Political Dialogues; with Letters on Chivalry and Romance* (1765), Number 19 on the list of the top 40 most heavily annotated works and a relatively early, pre-Revolutionary addition to the collection that has not previously been discussed by scholars, perhaps for good reason. Of these three, only the Price title was held in common by Adams and Jefferson.

I do not mean to suggest that Adams's notes have gone unread or unappreciated till now. Far from it; we can tell even by the single example of Franklin that Adams's notes were admired as it were for themselves, that is, for their content and style, even before his Presidency. Afterwards, editors, biographers, and historians regularly turned to Adams's library for evidence about the sources of his ideas and to the annotated books specifically for clarification of his opinions on political issues. The marginalia were especially well served by Zoltán Haraszti, the curator of the collection in the Boston Public for many years, who first of all wrote a series of articles that presented Adams's notes on different titles, and then in 1952 published his book *John Adams and the Prophets of Progress*, which provides a thorough, detailed, history-of-ideas analysis of the large body of commentary that Adams wrote in the works of eighteenth-century *philosophes* from Voltaire to Wollstonecraft.

Here are some typical examples of Adams's marginalia, taken from Haraszti's book. While you or I might be satisfied with underlining or highlighting and with the briefest of comments—"true," "NB," "not so,"— since margins are narrow and time is short, Adams evidently let himself go. To Wollstonecraft's plea on behalf of the woman who leaves a despised husband for "a more congenial or humane bosom," he responded, "Would you divorce her when she pleases? Would you have no women because some are incorrigible prostitutes? Would you have no husbands because some are brutal? Would you have no beauty because it often seduces? Would you have no writers because some like you are licentious?" (1962: 193–4). In the margins of a volume of Rousseau he wrote, "Credulity! Thou art ready to believe anything but the truth" (ibid. 90) and "Nonsense. Is it possible this man could believe this?" (ibid. 91). Shocked by a disrespectful remark of d'Alembert's about the Creator, he erupted with indignation: "Thou Louse, Flea, Tick, Ant, Wasp or whatever Vermin thou art, was this Stupendous Universe made and adjusted to give you Money, Sleep, or Digestion?" (ibid. 111). He challenged almost every one of the statements in a letter written to Price by Turgot, as in this single illustration: "Is it possible that the writer of this paragraph should have ever read Plato, Livy, Polybius, Machiavel, Sidney, Harrington; or that he should ever have thought of the nature of man or of a society? What does he mean [by] collecting all authority into one center? What does he mean by the center of a nation? Where would he have the legislation placed? Where the execution? Where the decision of controversies? Emptier piece of declamation I never read; it is impossible to give a greater proof of ignorance" (ibid. 145).

These notes and hundreds like them convey a strong sense of presence, thus bridging, narrowing, even seeming to close the gap of more than two centuries. As we read them we hear a distinctive voice—impetuous, assured, forthrightly aggressive. Sometimes the tone is gentler, more accommodating, as when Adams concedes of one statement in Turgot's letter, "This is a great point and a very knotty one" (ibid. 147), or when in a summary note he commends Wollstonecraft as "a lady of a masculine masterly understanding" who, had she had the benefit of practical political experience, might "have produced a history without the defects and blemishes pointed out with too much severity perhaps and too little gallantry in the notes" (ibid. 187). But the more striking, pugnacious manner is dominant, and it is understandable that biographers of Adams should have taken his marginalia as confirmation of his character—especially his contrariness, which they all find lovable. Modest as are his claims for the marginalia, Haraszti thought they might help to bring about a positive revision of Adams's public image. "More than for any other reason," he wrote, "Adams is unappreciated because he is the least known of the great Americans. The immense mass of his manuscripts is still locked away" (ibid. 9). Unlocking the marginalia was his way of showing some of Adams's most attractive qualities—his wide-ranging curiosity, his avidity for ideas, and especially his zest for debate. Later biographers agreed with him. In *Passionate Sage*, Joseph Ellis cited the notes in his description of Adams as typically "oppositional" throughout his life, a man who "instinctively mobilized" his mental resources "in opposition to established conventions, personal enemies, or fashionable ideas. He was only comfortable in dialogue and he was invigorated when the dialogue took the form of an argument," he says (1993: 87). David McCullough likewise represents Adams as an habitual note-maker who found it "part of the joy of reading . . . to have something to say himself" by talking back to the book (2001: 619). He mentions Wollstonecraft's work specifically as a book Adams "read at least twice and with delight, since he disagreed with nearly everything she said" (ibid. 619).

Valuable as they are, and good as they must have been for Adams's reputation, these character portraits innocently misrepresent, I think, both the man and the books. Psychologically, they presume that character is constant; they commit what is now thought of as the essentialist fallacy. Historically, they overlook the evidence of an evolution in Adams's approach to books and reading—though heaven knows they had enough to do without devoting detailed attention to that aspect of his development. Finally, from my point of view as a literary scholar, I have to say that they seem to have been unaware of the genre conventions that contributed to making the marginalia as appealing as they are.

In Adams's day, writing notes in books was a kind of performance. While books were relatively rare and costly, they were handled with respect. Their owners knew that they were likely to last and to be passed on to others, and therefore considered themselves as merely temporary custodians. Even in their custody, the books were likely to have more than one reader: they might be consulted by anyone in a circle of family, friends, colleagues— to whom the owner would be known even if the book did not bear his or her name in an ownership inscription. So notes were seldom truly anonymous and *nobody ever expected* marginalia to be private, composed for the writer's eyes only. For the same reason, they were seldom messy: other people would be reading them sooner or later. Adams is a case in point. The books at Adams's house in the town of Quincy were part of a family library. Though it seems to us, given the customs of our own time, that he must have written notes such as those I've quoted on the spur of the moment, spontaneously, yielding to an irresistible impulse, he didn't. Neither, so far as I can tell, did any of his generation. They made the decision to mark up a particular book for a particular occasion. There were a few methodical folk who adopted some form of annotation and applied it consistently to all their books—William Beckford, for instance, who copied little extracts that amused him onto the front and back flyleaves, leaving the pages of text pristine; and those serious collectors who invariably recorded the place and date of acquisition along with their ownership inscription in every volume—but Adams was not one of them. Though he left an interesting body of commentary in about a hundred extant books, that's a hundred out of three thousand or more. The image of him sitting reading with pen in hand, ready to pounce on an ill-considered statement, is an exaggeration based on an anachronistic view of the scribbling habit. The same is true of all the other notorious marginators of the day—Blake, Walpole, Coleridge, and Keats, for example. The great majority of the books they owned remained unmarked, for what they had was not a habit (though Coleridge did use the word) but a purposeful practice.

Furthermore, the extended critical note that we relish today is comparatively rare in Adams's library and a late development at that. I believe that the notes in the Price pamphlet (published in 1784 and a gift from the author) may be the earliest extant of their kind. That is not to say that *Observations on the Importance of the American Revolution* is the earliest annotated book, for Adams had been making notes for decades, only notes of different, more traditional and impersonal kinds. It is clear from his diary that during his Harvard years he had to struggle to concentrate, so he used conventional study techniques, such as underlining, in order to focus his attention. (He sounds like a hearteningly normal young man, though one with high standards, when he laments that "My thoughts are roving from Girls to friends, from friends to Court, to Worcester, to Piscataquay, Newbury, and then to Greece and Rome, then to France. Could I fix my attention, and keep off every fluttering Thought that attempts to intrude upon the present subject, I could read a Book all Day" [Adams, 1961: 1:86].) At least as early as 1755, when he turned 20, he kept a commonplace book into which he could copy passages from his reading (Adams, 1850: 1:39). Then on 26 June, 1760, as he prepared to tackle Montesquieu, his diary registered a breakthrough as he made this new resolution: "I have begun to read the Spirit of the Laws, and have resolved to read that Work, thro, in order and with attention. I have hit on a Project that will secure my Attention to it, which is to write in the Margin, a sort of Index to every Paragraph" (Adams, 1961: 1:142). What Adams was describing was not an invention of his own but the traditional academic technique of writing "heads," that is, copying in the margin a word or phrase from the text that provides a keyword for the passage. Access a page almost at random from the digitized copy of Hurd's *Dialogues* on the Boston Public Library website or through LibraryThing, and you will immediately recognize the patterns of underlining and heads that were common in Adams's books from this time on (see Figure 7.1). They may be single words taken from the text, such as "Selden" and "Bracton" from 2:199 or slightly longer phrases such as "Feudal Law and absolute Monarchy incompatible" from 2:124. This technique served Adams well.

On his first reading of Wollstonecraft 30 years later, Adams was still using it, as you can see on p. 402 of her book (Figure 7.2), where one

ablest lawyers in their endeavours to make the policy of *England* speak the language of *Rome*.

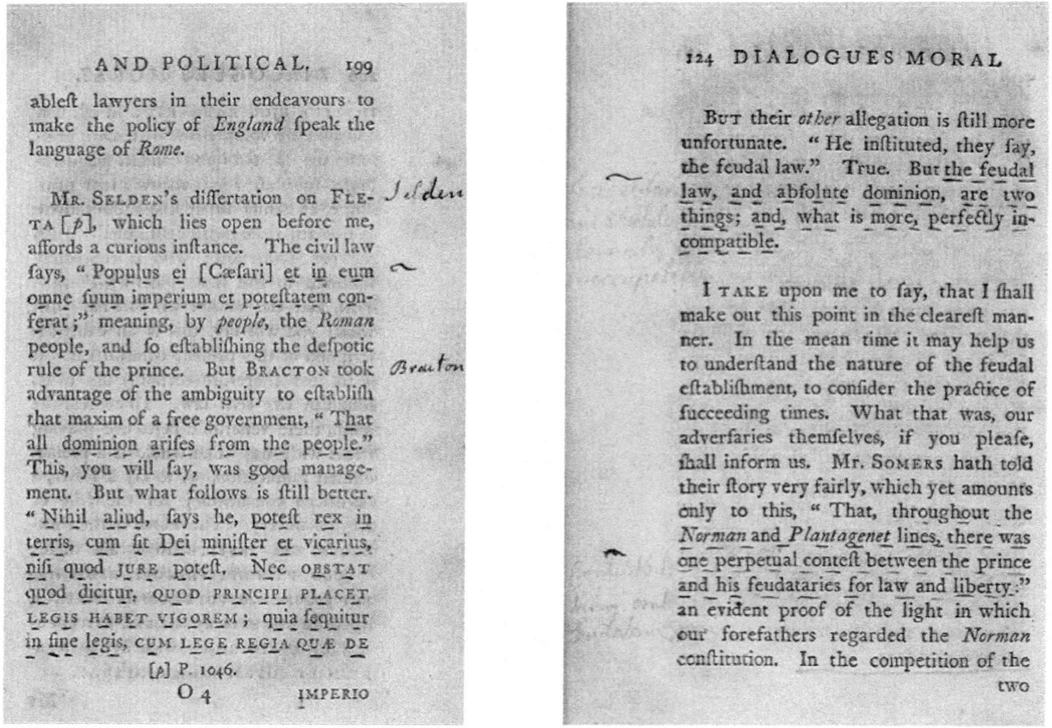

Mr. SELDEN's dissertation on FLE-TA [b], which lies open before me, affords a curious instance. The civil law says, "Populus ei [Caesari] et in eum omne suum imperium et potestatem conferat," meaning, by *people*, the *Roman* people, and so establishing the despotic rule of the prince. But BRACTON took advantage of the ambiguity to establish that maxim of a free government, "That all dominion arises from the people." This, you will say, was good management. But what follows is still better. "Nihil aliud, says he, potest rex in terris, cum sit Dei minister et vicarius, nisi quod jure potest. Nec obstat quod dicitur, quod principi placet legis habet vigorem; quia sequitur in fine legis, cum lege regia quæ de

[b] P. 1046.

O 4   IMPERIO

BUT their *other* allegation is still more unfortunate. "He instituted, they say, the feudal law." True. But the feudal law, and absolute dominion, are two things; and, what is more, perfectly incompatible.

I TAKE upon me to say, that I shall make out this point in the clearest manner. In the mean time it may help us to understand the nature of the feudal establishment, to consider the practice of succeeding times. What that was, our adversaries themselves, if you please, shall inform us. Mr. SOMERS hath told their story very fairly, which yet amounts only to this, "That, throughout the *Norman* and *Plantagenet* lines, there was one perpetual contest between the prince and his feudataries for law and liberty." an evident proof of the light in which our forefathers regarded the *Norman* constitution. In the competition of the

two

Source: Available on the Boston Library website or through LibraryThing.

Figure 7.1   Example of pages of Hurd's Dialogues

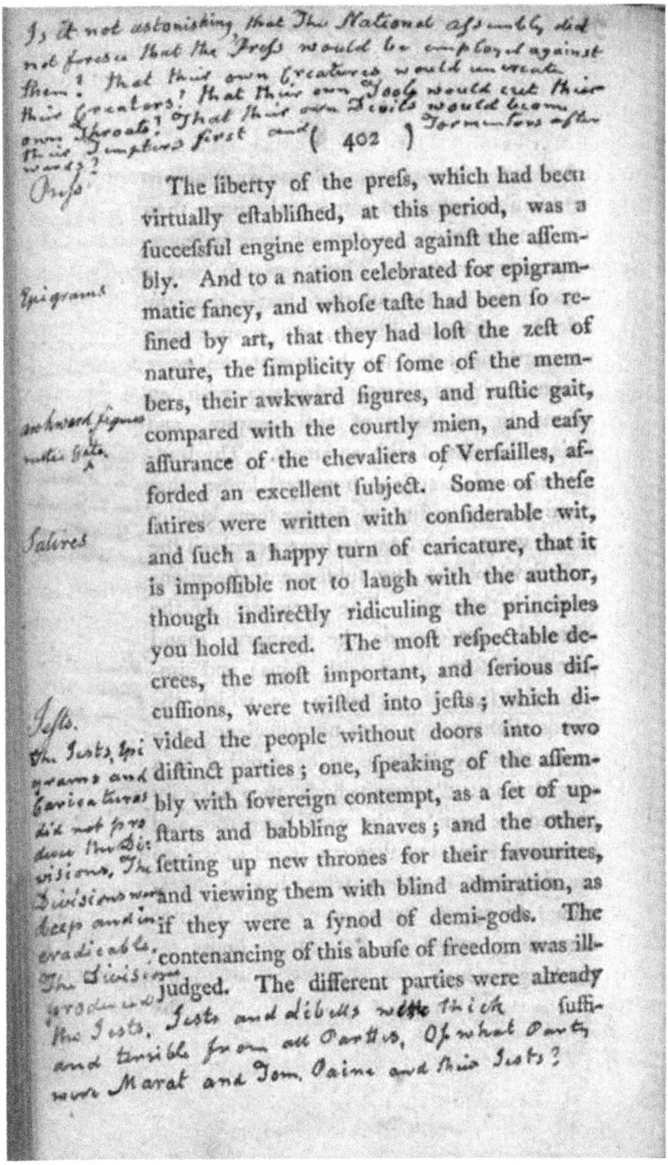

> Is it not astonishing that The National assembly did not foresee that the Press would be employed against them? That this own Creatures would uncreate their Creators? that their own fools would cut their own throats? that their own Devils would become Tormentors after their Temptors first and

(402)

Press

The liberty of the press, which had been virtually established, at this period, was a successful engine employed against the assembly. And to a nation celebrated for epigrammatic fancy, and whose taste had been so refined by art, that they had lost the zest of nature, the simplicity of some of the members, their awkward figures, and rustic gait, compared with the courtly mien, and easy assurance of the chevaliers of Versailles, afforded an excellent subject. Some of these satires were written with considerable wit, and such a happy turn of caricature, that it is impossible not to laugh with the author, though indirectly ridiculing the principles you hold sacred. The most respectable decrees, the most important, and serious discussions, were twisted into jests; which divided the people without doors into two distinct parties; one, speaking of the assembly with sovereign contempt, as a set of upstarts and babbling knaves; and the other, setting up new thrones for their favourites, and viewing them with blind admiration, as if they were a synod of demi-gods. The contenancing of this abuse of freedom was ill-judged. The different parties were already suffi-

Epigrams

awkward figures rustic Gate

Satires

Jests.
The Jests, Epigrams and Caricatures did not produce these Divisions. The Divisions produced the Jests. Jests and libels were thick and terrible from all Parties. Of what Party were Marat and Tom Paine and their Jests?

Source: Boston Public Library.

Figure 7.2   Adams's annotation on first reading Wollstonecraft's p. 402 with the single word "Jests" as the keyword at first, and a much longer personal comment added on a later reading

paragraph elicited the single word "Jests" as the keyword at first, and then a much longer personal comment on a later reading. The keyword method has several potential benefits. As Adams observed, at the time of reading it focuses the reader's mind by giving him something to do. Later on the words in the margin can act as a finding aid—just flick through the pages to find the quotation from Bracton—or as a quick summary to recall and reconstitute the original reading as it unfolded.

The conventional practices of the student were reinforced for Adams later on by the customary usage of the lawyer. Law books typically came with wide margins that left space for both the printed marginalia supplied by the editor or publisher, providing precedents and references to laws and statutes, and the handwritten supplements of the lawyers using them, whereby they kept up to date with new legislation and added cross-references to relevant cases. This professional discipline, like the student's study tools, helped Adams to keep his nose to the grindstone. (I find it touching—somehow admirable and pitiable at the same time—that prominently at the front of the third of four fat quarto volumes of Blackstone's *Commentaries on the Laws of England*, Adams wrote a motto from Horace that can be translated, "You must steer clear of the Siren Indolence.") Throughout his years as an active lawyer, Adams regularly made cross-references and similar additions to the books he worked with, as most lawyers did. The practice spilled over sometimes into unexpected places, as for instance another page in Hurd where he's slipped in cross-references to Blackstone, Robertson's History of Charles the Fifth, and Daines Barrington's "Observations on the Statutes," citing them by abbreviations which any lawyer of his day would have recognized at once (Figure 7.3). Incidentally, a good lawyer's books enriched with cross-references could bring many times the original price on the second-hand market. In 1813, when the London lawyer Francis Hargrave's library was purchased for the nation, a bookseller testified before the House of Commons that he had known books of this kind normally worth three guineas to sell for two hundred guineas, and books worth four or five shillings to sell for 40 pounds (Jackson, 2005: 105).

In the 1760s, as Adams acquired more books and felt more confident in possession of them, he began to write longer notes. They were not at first disputatious; Adams moved only gradually from note-*taking* to self-assertive note-*making*, from pupillage to independence. They supplemented the information available in the work in a modest way and might venture an opinion about its value in the manner recommended by Montaigne as far back as the sixteenth century. Such restrained, rather formal notes were the norm for Adams through the sixties and seventies. The Hurd that he acquired and presumably annotated in 1769 is a good example: it contains

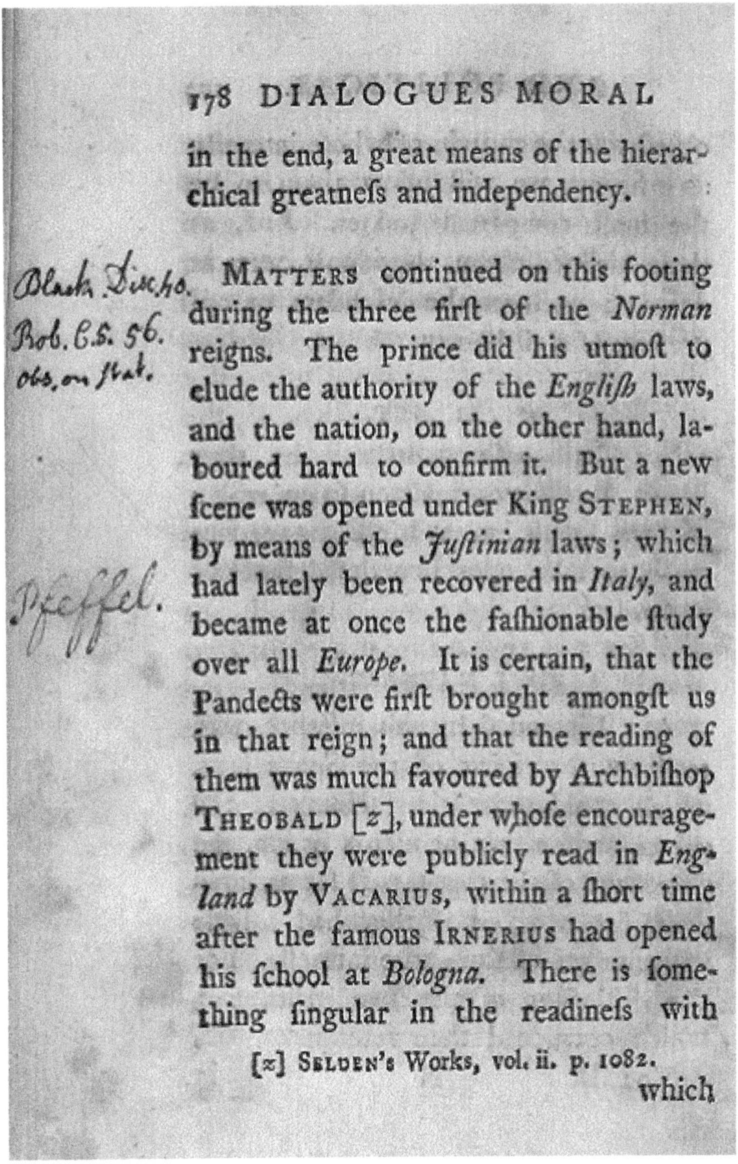

178 DIALOGUES MORAL

in the end, a great means of the hierarchical greatneſs and independency.

Black. Disc. 40. Rob. C.S. 56. obs. on Stat.

MATTERS continued on this footing during the three firſt of the *Norman* reigns. The prince did his utmoſt to elude the authority of the *Engliſh* laws, and the nation, on the other hand, laboured hard to confirm it. But a new ſcene was opened under King STEPHEN, by means of the *Juſtinian* laws; which had lately been recovered in *Italy*, and became at once the faſhionable ſtudy over all *Europe*. It is certain, that the Pandects were firſt brought amongſt us in that reign; and that the reading of them was much favoured by Archbiſhop THEOBALD [z], under whoſe encouragement they were publicly read in *England* by VACARIUS, within a ſhort time after the famous IRNERIUS had opened his ſchool at *Bologna*. There is ſomething ſingular in the readineſs with

Pfeffel.

[z] SELDEN's Works, vol. ii. p. 1082.

which

Source: Available on the Boston Library website or through LibraryThing.

Figure 7.3 Adams's annotation of a page in Richard Hurd's Moral and Political Dialogues: with Letters on Chivalry and Romance *(1765)*

a lot of underlining and some of the familiar heads, but just a few—by my count, only three—observations, and none of them sounds like a quarrel with the author. On the contrary, Adams supports what Hurd has to say, or expands on it a little. When Hurd laments the limited understanding that most of his contemporaries, even in Parliament, have about the forms and principles of government, Adams concurs, "The No. of Persons in any free Govt. who understand the Constitution is very small" (Hurd, 1765: 2:103); and when Hurd deplores the "false tenderness" that English people have to their monarchs, however culpable, when they suffer misfortune, Adams points out that "This is not peculiar to the People of England, in Holland it is equally Strong" (ibid. 2:109). These are the kind of anodyne notes that usefully reinforce and supplement the text; they are not vigorous expressions of opposition or a point-by-point refutation of an argument.

Paris seems to have set Adams free to express himself in the margins of his books—Paris, intensive book-buying, and perhaps the example of his peers. Haraszti notes with surprise that Voltaire's marginalia to Rousseau sound a lot like Adams's (1962: 92). Franklin, we know, had taken to writing comments in the margins of political pamphlets in the 1760s, not having done so before (Hayes, 2008: 442). In England at the same time, the philosopher Jeremy Bentham was scribbling down his objections to the arguments of Burke and the like (Jackson, 2001: 226). Pamphlets may have been easy starter texts to practise on, since they were thought of as ephemeral and therefore expendable. In any case, it is striking that all the distinctively Adamsish notes in Adams's books belong to the 1780s and later. The part of Price's pamphlet that most occupied Adams was a letter that Price had received from the French economist and statesman Jacques Turgot in 1778. Adams had met and admired Turgot but thought that although "he had an honest heart and great theoretical knowledge," he "was not a judicious, practical statesman"—and that it was primarily his lack of practical political experience (just what Adams prided himself on) that had led to his dismissal from the post of Comptroller General under Louis XVI (quoted Haraszti, 1962: 143). His notes respond point by point to the revelations and opinions of the letter, covering such issues as protectionism, national characters, and the future of the new independent American states. "The fate of America is now decided," according to Turgot, "she is independent now for ever. But will she be free and happy?" "Yes," stoutly responds Adams (Haraszti, 1962: 144). But there is no sense, he agrees, in expecting a New Jerusalem; human nature is the same in America as elsewhere. Adams's comments on Turgot seem to have been written at the first reading, probably at a single sitting; the earlier, friendlier ones do not anticipate the fundamental disagreement that emerged partway through, when Turgot appeared to Adams to be advocating centralized unicameral government—anathema to him. It's at that point that he burst out with the note I quoted earlier—"emptier piece of declamation I never read," etc. After that point, there are more notes correcting Turgot on matters of fact about local government in America and on basic political principles, and Adams's praise is more grudging. Still it is clear that he was intensely interested in what Turgot had to say. Two years later, he published his *Defence of the Constitutions of Government of the United States of America* explicitly to address Turgot's objections. Haraszti's study describes the composition of the *Defence* but does not address the relationship between Adams's notes to Turgot's letter and the content of the *Defence*. Probably he thought there was nothing to say about it. The *Defence* is a patchwork quilt of extracts from a variety of writers, stitched together with bits of commentary from Adams. Haraszti observes that this indigestible composition might be easier to take if it were laid out as he had laid out the marginalia, with the extracts followed by Adams's commentary—an interesting proposal that suggests there might have been some connection between the way that Adams read books and the way that he composed them. But what I find surprising is the fact that Adams did not make use of the notes he had already written about Turgot in the preparation of his response to the notorious Letter. (A word search of the *Defence* shows quite conclusively that he did not. The same is true of his annotated copy of Davila in relation to the *Discourses on Davila* that got Adams into so much trouble in 1790–91.) By this way of proceeding—by separating his immediate reaction as recorded in marginalia from the later labour of a published response—Adams was thinking and operating like a statesman, not like a writer. Those of his contemporaries who wrote for a living typically exploited their marginalia, they didn't let them go to waste. Coleridge's *Aids to Reflection* took shape as a series of meditations on passages in the works of Archbishop Leighton and overlapped a good deal with his actual marginalia; he drafted some of his Shakespeare lectures in copies of Shakespeare's works that he then carried into the lecture room. Benjamin Franklin made notes in the margins of his opponents' pamphlets in order to refute them in his own publications, and Kevin Hayes describes these notes as "first drafts of the political essays he wrote in the years leading up to the American Revolution" (2008: 442). But Adams—I find this very winning—read for ideas, not for copy that he could put to use later.

The final phase of Adams's life as a writer of marginalia came in his retirement, after 1800, when he returned to some of the books of political theory and recent history that he already knew quite well and wrote most of the copious, challenging notes that interest us today. "Books and Agriculture may fill the Mind" after one has given up power, he observed in a note to Mme de Staël's treatise on the influence of the passions on the happiness of individuals and nations (1796: 99). That was certainly his own programme. Reading and reflection were necessary to his well-being. In the very last years, from about 1820 when he was in his mid-eighties, according to the recollections of the teenaged grandson who was called on to read to him in French at that time,

> he would cheerfully listen to any book, however trifling, which might at the moment be attracting the fancy of younger generations. The brilliant fictions of Walter Scott, then in the height of their popularity, the sea stories of Cooper, and even the exaggerated, but vigorous poetry of Byron, were all welcome, in the intervals when he could not obtain what he better relished, the reminiscences of contemporaries, or the speculations of more profound writers in England and France.
>
> (Adams, 1850: 1:633)

But at a slightly earlier stage, while he could still see to read and hold a pen to write, he undertook the rereading of the distinct set of books isolated by Haraszti. Adding to the heads and briefer comments that he had written earlier, he produced running commentaries that I believe he more or less consciously intended as part of his intellectual legacy. John Adams was well aware of the conventions governing such informal genres as the letter and the marginal note.[1] He knew what he was doing; he wrote these notes to be read after he was gone. He must have calculated that if the books went no further than his own family and descendants, at least *they* would see his version of the great events in which he had played a part, and the great ideas that had driven him. He would distance himself from the godless rationalists who had promoted revolution in France and at the same time correct the misrepresentations of his character and role that were already circulating in America. Why else make a point of noting, when Wollstonecraft says how important it is after a government has fallen to form the plan of a new constitution and present it to the people, "I had preached this doctrine a whole year in Congress in 1775 and 1776 before I could prevail upon that Body to pass my Resolution of the 15th of May 1776 recommending that Measure to the People of the States" (Haraszti, 1962: 221, corrected against the original, 403). Adams can hardly have written this note to remind himself of what had happened; nor was he, on this occasion, correcting Wollstonecraft personally through her book; he was setting the record straight for posterity. This use of the margins of his books is consistent with other occupations of Adams's long years of retirement. He had planned to write an autobiography but gave it up to defend himself against an attack by Mercy Warren in her history of the American Revolution, publishing a long series of letters in the *Boston Patriot* in what David McCullough refers to as "his last passionate exercise in self-justification" (2001: 596). The letters that passed between him and Benjamin Rush from 1805 to 1813 reveal both men to have been preoccupied with their posthumous reputations, as the editors' title for a selection of them, *The Spur of Fame*, indicates (Adams and Rush, 1966). Adams also shared reflections and reminiscences with Jefferson in their marvellous late correspondence. He was in retrospective mode. The notes that he wrote in this period would become part of the public record. When he made provision for his books in 1822 by giving a deed of land and most of his library to the town of Quincy, towards the foundation of an academy, he did not exclude the annotated books. In keeping with the conventions of the time, he did not mind that strangers would read the notes in them; he knew the notes would be perceived as enhancements. For readers of his time, as for generations before them, the privilege of ownership entailed responsibility, and if books were to be altered, it should be by way of improvement. These assumptions did not change until after Adams's death, when technologies and trade practices combined to bring down the price of books. With mass production, personal ownership of books (as opposed to sharing or borrowing) became the norm at all levels of society, and standards of note-making that had been enforced by educational tradition and public accountability were relaxed. We cannot think wider access a bad thing and even for the history of marginalia, completely private ownership had its advantages—but Adams and his contemporaries had no notion of such conditions.

Adams left the notes in his books as part of what was to become the public record of his life and achievements overall. Our focus at the moment is much more specialized: we ask what contribution the marginalia can make to the profile of Adams as a reader. The short answer is, not as much as we might think, and not exactly what we might expect. If we want to know what he read and when he read it, how he read, and what books were most important to him, the annotated books ought to be a goldmine. Many of them contain ownership inscriptions with Adams's name and the date of acquisition; a few score have routine marks of disciplined study; a dozen or so contain extended commentary. We might assume that there is a direct correlation between quantity of annotation and personal value— that Adams singled out the books that were most important to him for this close scrutiny—but we would be mistaken. What the copious notes indicate is that at a certain, late stage in his life, he occupied and entertained himself by rereading a special set of books that for the most part he disagreed with and meant to dissociate himself from. The other, less heavily and more conventionally annotated volumes prove that he did at some point read those works too—and even that is something, because we all have in our libraries books that we might have owned for many years but scarcely opened, and the fact that a book has been carefully preserved in Adams's library does not prove that he read it, whereas study notes certainly do. But those notes are not of a kind to reveal what he *thought of* the works he was temporarily engaged with. Some of the books that must have been most formative for him—the works by "Plato, Livy, Polybius, Machiavel, Sidney, Harrington" whom he mentions as standard in the note to Turgot that I quoted earlier—are still in his library but are practically unmarked. Five Plato titles appear to contain only one short substantive note, though we are aware, thanks to other sources, that Plato at one stage absorbed a lot of his time, and that he had decided views about his philosophy. In a letter of 1814, he told Jefferson how much trouble Plato had cost him 30 years earlier, when he had compared translations in three languages with the Greek originals, only to end up disappointed and disgusted. "Two Things only did I learn from him. 1. that Franklins Idea of exempting Husbandmen and Mariners etc. from the depredations of War were borrowed from him. 2. that Sneezing is a cure for the Hickups" (Adams, et al., 1959: 2:437). He concluded, he says, that Plato was as mad as his modern counterparts Helvétius and Rousseau. But if his own approximate dating is anywhere near correct, he studied Plato about the same time as he wrote his notes in the Price pamphlet but did not choose to annotate Plato in the same way.

In 1776—to take another example of the limitations of the record of existing marginalia—Adams acquired two copies of Paine's electrifying pamphlet *Common Sense*, one for himself and one for his wife Abigail, but the one copy that remains with the Adams collection is unmarked. In the 1790s he teased Abigail about being a "disciple" of Wollstonecraft, in an obvious allusion to the *Vindication of the Rights of Woman*, published in 1792 (Adams and Adams, 2007: 351); but the only work of hers that remains in the Adams collection is the heavily-annotated account of the Revolution (1794) that I have been quoting from. We also have to consider all the other things that Adams read of which no physical trace remains—books belonging to libraries or borrowed from friends; government reports and documents; newspapers and periodicals; and all the fiction and poetry (the Scott, Cooper, and Byron mentioned by his grandson, for instance, none of them represented in the existing library catalogue) that were read aloud for pure pleasure in the family circle. Like all of us, he read far more books than he ever owned. His letters and diary provide a better guide to the full extent of his reading than the marginalia or even the library, taken as a whole, can do, though both play a strong supporting role.

Nor do the copious notes in Wollstonecraft, Condorcet, Rousseau, and others give us direct insight into the psychology of the reading process in Adams's case. In the first place, they were written at a particular time for a particular occasion and, as I have pointed out, there was more than a hint of performance involved. We have also to consider that the process cannot have been the same at all times. Like the rest of us, Adams read different books, at different times, in different states of mind. He even read the same books different ways at different times: the pages of Wollstonecraft and others show a relatively docile first reading with no more reaction than keyword "heads" as well as the more combative later readings.

Nevertheless, the preservation of the library is a boon and the presence of marginalia a blessing to those of us engaged in reconstruction of the past, whether our efforts are Adams-centred or not. Adams's notes may be of limited value in telling us what, when, and how he read his books, but they are exceedingly helpful in showing how he *used* them, to wit, variously at various times. Writing marginalia gave him something that he needed from his reading: at first, discipline; later, a means of sharing ideas with his contemporaries; and towards the end of his life, a way to set the record straight for posterity. The most heavily annotated volumes, few though they are, offer dramatized readings in which Adams appears to be thinking out loud. Even the least colourful examples—the Hurd, for instance—have the effect that Haraszti hoped for half a century ago: they familiarize Adams, they make us feel closer to him. This is a common effect of marginalia, not altogether uncalculated; but it also has its mystical side. Later readers who are sensitive to that sort of thing sometimes express themselves in terms of hearing voices (Lockhart said that about coming upon Scott's marginalia [Jackson, 2005: 196–7]) or of possession. Turning the pages of the books that Adams marked, we feel that we are reading over his shoulder, sharing an experience with him. Our attention rises a notch when we come upon a passage underlined or slow down to read a brief remark. We can see how some parts of the work aroused in him a sudden interest, even if it shows only in a heavy concentration of keywords; and conversely, how long stretches went unremarked upon. In Hurd's "moral and political dialogues," Adams underlined or drew vertical lines in the margin to mark quotable sentences here and there, but two dialogues "On the Constitution of the English Government" in the second volume and one "On the Uses of Foreign Travel" in the third received sustained attention, whereas the "Letters on Chivalry and Romance" at the end of the volume were marked with dutiful heads for 50 pages but then even those came to an end. Did he ever finish those "Letters"?

Which brings me to the final question. Adams's marginalia may not have all the answers but they do help us to reconstruct how he, then, read and used his books; how do we, now, read him? I have been concentrating on the internal, invisible barriers between him and us, specifically our assumptions that marginalia must be private, spontaneous, compulsive, and transparent. There are material barriers too, despite centuries of professional efforts to overcome them. Very few people are or ever have been privileged to handle the actual books from Adams's library, though they were institutionalized even before his death. For public custodians of these objects, the challenge has been to make these minor but attractive writings publicly available and thus to provide a more rounded image of the author. They have met this challenge time after time in a most responsible way, but of course could only do as much as the technologies and the print conventions of their day allowed them to do. I don't doubt that the present seemingly miraculous solution will come to be seen as inadequate in its turn—but let's hope, not for another century or so.

The trouble with marginalia is that they reverse the normal dynamic of text and reader. If the marginalia are interesting enough, for whatever reason, they call attention away from the book in which they were written and may displace it altogether, particularly when marginalia are quoted as detached statements—as they typically are—to make a point or confirm an argument. This is the "nuggets" approach. If the author of the marginalia is important enough or if the body of marginalia is substantial enough to warrant publication en masse, the notes may be gathered together with other miscellanea in a collected edition, as Scott did for Swift's snappy "remarks" in 1814. But editors realized very early on that most notes make very little sense without the passage that prompted them; in the examples of Adams's marginalia with which I began, I had to look quite hard before finding any that could stand alone, and even so, in some cases I was obliged to explain the context, if not to quote directly from the work commented on. So it has been generally accepted—as it was even in Adams's day— that both sides of the dialogue must be heard, though the annotator predominates and has the last word.

Various experiments have been tried, to get the balance right. When the original annotated volume circulated among the owner's friends, copies could be taken by transcribing the notes either onto separate sheets (as Coleridge's family editors did after his death) or into another copy of the same work (as Crabb Robinson did for some of Blake's marginalia). Franklin's copy of Adams's notes in the Price pamphlet combines these two approaches, the notes being copied on separate sheets and pasted in at the back, but keyed to a series of numbers embedded, handwritten, in the text. Print solutions include subordinating the notes as footnote commentary to the text, printing in double columns with the original text on one side and the marginalia on the other, and printing in two colours (as we did with the Coleridge edition). Scott, presenting Swift, provided a brief account of the context or a direct quotation from the text to introduce his notes, and the twentieth-century editors of the Franklin papers used much the same system when they published his marginalia. Haraszti ingeniously reformatted Adams's notes as dramatic dialogue, the two speakers taking turns so that they seem to be engaged in repartee, Adams as the wit and the original author liable to play the stooge.

All these devices, practical and satisfying as they seem for a while, have hidden drawbacks. They don't and can't distinguish between notes written at different times, for instance on multiple rereadings; or between notes written at different times on a single reading, for instance between the comments made during reading and the general summary written afterwards, which often appears as the first note at the front of the book. They can only represent the book in its final state, not in process. They naturally don't show all the unmarked pages—what would be the point?—but those pages may also tell a story of waxing and waning attention, as in the case of Adams's copy of Hurd. They attach each note to at best one passage, not too long, from the original work, whereas the note may be a response to a long section or to a cumulative argument, and it takes a very dedicated researcher to pay as much attention to the original author's argument as to the annotator's counter-position.

Most significantly, all these methods involve editorial selection. We don't know whether Adams's copy of the Price pamphlet contained underlining or heads (though it is likely that it did), because Franklin was interested only in the substantive notes. Haraszti mentions the presence of other marks in the books he describes, but they did not concern him either: he wanted to show Adams zestfully engaged in intellectual combat. Haraszti gives no page numbers, so it is virtually impossible to reconstitute the annotated text from his presentation; of course he did not intend his work to function as an edition. The transcriptions available today through the Adams Library at the Boston Public Library likewise mention the presence of other marks but rarely include them (and the transcriptions, though very helpful, are not yet absolutely accurate). But then they did not need to include them, because the books themselves have been or are being digitized.

The ideal situation for the reader wishing to track Adams's progress through his books is to be able to examine the very volumes he used, with aids such as the Boston Public and LibraryThing have already made available: notes about the author, partial transcriptions of the marginalia with keyword searchability (though I haven't been able to get that to work yet), lists of the most heavily annotated books, and a chronology of books inscribed or otherwise dated by Adams himself. But that way is expensive, time-consuming, and bad for the books. The next best, hitherto, has been a scrupulous scholarly edition that is properly introduced, footnoted, and indexed, not just a diplomatic transcription. But that is labour-intensive, infinitely more expensive, and subject to the limitations that I have described. It's not clear that Adams's marginalia merit such special treatment, and the Adams Papers Project so far as I know is not contemplating it. The new digitization project is a marvellous alternative to a printed edition because it is comparatively cheap, it does not prejudge what use might be made of the annotated books, and it includes every page, not just every marked page, so that the reader can follow Adams's reading step by step and (if she so desires) read Hurd, Turgot, and Wollstonecraft at the same time. It is our best shot at a facsimile edition. Since it is in electronic form, it is potentially highly adaptable and expandable: we can fantasize about links to improved transcriptions, editorial explanations, and commentary, perhaps introduced on a wiki basis. We'll have to wait and see what happens to online resources in general as well as to this particular worthy project. In the meantime, it pleases me to consider that when Franklin had Adams's marginalia transcribed into his own copy of Price's pamphlet he was doing the same thing as we are doing now, commissioning *his* best shot at a facsimile edition; and that adding Adams's annotated books to a social-networking site is *our* best shot at giving them free circulation among like-minded friends. (Even the finicky Jefferson owned a volume of Franklin's annotated pamphlets.) The gap between then and now may not be all that wide after all.

NOTE

1. Witness his letter about epistolary style, written to Abigail Adams on 7 July 1776 (Adams and Adams, 2007: 126–8).

REFERENCES

Adams, Abigail and John Adams. *My Dearest Friend.* Ed. Margaret A. Hogan and C. James Taylor. Cambridge: Belknap Press, 2007.

Adams, Abigail, John Adams, and Thomas Jefferson. *The Adams-Jefferson Letters: The Complete Correspondence between Thomas Jefferson and Abigail and John Adams.* Ed. Lester J. Cappon. 2 vols. Chapel Hill: U of North Carolina P, 1959.

Adams, John. *Works.* Ed. Charles Francis Adams. 10 vols. Boston: Little, Brown, 1850–1856.

Adams, John. *Diary and Autobiography.* Ed. L.C. Butterfield. 4 vols. Cambridge: Belknap Press, 1961.

Adams, John and Benjamin Rush. *The Spur of Fame: Dialogues of John Adams and Benjamin Rush, 1805–1813.* Ed. John A. Schutz and Douglass Adair. San Marino: Huntington Library, 1966.

Ellis, Joseph J. *Passionate Sage: The Character and Legacy of John Adams*. New York and London: W.W. Norton and Company, 1993.

Haraszti, Zoltán. *John Adams and the Prophets of Progress*. Cambridge: Harvard UP, 1962.

Hayes, Kevin J. "Benjamin Franklin." *Oxford Handbook of Early American Literature*. Ed. Kevin J. Hayes. Oxford: Oxford UP, 2008. 431–50.

Hurd, Richard. *Moral and Political Dialogues, with Letters on Chivalry and Romance*. London, 1765.

Jackson, H.J. *Marginalia: Readers Writing in Books*. New Haven: Yale UP, 2001.

Jackson, H.J. *Romantic Readers: The Evidence of Marginalia*. New Haven: Yale UP, 2005.

McCullough, David. *John Adams*. New York: Simon and Schuster, 2001.

Price, Richard. *Observations on the Importance of the American Revolution*. Boston, 1784.

Staël, Anne-Louise-Germaine de. *De l'influence des passions sur le bonheur des individus et des nations*. Lausanne, 1796.

Swift, Jonathan. *Works*. Ed. Walter Scott. 19 vols. Edinburgh: Constable, 1814.

Wollstonecraft, Mary. *An Historical and Moral View of the Origin and Progress of the French Revolution*. London, 1794.

8. 'Soiled by use' or 'enlivened by association'? Attitudes toward marginalia

William H. Sherman*

There are few subjects that divide people like the practice of writing in books. Some readers wouldn't dream of picking up a text without taking pen, pencil or highlighter in hand, while others find even the faintest underlining distasteful or offensive. Some collectors seek out books that carry the signs and scars of the histories that have delivered them to us while others prefer their volumes to look as much as possible like they did when they were first produced. Historians of books and readers have long since started to study the evidence preserved in the margins of books, but they have barely begun to recover and interpret the history of attitudes toward them.[1] Where can we find expressions of these values, and what kinds of tools do we need to make sense of them?

There is no better place to start than the sale or auction catalogue, where cultural values are translated into financial valuation. And here we find a sharp divergence in the treatment of annotated books. Take these two examples from the middle of the twentieth century:

> black letter, each title within a woodcut border; the blank margin . . . skilfully renewed; each work rather soiled by use but sound copies . . .
> —Sale catalogue, Bernard Quaritch Ltd (January, 1952)

> This volume, printed during the reign of Elizabeth I, has been well and piously used. Marginal notations in an Elizabethan hand—comments and scriptural quotation—bring to life an early and earnest owner.
> —Exhibition catalogue, *The Book of Common Prayer* (1953)

These two descriptions offer different views of—and vocabularies for—signs of use in rare books. One volume has been 'rather soiled by use' while the other has been 'well and piously used' by 'an early and earnest owner'. What makes them the perfect point of departure for the issues I want to explore in this essay is the fact that they are both describing the same volume—that is, the same copy of the same book. It is a small folio, now housed at the Huntington Library, containing the 1586 *Book of Common Prayer* and the 1583 Psalter (Figure 8.1).[2] It was among the unusual collection of more than 700 rare prayer books assembled by the Los Angeles-based businessman James R. Page and donated to the Huntington (on whose Board of Trustees he had served). The first description above is from the January 1952 catalogue of the antiquarian book-dealers Bernard Quaritch Ltd, from whom Page acquired the volume for $210.[3] The second text is from the catalogue accompanying a 1953 exhibition at the Huntington, where Page's prayer books were first displayed (Bowen, 1953, 6).

What the sale catalogue describes as dirt, then, is what the exhibition catalogue identifies as a thorough set of manuscript notes. The unidentified reader who produced them took up this volume with pen in hand many times, entering in the margins short summaries of important points, corrections of typographical errors, and references to other texts, and filling the blank spaces between sections of text with extended discourses on points of piety and liturgical practice.

Prayer books were, not surprisingly, among the most heavily used books in the early modern period, and—along with copies of the bible and texts on childbirth and household medicine—the most likely repositories for manuscript family histories. The 'soil' on the title page and flyleaf of another copy of the *Book of Common Prayer* at the Huntington Library preserves the signatures, mottos, scribbles, and tabular record of births and deaths in the Wood family of Weardale (Durham) and Brafferton (Yorkshire) from 1643 to 1661.[4] The phrasing in the Quaritch catalogue reflects a preference for clean copies that is so universal today it may hardly give us pause for thought. While many of us now write in at least some of our books, very few of us were given the message that it was the right thing to do, much less trained to do it in school. But the desire for pristine texts is not (as we shall see) universal, and Renaissance scholar and collector of marginalia Stephen Orgel has gone so far as to describe it as 'one of the strangest phenomena of modern bibliophilic and curatorial psychology'(Orgel, 2000, 92). While it is neither as modern nor as strange as Orgel suggests—indeed, it has been the dominant position in librarianship and the book trade for several centuries—the story turns out to be, and always to have been, surprisingly full of opposing values and practices.

The preference for clean copies has a long history, with significant implications for those who preserve, collect and study the books that come down to us from the past. It has deep roots in the aesthetics and economics of both scribal culture and print culture, and it informs both the ethics of possession and the etiquette of use. The bias against writing in books

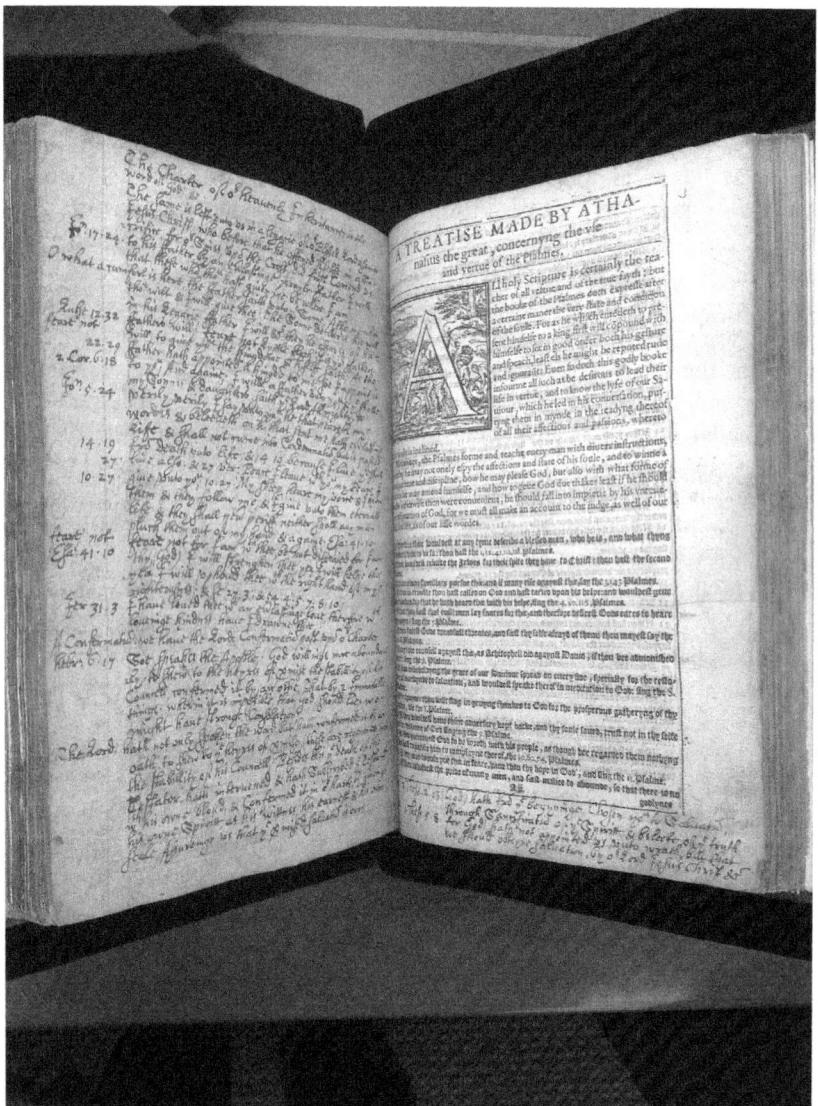

Source: Courtesy of The Huntington Library, San Marino, California (copyright William Sherman).

Figure 8.1   A heavily used 1583 Psalter from the James R. Page Collection (RB438000:87F)

is bound up with a variety of taboos and transgressions: Virginia Woolf described it as a sexual violation of both the text and its future readers, and other negative analogies compare annotations to sacrilege, noise, and parasites (Jackson, 2001, 239–240).[5] A wide range of recent psychological and sociological theories can provide some purchase on the anxieties provoked by marginalia: they can be related to the ideology of the passive reader identified by historians of reader-response; to the fear of clutter discussed by Adam Phillips; and to the general discourse of messiness and 'matter-out-of-place' that, as Mary Douglas has explained, governs a wide range of behaviours involving consumption.

As Holbrook Jackson put it in his classic compilation of book behaviour and misbehaviour, *The Anatomy of Bibliomania*, 'Scholars do not hesitate to mix books with eating apparatus'(Jackson, 1950, 424). One of the least hesitant scholars was evidently the critic and poet William Empson—best known as the author of *Seven Types of Ambiguity* and *The Structure of Complex Words* but also one of his generation's fiercest (and messiest) readers of Renaissance drama. According to his former lodger, the translator and playwright John Henry Jones, Empson was once forced to buy the London Library a new copy of Marlowe's *Doctor Faustus*: when he returned the original they found it covered not only with his marginal notes but with the jam from his morning toast (Jones, 1989). When I cited this anecdote in a *TLS* review, Jones himself wrote in to elaborate:

> The work in question was W.W. Greg's parallel-text edition of Marlowe's Doctor Faustus, and the librarian . . . was hardly straining at a gnat [sic] in demanding a fresh copy—the book was virtually done to death in Empson's zeal to demolish Greg's argument in favour of the B-text, a process which . . . was maintained throughout all quotidian activities.
>
> (Jones, 2001)

When books are public property (as in libraries or schools, where volumes move rapidly from one reader to another) writing in their margins is considered antisocial behaviour, certainly a breach of decorum and possibly a breach of the law. Every reader in the Bodleian Library must swear an oath which not only famously forbids them to 'kindle . . . any fire or flame' but also 'to mark, deface or injure in any way, any volume [or] document . . .' The Cambridge University Library has placed a sign on every desk that reads: 'MARKING BOOKS IS FORBIDDEN' (though many of these have themselves been covered with graffiti). And the Clark Library in Los Angeles warns readers against 'removing or adding' any text. In his letter about Empson, Jones concluded by castigating 'the arrogant twerps who deface public and university library books with their mindless graffiti', observing (with just a little exaggeration) that 'Users of the [University of London] library will know that a "clean" book, unless it is a first-time issue, is a great rarity . . .'

In her recent book on marginalia from the eighteenth century to the present, Heather Jackson explains that the rise of the 'clean book' is indeed associated with the growth of circulating libraries. The efforts of libraries to keep their books in good shape are understandable, but the current obsession with cleanliness poses some difficult questions about the role of libraries in the empowerment of readers. Lending libraries undoubtedly helped to spread literacy and learning to new groups of readers, but in turning marginalia from a tool to a transgression they also deprived those readers of one of their most powerful methods for conversing with authors and other readers.

Consider, for instance, the comfort that Charles Lamb took in reading library books in the early nineteenth century:

> How beautiful to a genuine lover of reading are the sullied leaves, and worn-out appearance, nay, the very odour . . . if we would not forget kind feelings in fastidiousness, of an old 'Circulating Library' Tom Jones, or Vicar of Wakefield! How they speak of the thousand thumbs, that have turned over their pages with delight!—of the lone sempstress, whom they may have cheered . . . after her long day's needle-toil, running far into midnight, when she has snatched an hour, ill-spared from sleep, to steep her cares, as in some Lethean cup, in spelling out their enchanting contents! Who would have them a whit less soiled?[6]

The novelist Robertson Davies is one of those who would, as he explained in his 1995 essay on 'How to Be a Collector':

> As a boy I sometimes made use of a library which was also used by uncommonly dirty people; many of the books were heavily thumbed, and others showed evidence of bread and butter—even peanut butter; I remember one volume in which a reader had used a dirty pipe-cleaner as a bookmark . . . To be frank with you, I have never much liked public collections and of late years have avoided them totally. If I want a book, I buy it, and if it cannot be bought, I find a way of doing without.
>
> (Davies, 1997, 72–73)

While few of us would go quite as far as that, Davies is giving voice to something deep within the bibliographical unconscious, and not so deep in modern class consciousness. The desire for clean books now comes almost instinctively to modern readers and owners. Heather Jackson (2001) tells the story of 'a small boy taken against his will by his father to one of Maurice Sendak's book signings. Pushed forward to get his book signed, the boy looked at Sendak imploringly and said, "Please don't crap up my book!"' (p. 235). This may simply reflect the desire to make, and keep, a book one's own—which is also, ironically, one of the most common motives for writing marginalia, whether of the simple 'I was here' variety or the more complicated kinds that register a present or future personal interest.

As these examples suggest, the aversion to writing in books has been extended from publicly to privately owned books; and it has also been projected by modern scholars back onto pre-modern readers. A case in point is Ethel M. Portal's 1915 *British Academy Lecture* on the abortive plans for an academy at the court of King James I. She regrettably informs us that James 'was said to have kept his books in a ragged and untidy condition, and to have scribbled in their margins'. Portal quotes the contemporary advice of Henry Peacham, 'Have a care of keeping your bookes handsome and well bound', but she ignored the fact that Peacham went on to say, 'For your owne use spare them not for noting or enterlining' (1622 cited in Portal, 1915–16, 191).[7] A more complicated example comes from May McKisack's account of the Elizabethan library of Archbishop Matthew Parker. Parker used his position in the church to acquire countless manuscripts during the dissolution of the monasteries: he and his team of scholarly secretaries systematically collated and regularly annotated these books, and their pioneering work led to the production of the first printed books using Anglo-Saxon type. But McKisack's description of Parker's practices—'Virtually all the historical manuscripts in the collection contain addenda in the hands of Parker or his scribes . . . tables of contents, sometimes a sketchy index, marginalia innumerable'—culminates in the judgement, 'Deplorable methods no doubt . . .' (McKisack, 1971, 36).[8]

Parker's active interventions in the texts in his collection look less deplorable if they are approached not by looking backward from late print culture but by moving forward from medieval scribal culture (in which readers were, to some extent, expected to customize their books) and from the ancient scriptural tradition (in which even the holiest words were surrounded by layers of later commentary). That said, Parker's attitude was markedly different from that of Bishop Richard de Bury, whose fourteenth-century book *Philobiblon* was one of the earliest and most influential guides to book collecting. In chapter 17, 'Of showing due Propriety in the Custody of Books', Richard suggests that 'next to the vestments and vessels dedicated to the Lord's body, holy books deserve to be rightly treated by the clergy, to which great injury is done so often as they are touched by unclean hands.' He describes the disrespectful treatment common among the novice reader:

> His nails are stuffed with fetid filth as black as jet, with which he marks any passage that pleases him . . . He does not fear to eat fruit or cheese over an open book, or carelessly to carry a cup to and from his mouth; and because he has

no wallet at hand he drops into books the fragments that are left . . . Aye, and then hastily folding his arms he leans forward on the book . . . and then, by way of mending the wrinkles, he fold back the margin of the leaves, to the no small injury of the book . . . But the handling of books is especially to be forbidden to those shameless youths, who as soon as they have learned to form the shapes of letters, straightaway, if they have the opportunity, become unhappy commentators, and wherever they find an extra margin about the text, furnish it with monstrous alphabets . . . a practice that we have frequently seen injuring the usefulness and value of the most beautiful books.

(Bury, 1960, 157–159)[9]

Marc Drogin's study of the anathema—or 'book curses'—in medieval manuscripts explains that the scribes who copied them were often haunted by visions of grubby hands besmirching the pristine products of their labours:

a typical inscription read 'Quisquis quem tetigerit/Sit illa lota manus [Please wash your hands / Before touching this book]'.

(Drogin, 1983, 17)[10]

Such attitudes reflect an awareness that when books are made of decent materials, and are handled properly, they are likely to outlive their early owners and become available for future buyers and readers. We might therefore expect the preference for clean copies to be nothing less than common sense among those who trade in rare books where—as in the trade of used goods of any kind—those that are in better condition tend to fetch a higher price than those that are worn. In fact, it's clear that the ideal book, among many collectors, is an un-used book. Consider the position of readers (and their marginalia) in the standard terms used to describe the condition of used books:

MINT As new, unread.
FINE Close to new, showing slight signs of age but without any defects.
VERY GOOD Indicates a used book that shows some signs of wear but still has no defects.
GOOD Used for a book which shows normal wear and aging, still complete and with no major defects.
FAIR A worn and used copy, probably with cover tears and other defects.
READING COPY [or WORKING COPY] A poor copy with text complete but not much else going for it.

(Ahearn, 1989, 49)[11]

The ultimate mint copy might still have its pages uncut, which not only ensures that it is an un-used book but makes it a virtually un-usable one. Not surprisingly, collectors and booksellers have used various methods to improve the condition of the books that come into their hands; and in some cases, this has clearly involved removing the handwriting of earlier owners. Among the annotated books at the Huntington, I found examples of signatures and notes that had been crossed out, washed away and even cut out of the margin—often trimming the entire margin but sometimes excising only handwritten notes, leaving a jagged edge that reveals the extent and location, but not the content, of the annotations.

Some of these 'cleanings' were no doubt done by subsequent readers rather than booksellers or binders. But within the book trade, there has been a history of aggressive practices involving bleaching the pages and trimming their margins down to the very edge of the printed text—sometimes even re-mounting every page in a frame of new paper. This history is extremely difficult to reconstruct, since these practices have rarely been documented and still remain to be studied in their own right (by historians of the book, booksellers, conservators, or—ideally—all of them together); but such operations seem to have been common in the eighteenth and nineteenth centuries and are by no means unknown in the twentieth (Hulvey, 1998, 161). Roger Stoddard has recently offered a particularly vivid description of these trends in conservation and collecting which has chilling ramifications for the history of reading: 'Rare is the binder who has deliberately preserved historical evidence. Old covers and endpapers are jettisoned along with their library marks, ownership marks, booksellers' marks, index notes, annotations, documents, or verses ... Then stains, both finger marks and marginalia, are bathed away in bleach before the results are squeezed flat in a standing press, obliterating from paper the bite of type and ornament and the dents and scratches scribed or pressed blind without pigment' (Stoddard, 2000, 32).[12] Although this may sound mild compared to bleaching or cutting pages, it too can remove evidence of past reading: two types which are mentioned by Richard de Bury are marking pages by folding their corners, and marking passages by running a fingernail down their margins.[13]

The treatment received by Item 87 in the *James R. Page Collection* (the book I began with) was apparently more benign. Turning back to the passage from the Quaritch catalogue, we can see that the frayed margins of some of the leaves have been 'skilfully renewed': this involved reinforcing them with patches of blank paper, thus making every page a uniform size. The language here suggests an attempt to make the book new again, to take it back through time by undoing the signs of its subsequent use. The ideal copy becomes, paradoxically, a historic book with most of the traces of its history removed.

What makes the conservator's decision of what to preserve, what to repair, and what to discard so difficult is that the value of particular types of physical evidence is not always clear and is subject to change through time. As Nicholas Hadgraft put it in condemning the repairs favoured by what he calls 'tidy-minded' librarians, 'Conservation . . . can . . . remove evidence which we are only just beginning to appreciate . . .' (Hadgraft, 1995, 27–28).[14] One of Quaritch's most recent catalogues offers what may be one of the most poignant cases of misguided 'restoration' in the modern book trade. It describes a first edition of Milton's *Areopagitica* with two manuscript notes that are 'very faint . . . all but washed out during some restoration in the past'. Comparison with other copies reveals that these notes were most likely corrections in the hand of Milton himself (Orgel, 2000, 92). In this (hopefully) extreme case, the desire to take a book back to its original state—or our image of its original state—has obliterated the very hand of the author who produced it.

Aggressive restoration has not been endorsed by all dealers, conservators, and collectors: indeed, a book that has had no restoration is now known in the book trade as an 'honest book'.[15] Heather Jackson (2001) suggests, in fact, that up to about 1820 marginalia were not only tolerated by booksellers but seen as a potential selling point: 'In catalogues that I have examined dating from the 1740s to the 1820s, the presence of notes is recorded only as an asset . . .' (p. 271). After this date, Jackson observes that prohibitions against the marking of books get stronger, and suggests that 'annotating readers went underground' (p. 73). It is tempting to assume that collectors' tastes changed accordingly, but there have been some important exceptions. For James R. Page, readers' marks still added to, rather than detracted from, the value of the book: as he put it in an interview with the *Los Angeles Times* during his 1953 exhibition, 'Many of the books in my collection are enlivened by the marginal notes and comments made by the many people, from distinguished and well-known people to otherwise unknown persons, through whose hands they passed . . .'[16] The rare book dealer Bernard M. Rosenthal—whose collection of annotated Renaissance books was recently acquired by the Beinecke Library at Yale—has explained that when he started buying books in the 1950s, early printed books stained with the occasional fingerprints of a fifteenth-century pressman, or filled with scribblings by a contemporary student . . . did not have the same appeal to the bibliophiles as the flawless, virginal copy—even now one sometimes finds dealers' and auction catalogues in which the presence of manuscript annotations is mentioned in the same breath with the defects, e.g. 'some water stains, occasional manuscript notes, else fine.'

For Rosenthal, buying annotated books turned out to make good economic sense: it was a way to compete with buyers who had more money. But, as with Page, it gradually gave him a different set of attitudes toward the annotations themselves. Rosenthal became 'obsessed, by the idea of some day . . . producing a catalogue of books in which the presence of annotations would not merely be mentioned, but . . . ranked on the same level as the printed text and dignified by proper descriptions . . .' In 1997 Rosenthal published just such a catalogue of 242 annotated books, with remarkably detailed descriptions of the length, content, and appearance of the marginalia (Rosenthal, 1997).[17]

There is evidence, too, that Rosenthal's attitudes are being shared by a growing number of people in the rare book community—and particularly by librarians eager to rethink the mission of 'departments of special collections'. In a polemical essay in the inaugural issue of the rare book librarians' journal *RBM*, Daniel Traister asked what would be so bad about giving readers a freer hand in rare book collections and even putting the books back into general circulation:

> our students and faculty [would] take it as their God-given right to . . . take the books home, sneeze on them . . . drop spaghetti sauce on them, and do all the other horrible things people do to books all the time. And, by the bye, which they have done to books at all times since there were books, even going so far as to write on them. (I cannot be the only person in our field who thinks that the emphasis on pristine condition in collecting modern first editions is misplaced, indicative merely of the fact that the book has never been [yuck!] read. One of the things that excites me about older books is precisely marks, comments, marginalia, showing that they have had early readers and occasionally even indicative of those readers' responses.
>
> (Traister, 2000, 66)[18]

Surprisingly enough, the man who gave his books and his name to the Folger Shakespeare Library in Washington DC seems to have agreed with Traister. During the early decades of the twentieth century, Henry Clay Folger became infamous for his relentless pursuit of Shakespeare *First Folios*, but he also had a reputation as a collector of annotated books.

On 9 July 1931, a British bookseller named N.M. Broadbent wrote to the newly appointed director of research at the Folger Library, Dr Joseph Quincy Adams, to describe some books he had sent to Folger containing annotations by sixteenth- and seventeenth-century readers.

Broadbent suggested that 'The subject of book annotations has, as far as I know, received no attention as yet from men of letters, but it is surely worthy of the deepest study.' While 'the late Sir Israel Gollancz was attracted to the subject' he did not have time to pursue it, and as 'a branch of book collection' Broadbent believed it to be 'peculiar to Mr. Folger—all other great collectors appearing to be unaware of the great importance of these books.'[19]

Among the books Broadbent had sold to Folger, he wanted to draw Adams's attention to one of particular importance: it was a copy of

Cicero's *De Oratore*, published in Venice in 1569. The marginal annotations by a contemporary reader feature a complex code of symbols.
While similar marks appear in other annotations from the period, this
may be the first known case where the reader had provided a key to their
meanings: on the last page of the volume, there are two tables listing the
symbols and explaining what they signify.[20] The symbols amount to a fairly
elaborate system for tagging passages touching on particular topics and
employing various rhetorical devices: a trident was used for passages of
argumentation or reasoning and the sign for Venus signalled an interest in
love, and '*amp*[*lificatio*]', 'metap[hor]', and 'sim[ile]' are all signified by a
symbol that looks like a flower. Broadbent spotted the 'trefoil' (or clover)
symbol that had also been found in some of Francis Bacon's notes, and
claimed that this was the key to the annotational system devised by Bacon
for digesting the material he read. He suggested that the same system was
shared by Ben Jonson, and in the letter to Adams he identified the notes
in the Cicero volume as being in Jonson's own hand. Adams duly endorsed
Broadbent's letter, 'Key to Annotated Books by Bacon and Jonson'.

Broadbent's letter prompts a brief return to attitudes toward marks in
books during Bacon's and Jonson's own day. The fact that early marginalia are so common in Renaissance books—despite all of the human and
natural forces at work to remove them—suggests that it was not just great
scholars like Bacon and Jonson who wrote in their books. A wide range
of readers were encouraged to mark their books as a way of making them
more useful for their present and future needs, and in the early modern
period marginal annotations played a prominent role in pedagogical
theory and professional practice.[21]

Records of professors and students at the universities of Renaissance
England and France testify to their use of marginalia for parsing Latin sentences and storing useful phrases, but educational textbooks from the period
make it clear that the same practices were introduced at a much earlier age.[22]
In 1612, the schoolmaster John Brinsley published his *Ludus Literarius: Or,
the Grammar Schoole*, an influential handbook for introducing students to
reading and writing. In several places Brinsley touches on marginalia and
offers some remarkably detailed instructions for 'marking' books:

> difficult words, or matters of speciall obseruation, [which] they doe reade in any
> Author, [should] be marked out; I meane all such words or things as eyther are
> hard to them in the learning of them, or which are of some speciall excellency,
> or vse . . . For the marking of them, to doe it with little lines vnder them, or
> aboue them, or against such partes of the word wherein the difficulty lieth, or by
> some prickes, or whatsoeuer letter or marke may best helpe to cal the knowledge
> of the thing to remembrance.
>
> (Brinsley, 1612, 46)[23]

'As they proceed to higher fourmes,' Brinsley continues, they should 'marke onely those [passages] which haue most difficulty, as . . . Deriuations, figuratiue Constructions, Tropes . . . and the like'—precisely those features signalled by the key of symbols in the Folger's 1569 Cicero.

Not every Renaissance reader felt comfortable with entering such notes in their books, however, and Brinsley offered students several ways to avoid 'marring' their books. First, they could make their writing neat and inconspicuous, using 'a fine small hand [which] will not hurt their bookes' (124). They could also choose to use pencil rather than pen for some of their notes, since they could later be erased:

> For the manner of noting, it is best to note all schoole books with inke; & also all others . . . whereof we would haue daily or long practice, because inke will indure: neither wil such books be the worse for their noting, but the better, if they be noted with iudgement. But for all other bookes, which you would haue faire againe at your pleasure, note them with a pensil of black lead: for that you may rub out againe when you will, with the crums of new wheate bread.
>
> (Mogg, 1985, 46–47)[24]

For very young readers, who were not yet capable of writing a fine small hand, Brinsley suggested that they 'may make some secret markes . . . at euery hard word; though but with some little dint with their naile' (47). And finally, those who wanted to keep their books completely clean could use 'a little paper book' to write their notes in (124).

The issues raised by Broadbent's claims for the 1569 Cicero need to be put, finally, in two additional contexts. First, Folger assembled his collection and cultivated his interest in annotated books, toward the beginning of what Robert Alan Shaddy has recently called the Anglo-American 'cult of collecting' (Shaddy, 1994). While this cult was certainly concerned with turning newly acquired corporate cash into old-world cultural capital,[25] Shaddy suggests that the movement is also marked by what he describes as the language of 'sentimental attachment'. Within the field of book collecting, there was a particular fascination with books that had 'a documented connection to famous people from the past—so-called "association copies"'(Arnold, 1923). The associations were usually documented by a signature or dedication, but also by marginalia (if they were in a verifiable hand). Raymond Blathwayte explained the attraction of the association copy in a 1912 article on 'The Romance of the Sale Room':

> As the years roll on the value of a book is often gauged by its associations, by its own individual history, by some special fact of interest connected with its owners, and, most especially of all, by any autographic value which those owners may have attached to it. There are books today which, by reason of

pencilled margins or autographed presentations, possess a hundred times their original value or the value they would otherwise have possessed, and your true book collector is well aware of this.

(Blathwayte, 1912, 939)

It is not hard to see how the signature and marginalia of a famous writer like Bacon or Jonson would be seen as a source of added value, and how such an association could become a greater source of value than the physical condition of the book. William Harris Arnold, who created one of the period's most impressive libraries of association copies, suggested that the collector of early editions should strive:

to procure them in their pristine state . . . but, when a book bears evidence of a distinguished association, the material condition of the volume becomes a matter of secondary importance . . . A volume of the very slightest consequence may be transformed into an object of precious regard just by a bit of writing on one of its leaves.

(Arnold, 1923, 37)

In one extraordinary case, the evidence of association which transformed a book was not a bit of writing but a bit of soil on one of its leaves. Blathwayte told this story of a volume made more valuable after a particularly important reader dropped it in the road:

Charles I borrowed a volume of tracts from Thomason, the stationer, and clumsily let them fall into the mud, whereby their then value was considerably depreciated. To-day the British Museum regards those stains as out-weighing by far the intrinsic value of the quaint old verbosities they so sadly dim.

(Blathwayte, 1912, 940)[26]

One of the standard guides to book collecting captures the current appeal of—and limits to—such association: 'If the name is that of a well known person, it adds to the value of the book, converting it into an "association copy". If the name is unknown, it is best that it should be unobtrusive, neat and not on the title-page' (Brook, 1980, 88). Some collectors, however, did not restrict their interest in a book's associations to the signatures and notes of famous people, and extended it to any sign of life left behind by the hands of any past reader. An eloquent justification of this approach—and one that anticipates the sentiments of Page and Rosenthal—can be found in the tribute paid in 1941 by Princeton English professor Charles Grosvenor Osgood to the library of A. Edward Newton (which was almost entirely devoted to association copies):

Who in all the centuries have touched this book as I am touching now? Or how many generations has it passed, quiet and undisturbed, on a darkened shelf, enclosing its own dateless life, while the life of men swirled and eddied, around it unconcerned? . . . To the rightful owner the value of an old book is not a mere matter of date and scarcity. From all its previous owners and readers, known or unknown, has accrued to it a certain potential of humanity which is more than a mere matter of sentiment.

(Parke-Bernet, 1941)[27]

If it was relatively easy to obliterate the signs of former owners, it was even easier to create associations with them after the fact—or to invent them altogether. The most celebrated example of forced—or forged— associations involving a Renaissance author is the so-called Ireland Shakespeare Forgeries, in which William Henry Ireland faked signatures, letters and even works by Shakespeare.[28]

But the methods for engineering associations need not be as devious as outright forgery, and one interesting book associated with Ben Jonson points to more ambiguous, and understandable, motives. On the title page of the Huntington Library's copy of *George of Montemayor's Diana* (published in London in 1598) Ben Jonson clearly inscribed his signature ('Sum Ben: Jonsonij') and his motto ('tanquam explorator').[29] This inscription is genuine, but its association with this volume is not: at some point in its history, the title page was detached from the copy Jonson originally owned and pasted into this one.

Broadbent's association of the 1569 Cicero with Jonson and Bacon needs to be put in the context not just of this passion for association copies in the early twentieth century but of the so-called 'Baconian' movement that flourished alongside it. In arguing that it was Francis Bacon who wrote the plays now attributed to Shakespeare, the Baconians found his signature everywhere (including countless instances, in codes and ciphers, within the texts of Shakespeare's plays). In 1912, Broadbent's contemporary W.T. Smedley claimed to have worked with his fellow Baconian W.M. Safford to recover nearly 2,000 books annotated by Bacon (Smedley, 1912). An article from 1943 in the journal *Baconiana* (entitled 'The libraries of Bacon and Jonson: How they marked their books') offered a complete listing of what it claimed were the marks used in annotations by Bacon and Jonson, and mentioned that the books on which it was based 'were collected by the late Mr. W.T. Smedley, and are now preserved in a famous American library [i.e. the Folger]'(Rose, 1943).[30] At the time, this earned Folger the admiration of the book-collecting community: a short article in a journal called *The Librarian and Book World* reported that Folger's 'most astounding achievement' as a collector consisted not in assembling more than half of the world's copies of Shakespeare's *First Folio* but 'in the re-formation of considerable portions of the libraries of Ben Jonson and Francis Bacon, including the acquisition of the famous collection en bloc of W.T. Smedley and W.M. Safford'(Immerito [pseud], 1932). This notice was signed 'Immerito', which is the same pseudonym used by Smedley in an earlier article in the journal *Baconiana*, so it is distinctly possible that he penned the tribute himself.

Smedley, Safford and Broadbent may just be the tip of a Baconian iceberg in the twentieth-century rare book trade. In his discussion of Bacon in the *Index of English Literary Manuscripts*, Peter Beal concludes:

> In so far as it relates to Bacon, Safford's collection was based on nothing more than fanciful conjecture. Many men besides Bacon were in the habit of marking their books, and also of using the marginal trefoil which is found in certain of Bacon's MSS. Without clear evidence of provenance or positive palaeographical identification it would be impossible to distinguish Bacon's books from those of his contemporaries.
>
> (Beal, 1980, 20)[31]

Some of the marks found in the Folger's 1569 Cicero are similar to those used by both Bacon and Jonson, but they are also used by other readers, and the hand used to inscribe them does not bear a close resemblance to the hand of either Jonson or Bacon. There does not seem to be any evidence whatsoever to connect the 1569 Cicero with Jonson or Bacon.

My purpose in exploring it at such length has not been to put either Folger or the dealers who sold books to him into a negative light. Like Page's and Rosenthal's special appreciation of annotated copies, and Arnold's and Newton's passion for association copies, Folger's dealings with Broadbent and Smedley raise the larger and more interesting question of what exactly gives old books their value in the present. Are annotated books 'soiled by use' or are they 'enlivened by association'? Are books from the past precious relics, in which marginalia are dirt or desecration, or are they inanimate objects which are only brought to life by traces of the human hands and minds that used them?

The books and readers I have examined here point to two different economies of collecting and two opposing philosophies about how to treat the books we find valuable. It's possible, and in some ways useful, to read these positions in relation to the terms offered by Karl Marx at the very beginning of *Capital*, where he suggests that the value of any commodity will be split into two factors. The first is what he calls their 'use value' (that is, their utility or their ability to satisfy some function useful to humans). The second is their 'exchange value' (their marketability, or the money they will fetch when sold). There are certainly examples, here, of the fetishism of the commodity that Marx critiqued—the emptying of the tangible and the masking of the social in the name of abstract exchange. But the commodity Marx uses in his discussion is the manufacture of coats from linen, and books seem to be a special kind of commodity in which the definitions of, and distinctions between, use value and exchange value get a little blurry.

Even those of us who are not in a position to approach books as commodities have to choose between two opposing systems of value and a wide range of possible reading behaviours. Anne Fadiman has recently suggested that people who value books fall into two categories. Those she calls 'courtly lovers' read a book with 'Platonic adoration, a noble but doomed attempt to conserve forever the state of perfect chastity in which it had left the bookseller.' For those she calls 'carnal lovers', on the other hand, 'a book's words [are] holy, but the paper, cloth, cardboard, glue, thread, and ink that contained them [are] a mere vessel, and . . . Hard use [is] a sign not of disrespect but of intimacy' (Fadiman, 1998, 31–32). While it's probably clear that my own sympathies lie with the carnal lover, the courtly lover asks some difficult questions: Would you really be happy to see a copy of Shakespeare's *First Folio* dipped in spaghetti sauce? And while rare marginalia may be as interesting as rare books, what about newer ones? At some point, don't they start to look too much like our own notes? On the other hand, we're now closer in time to the *First Folio* than Archbishop Parker was to most of the manuscripts he annotated. And if we do not leave marks in our books, what kinds of evidence will future historians turn to? You may, depending on your answer to the questions I have been posing, wish to respond in the space below.

NOTES

*　　Thanks to Laurence Droy (University of Leicester) and Emma Perry (TCRU, Institute of Education) for their help in formatting the text for this chapter.

1. See Stoddard RE. (1985) *Marks in Books, Illustrated and Explained*, Cambridge, MA: Houghton Library; Jackson HJ. (2001) *Marginalia: Readers Writing in Books*, New Haven: Yale University Press and Sherman WH. (2008) *Used Books: Marking Readers in Renaissance England*, Philadelphia: University of Pennsylvania Press.
   This essay is based on Sherman W. (2003) 'Rather soiled by use': attitudes toward readers' marks. *The Book Collector* 52: pp. 471–490 which was revised and expanded as Chapter 8 of *Used Books: Marking Readers in Renaissance England*.

2. The *Book of Common Prayer* is STC 16311.3 and the Psalter is STC 2463. The shelf-mark at the Huntington Library is RB 438000:87F.

3. The text is now taped to a flyleaf at the front of the book. The details of the purchase are noted in Page's acquisition records in the Huntington Library's institutional archives.

4. Henry E. Huntington Library, R[are] B[ook] 61457; STC 2241.

5. See also her earlier essay, Jackson HJ. (1992) Writing in books and other marginal activities. *University of Toronto Quarterly* 62: pp. 218–231.

6. Lamb C. 'Detached thoughts on books and reading', *The London Magazine*, July 1822.

7. Citing Peacham H. (1622) *The Compleat Gentleman*, London. I am grateful to Ian Donaldson for bringing this passage to my attention.

8. For a more measured assessment of Parker's interventions, see Graham T. (1997) The beginnings of Old English studies: evidence from the manuscripts of Matthew Parker. In: Sati S (ed) *Back to the Manuscripts*. Tokyo: Centre for Medieval English Studies, pp. 29–50.

9. On the presence of 'monstrous alphabets' in the margins of medieval books see Camille MB. (1992) *Image on the Edge. The Margins of Medieval Art*, London: Reaktion.

10. I am grateful to Elizabeth Eisenstein for reminding me of this passage.

11. Cf. Bernard P, Bernard L and O'Neill A. (1994) *Antiquarian Books: A Companion For Booksellers, Librarians and Collectors*, Aldershot: Scholar Press.

    The entry for 'Reading Copy' reads 'This apparently otiose description is generally taken to mean that a book offered in a catalogue is little more than complete, and thus "readable", though not in suitable condition for a collector. "Working copies" are usually even worse' (p. 349), and 'Marginalia' is defined as 'Anything written in the margin of a book after it was published . . . Although marginalia can be of considerable interest and importance—Boswell's annotations to the works of Johnson, for instance—many, particularly in more recent books, are no more than defacements' (p. 277).

12. Randall McLeod has recently shown how the un-inked impressions left behind by 'bearing type'—which was used to balance the printing surface in the hand-press period—can provide important clues about the production of printed books (see McLeod R. (2000) Where angels fear to read. In: Bray J, Handley M and Henry AC. (eds) *Ma(r)king the Text: The Presentation of Meaning on the Literary Page*. Aldershot: Ashgate, pp. 144–194.)

13. On the latter see Jackson K. (1999) *Invisible Forms: A Guide to Literary Curiosities*, London: Picador and Brinsley J. (1612) *Ludus Literarius: Or, the Grammar Schoole*. London: Thomas Mann.

14. Cf. Petersen E. (1995) The archaeology of texts and codices. In: Fellows-Jensen G and Springborg P (eds) *Care and Conservation of Manuscripts 3*. Copenhagen: The Royal Library, pp. 125–129 and Page RI. (1995) The ideal and the practical. In: Fellows-Jensen G and Springborg P (eds) *Care and Conservation of Manuscripts 4*. Copenhagen: The Royal Library, pp. 122–130.

15. I owe this point to David McKitterick.

16. *Los Angeles Times* (7 June 1953), IA: 6. The clipping can be found in the Huntington's Institutional Archives (folder 12.14.2.4).

17. The comments quoted in this paragraph can be found on p. 9.

18. A more conservative discussion of the question can be found in Ringrose J. (1990) Making things available: the curator and the reader. *The Book Collector* 39: pp. 55–73.

19. Letter from Broadbent to Adams, 9 July 1931 (Folger Shakespeare Library, Catalog Office Closet, Correspondence Files, 'Special Collections and Subjects', folder for 'Broadbent'), pp. 1–4. An earlier letter from Broadbent to Folger himself (dated 2 May 1927), offering him his entire collection of annotated books for £7,500, is also in this folder. I am grateful to the staff at the Folger Library (and particularly to Suellen Towers and Elaine Shiner) for bringing these materials to my attention.

20. Marcus Tullius Cicero, *De Oratore* libri III (Venice: ex Bibliotheca Aldina, I 569), Folger Shakespeare Library shelf-mark PA6296.D6 1569 Cage.

21. See my essay, Sherman WH. (2002) What did Renaissance readers write in their books? In: Andersen J and Sauer E (eds) *Books and Readers in Early Modern England: Material Studies*. Philadelphia: University of Pennsylvania Press, pp. 119–137.

22. See the references in Sherman WH. (1997) *John Dee: The Politics of Reading and Writing in the English Renaissance*, Amherst: University of Massachusetts Press and Kintgen ER. (1996) *Reading in Tudor England*, Pittsburgh: University of Pittsburgh Press. Ch. 2.

23. Appropriately enough, the Huntington's copy of this text (shelf-mark 29028) has been very heavily annotated.

24. This practice is still in use today. In his guide, *How to Buy Rare Books* (Oxford:

Phaidon-Christie's, 1985), William Rees-Mogg offers the following advice under the heading of 'soiling': 'dust-soiling and dirty finger-marks can usually be partially or completely removed with a very soft eraser, or with fresh white bread used in the same way' (p. 139).

25. Michael Dobson has called Shakespeare's *First Folio* 'a high-prestige bequest to [American collectors'] fellow-citizens—or, to put it more cynically, a commodity of choice for humanist money-launderers' (Dobson M. (2001) Whatever you do, buy. Review of the Shakespeare first folio: the history of the book vol. I: an account of the first folio based on its sales and prices, 1623–2000 by West, AJ., *London Review of Books* 23, pp. 8–10).

26. This is, in fact, a cleaned-up version of the story: according to Joad Raymond, Thomason himself explained that he valued them more for the royal soil than the original text.

27. Unpaginated preliminaries to Volume I.

28. See for example, Grebanier BD. (1965) *The Great Shakespeare Forgery*, London: Heinemann.

29. Huntington Library RB 62717.

30. According to the Folger's acquisitions files, the books did not come directly from Smedley.

31. Henry Woudhuysen and Peter Beal himself provided useful information about Broadbent, Smedley and Bacon.

REFERENCES

Ahearn A. (1989) *Book Collecting: A Comprehensive Guide*, New York: G.P. Putnam's Sons.

Arnold WH. (1923) *Ventures in Book Collecting*, New York: Charles Scribner's sons.

Beal P. (1980) *Index of English Literary Manuscripts*, vol. I: 1450–1625, Part 1, Andrewes-Donne, London: Mansell.

Bernard P, Bernard L and O'Neill A. (1994) *Antiquarian Books: A Companion for Booksellers, Librarians and Collectors*, Aldershot: Scholar Press.

Blathwayte R. (1912) The romance of the sale room. *Fortnightly Review* November: pp. 939–950.

Bowen D. (1953) *The Book of Common Prayer*: the James R. Page Collection, Los Angeles: The Plantin Press.

Brinsley J. (1612) *Ludus Literarius: Or, the Grammar Schoole*, London: Thomas Mann.

Brook GL. (1980) *Books and Book-collecting*, London: Andre Deutsch.

Bury R de (1960) *Philobiblon*, ed. M. Maclagan, Oxford: Basil Blackwell.

Camille MB. (1992) *Image on the Edge: The Margins of Medieval Art*, London: Reaktion.

Davies R. (1997) *Happy Alchemy on the Pleasures of Music and the Theatre*, New York: Viking.

Dobson M. (2001) Whatever you do, buy. Review of the Shakespeare *First Folio*: the history of the book Vol. I: an account of the *First Folio* based on its sales and prices, 1623–2000 by West, AJ., *London Review of Books* 23: pp. 8–10.

Drogin M. (1983) *Anathema! Medieval Scribes and the History of Book Curses*, Totowa, NJ: Allanheld and Schram.

Fadiman A. (1998) *Ex Libris: Confessions of a Common Reader*, London: Penguin.

Graham T. (1997) The beginnings of Old English studies: evidence from the manuscripts of Matthew Parker. In: Sati S (ed) *Back to the Manuscripts*, Tokyo: Centre for Medieval English Studies, pp. 29–50.

Grebanier BD. (1965) *The Great Shakespeare Forgery*, London: Heinemann.

Hadgraft N. (1995) The significance of the archaeology of the book in the context of conservation work. In: Fellows-Jensen G and Springborg P (eds) *Care and Conservation of Manuscripts*, Copenhagen: The Royal Library, pp. 23–28.

Hulvey M. (1998) Not so marginal: manuscript annotations in the Folger incunabula. The papers of the *Bibliographical Society of America* 92: pp. 159–176.

Immerito [pseud.] (1932) The Folger Library Shakespeare Collection. *The Librarian and Book World* 21: pp. 262–263.

Jackson H. (1950) *The Anatomy of Bibliomania*, London: Faber and Faber.

Jackson HJ. (1992) Writing in books and other marginal activities. *University of Toronto Quarterly* 62: pp. 218–231.

Jackson HJ. (2001) *Marginalia: Readers Writing in Books*, New Haven: Yale University Press.

Jackson K. (1999) *Invisible Forms: A Guide to Literary Curiosities*, London: Picador.

Jones JH. (1989) Diary. *London Review of Books* 11: pp. 20–21.

Jones JH. (2001) Empsons toast, Letters to the editor. *TLS* 5125: p. 17.

Kintgen ER. (1996) *Reading in Tudor England*, Pittsburgh: University of Pittsburgh Press.

McKisack M. (1971) *Medieval History in the Tudor Age*, Oxford: Clarendon Press.

McLeod R. (2000) Where angels fear to read. In: Bray J, Handley M and Henry AC (eds) *Ma(r)king the Text: The Presentation of Meaning on the Literary Page*, Aldershot: Ashgate, pp. 144–194.

Mogg WR. (1985) *How to Buy Rare Books: A Practical Guide to the Antiquarian Book Market*, Oxford: Phaidon-Christie's.

Orgel S. (2000) Margins of truth. In: Murphy A (ed) *The Renaissance Text: Theory, Editing, Textuality*, Manchester: Manchester University Press, pp. 91–107.

Page RI. (1995) The ideal and the practical. In: Fellows-Jensen G and Springborg P (eds) *Care and Conservation of Manuscripts 4*, Copenhagen: The Royal Library, pp. 122–130.

Parke-Bernet G. (1941) *Rare Books, Original Drawings, Autograph Letters and Manuscripts Collected by the Late A. Edward Newton*, New York: Parke-Bernet Galleries.

Peacham, H. (1622) *The compleat gentleman fashioning him absolute in the most necessary & commendable qualities concerning minde or bodie that may be required in a noble gentleman*, London: John Legat for Francis Constable.

Petersen E. (1995) The archaeology of texts and codices. In: Fellows-Jensen G and Springborg P (eds) *Care and Conservation of Manuscripts 3*, Copenhagen: The Royal Library, pp. 125–129.

Portal EM. (1915–16) The Academ Roial of King James I. *Proceedings of the British Academy*: pp. 189–208.

Ringrose J. (1990) Making things available: the curator and the reader. *The Book Collector* 39: pp. 55–73.

Rose GR. (1943) The libraries of Bacon and Ben Jonson: how they marked their books. *Baconiana* 27: pp. 57–59.

Rosenthal BM. (1997) *The Rosenthal Collection of Printed Books with Manuscript*

Annotations: a catalog of 242 editions mostly before 1600 annotated by contemporary or near-contemporary readers, New Haven: Yale University Press.

Shaddy RA. (1994) A world of sentimental attachments, the cult of collecting, 1890–1930. *The Book Collector* 43: pp. 185–200.

Sherman WH. (1997) *John Dee: The Politics of Reading and Writing in the English Renaissance*, Amherst: University of Massachusetts Press.

Sherman WH. (2002) What did Renaissance readers write in their books? In: Andersen J and Sauer E (eds) *Books and Readers in Early Modern England: Material Studies*, Philadelphia: University of Pennsylvania Press, pp. 119–137.

Sherman WH. (2003) 'Rather soiled by use': attitudes toward readers' marks. *The Book Collector* 52: pp. 471–490.

Sherman WH. (2008) *Used Books: Marking Readers in Renaissance England*, Philadelphia: University of Pennsylvania Press.

Smedley WT. (1912) *The Mystery of Francis Bacon*, London: Robert Banks & Son.

Stoddard RE. (1985) *Marks in Books, Illustrated and Explained*, Cambridge, MA: Houghton Library.

Stoddard RE. (2000) Looking at marks in books. *The Gazette of the Grolier Club New Series* 51: pp. 27–47.

Traister D. (2000) Is there a future for special collections? And should there be? A polemical essay. *RBM* 1: pp. 54–76.

Afterword: the craft of paradata, marginalia and fieldnotes

Rosalind Edwards, Ann Phoenix, Henrietta O'Connor and John Goodwin

This edited collection, as we noted in our Introduction, has broken new ground in bringing together a diverse range of disciplinary and methodological discussions of the materials that 'go alongside' or are by-products of activities such as research data collection and analysis, and the process of reading. Taken together, the chapters show what we argued in the introductory chapter (Chapter 1): that although paradata, marginalia and fieldnotes have arisen and been popularised in different fields, it is extremely fruitful to consider them together.

Each of the chapter contributions demonstrate the value of rendering visible the acts of data collection and coding, or the intellectual processes associated with reading, through the craft of studying paradata, marginalia and fieldnotes. This performative focus produces a more holistic understanding of the research process, data and analysts' or researchers' positioning in relation to the data or research material, although it is important to recognise that it is necessarily partial, rather than complete. The study of paradata, marginalia and fieldnotes can make evident ethical issues and complex social relations that can be taken-for-granted or eschewed in analyses that focus on the main content of research material. This is discussed further below.

As data in themselves, paradata, marginalia and fieldnotes have captured the interest of people working in quite different disciplinary fields. Amongst the contributors to this volume we have social statisticians (Durrant, Maslovskaya), extensive and intensive survey researchers (Fahmy, Bell, Kilburn), social psychologists (Phoenix, Boddy), sociologists (O'Connor, Goodwin, Edwards), historians and literary scholars (Elliott, Jackson, Sherman). Their chapter discussions demonstrate that by-products in all their various forms have been subject to practices from across methodological approaches: quantitative and qualitative, using various methods of analysis, including here for example, binary logistic (Chapter 2), thematic

(Chapter 5), genre and historical narrative (Chapters 7 and 8), or mixed methods and complementary analyses in various combinations (e.g. systematic coding and thematic analysis in Chapter 3, and thematic and narrative analyses in Chapter 4). Several make use of visual methods, using images to deepen and illustrate their analytic arguments.

We have seen in the foregoing chapters that these materials can be brief, written calculations, digitally recorded computer keystrokes, extensive pieces of written narrative or digitally recorded verbal exchanges. They can function as both primary and secondary analysis and are often intertextual, drawing in meanings from other publications and social knowledge (Kristeva, 1980). Their form reflects developments in the spectrum of technologies available for the creation and collection of paradata. These may range from markings on paper, audio recording on magnetic tape, to the digitisation of actions and sounds and their storage in computer files. Indeed, as mentioned by H.J. Jackson in her chapter, the online technologies of digitised materials mean that multiple analysts may be exploring the same by-product at the same time or in various time zones. Digital technologies may have other implications in terms of the future of paradata and marginalia, as we note below.

In this concluding chapter of our edited volume we consider some of the important ideas about the value of studying paradata, marginalia and fieldnotes that run across the quite diverse contributions to this collection. What knowledge about the craft may be carved out of the interface of disciplinary and methodological approaches and concerns that constitute this collection? No matter what the substantive topic of the activity of which these materials are a by-product, the disciplinary field in which the researcher who studies them is steeped, or the analytic method they deploy, there are recurrent messages about the practice of the craft emerging from the chapters.

One fundamental feature of the study of paradata, marginalia and fieldnotes demonstrated in the chapters in this volume is that such materials are now acknowledged as significant and are considered a legitimate field of enquiry. By-products have moved from being background shadows of research practice to a place in the spotlight across the social sciences and humanities. Paradata and fieldnotes are no longer the taken-for-granted material that goes along with the process of data collection, as the unintentional automatic features of computer-assisted personal interviewing noted by Gabi Durrant and Olga Maslovskaya (Chapter 2), or as the 'private' aide memoires made about people and places by an observant field researcher such as Pearl Jephcott, discussed in Henrietta O'Connor and John Goodwin's chapter (Chapter 6). And as William Sherman demonstrates (Chapter 8), marginalia have not and are not always or necessarily, judged to be undesirable markings made by readers that 'soil' the pages of manuscripts and books. Rather than 'by-products', these materials are now acknowledged as informative 'products', or data, that are illuminative in and of themselves.

In the social sciences, an interest in by-products as data and the craft of studying them is perhaps more recent, associated with the increasing attention paid to methodological issues involved in research (Brannen and Edwards, 1998). Research methods have become a subject of study in their own right. They are now regarded as a self-standing set of skills that form the focus of taught courses, seminars and workshops, and are an important, substantive publishing field in both journals and books – as this volume attests. While fieldnotes have always been a feature of good research practice for qualitative researchers, there has been a 'reflexive turn' in social research, recognising and analysing the researcher's role in constructing the research process and findings. In turn, this has led social researchers not only to ponder more on the implications of their own research conduct for the production of knowledge, but also to study the practices of their peers, not only in the present but also in the past (as in Chapter 4 by Phoenix and colleagues, Chapter 5 by Kilburn and Chapter 6 by O'Connor and Goodwin). In the field of survey methods, the shift to computerisation has enabled an enduring concern with consistency, reliability and efficiency in data collection to be pursued through electronic capture and analysis of paradata for quality control and process development (as demonstrated in Chapter 2 by Durrant and Maslovskaya and Fahmy and Bell's Chapter 3). In the humanities, attention to 'marks in margins' is perhaps more long-standing in historical and literary studies, certainly in the case of marginal markings made in books by famous figures (as in the discussions by Jackson and by Sherman). Acknowledgement of the varied insights to be gained through the study of marginalia is more recent.

The value of the by-products is seen to lie in their contributions to understanding in various ways. This can be in terms of analysing paradata to improve the data quality of surveys. For example, Durrant and Maslovskaya look at the use of macro-level paradata for better understanding of non-response in surveys. This use is not only as part of efforts to enhance data quality by modelling non-response, but also to reduce inefficiencies and costs by, for example, informing effective calling strategies. Eldin Fahmy and Karen Bell have similar quality concerns in their analyses. They make a case for the value of bringing together behaviour coding of the automatically captured paradata associated with question and response problems with a thematic coding of verbatim transcripts of audio-recorded interviewer–respondent exchanges that are integral to the actual administration of the survey. Analysis of both these forms of by-products of survey administration offers insights into what actually goes on in survey interviews to inform the development of instruments. It is here, argues Daniel Kilburn, that the fundamental rationale for analysis of paradata lies – in its unique potential to render the research process visible. Analysis of various forms of survey paradata provides invaluable insights into how information about interviewees' situations is collected in ways that extend beyond the scripted questions. It illuminates how the condensation of the data into coded responses, and thus the knowledge produced in surveys, is contingent on the methodological instruments. Going further, O'Connor and Goodwin make a passionate case for the crucial importance of field and marginal notes for secondary analysts, without which their understanding of the original study would be constrained and defective. They demonstrate how the range of materials that 'went alongside' the youth employment research studies they (re)analysed was full of illuminative potential.

A further contribution of the study of by-products, in the form of marginalia and fieldnotes in particular, is the illumination of methodological or substantive specificities of a particular period, place, research study, and/ or person. For example, Ann Phoenix and colleagues' narrative analysis of the marginalia in the booklets from Townsend's 1967–68 poverty survey reveals the historical specificity of ethical conduct, where at that time it appeared to be customary for field interviewers to insist robustly that respondents take part in the survey and answer the questions in ways that would not formally be acceptable now. Using the same dataset, Kilburn discusses the importance of identifying the taken-for-granted but particular housing conditions of the period. O'Connor and Goodwin give a clear sense of how paradata can convey this more fully than the data themselves. They note the sense of time period conveyed in the descriptions of people's appearance and character and their living conditions contained within the marginalia and fieldnotes they looked at. They also point to the normative research and social assumptions of the time, apparent in marginalia, in how social researchers viewed themselves and the questions that they could and should ask, for example, on suppositions about family composition. Jackson notes that the presence of a sustained body of marginalia is a blessing for those engaged in reconstructing the past, and attempting to understand the intellectual development and complex personality of a celebrated individual. Sherman identifies the different economies of collecting rare books and the opposing philosophies about how to treat the books we find valuable. He shows us the historical and contextual shifts in whether marginal annotations are considered deplorable and in need of eradication, or appreciated as an asset.

The value inherent in studying paradata, marginalia and fieldnotes is often linked to the person who created them, as in the case of the marginalia created by major figures such as President John Adams (explored in Jackson's chapter). Durrant and Maslovskaya note interest in the survey interviewer's collection of paradata, for example, in recognition of their crucial role in gaining contact and responses from the sample members. This points us towards the way that, more than association with a particular originator, paradata, marginalia and fieldnotes are, intentionally or unintentionally, relational. Relationships are integral to paradata, marginalia and fieldnotes, both constituted through their production and reflected in their study. Clearly, whether they are explicit about this or not, researchers pursuing the craft of studying paradata, marginalia and fieldnotes are studying often complex sets of relationships.

In this volume, we can discern seven main sets of relations invoked by our contributors:

- *Between a field interviewer and their interviewee*
  The by-products of research point to the relational exchanges that are integral to the collection of data. Fahmy and Bell consider the interactions between survey interviewers and survey respondents in the conduct and delivery of survey interviews in the field. They approach the interview setting as a social interaction that is subject to conversational norms, and reveal the necessary relational work that underlies the production of the survey data through the posing and answering of questions. Other contributions that highlight the relations between interviewer and interviewee include Phoenix and colleagues' demonstration of the way that narratives evident in survey marginalia construct the interviewer, the interviewee, their relationship and wider relationships with the survey team. The paradata and marginalia they explore convey the interviewer's feelings about the interview and the interviewee, and their moral stance in relation to the interviewee's circumstances. Kilburn pursues an aspect of these relations in depth in his consideration of the explicit and implicit dissonance between interviewer and interviewee. He shows the contestation apparent in marginal notes where field interviewers' perceptions of an interviewee's circumstances do not correspond to those of the interviewee themselves.

- *Between a field interviewer and the core research team*
  The actual process of data collection may be undertaken by contracted field researchers who then pass that material to the (academic) research team who have designed the study and will analyse the data. Phoenix and colleagues' analysis of the narratives embedded in

survey interviewers' marginalia shows how they position themselves as professionals who are accountable to the central research team, justifying how they pursued and interpreted the survey responses, for example. Similarly, Kilburn's examination of the field interviewers' marginalia shows how hastily-made notes during the administration of the survey were later worked up into amplificatory descriptions to convey further information to the core research team when the interviewers felt that the survey categories did not do justice to the interviewee's situation.

- *Within research teams*
  Where research is conducted amongst teams of people, the materials that 'go along' with the research process can be particularly revealing of relationships amongst the team. O'Connor and Goodwin provide a tantalising glimpse into the intricate web of relations in the classic youth employment studies they explored. Through the examination of the by-products of the research studies, they uncover the tense and disputatious as well as creative relations between the eminent researchers ostensibly working together in leading a project, and between these senior colleagues and the early career members of their research teams.

- *Between the creator of paradata, marginalia or fieldnotes and themselves*
  There are moments when the by-products of research and reading activities appear to be an analytic commentary in which the creator attempts to explain to themselves how they should understand a situation or argument. A good example is provided by O'Connor and Goodwin's analysis of the way that Jephcott's richly detailed ethnographic fieldnotes provided a textual and visual record of her observations that served as context for her social research. This fits with the ways in which ethnographic fieldnotes function to contextualise research and remind researchers of issues important to analysis.

- *Between a reader of a text and another reader of that text, known or unknown*
  The creation of marginalia are not just associated with primary practices, but, in the materials considered by Jackson and Sherman, are a form of secondary practice. They are annotations to a primary text; responses to the text that are created by the reader of that text. In a further layer, they may not be produced (only) as conversation with one's self in response to reading but composed with other readers in

mind and with an eye to posterity, as Jackson suggests on the basis of Adams's vivid annotations in the books in his library. Indeed, Sherman describes marginalia as a powerful method for conversing with other readers, something sometimes seen in student texts borrowed from the library.

- *Reader engagement with writers, material and meaning*
  A related way in which writing in books or on interview or questionnaire booklets functions is in the engagement with the text, the writer or the intended meaning, sometimes operating as critical comment (Wagstaff, 2012). The chapter by Phoenix and colleagues illustrates how this form of writing can give analytic insights into the concerns and identities of the writer, as does Jackson's chapter (see also Moran, 2011) as well as how they actively struggle to clarify intended meanings.

- *Between the creator/s of the paradata, marginalia or fieldnotes and the researchers who analyse it*
  In this collection, the by-products of the activities of research and reading are subject to (secondary) analysis by people other than those who created them, who are thereby propelled into some form of relationship with those originators. Both Durrant and Maslovskaya's, and Fahmy and Bell's contributions have the potential to convey a sense of being at the interview, alongside the survey interviewee and field interviewer who are creating the paradata. Jackson remarks on the way that marginal notes generate a strong sense of presence, bridging the gap between creator and researcher over time. She includes reference to her emotional reactions, finding Adams variously admirable, pitiable and winning. O'Connor and Goodwin term the by-products they explored 'irresistible', with the acts of handling and reading them sparking interest in the originators and their practices. Indeed, some form of relationship between themselves as social researchers and the creators of the paradata, marginalia and/or fieldnotes that they study – and the fascination of the analysis – is evident in all the chapter contributions to this volume.

With reference to the fascination of analysis, another and recurrent message across the contributions to this unique collection is that paradata, marginalia and fieldnotes are often messy and evocative, reflecting complex structures and operating at multiple levels that deserve and require a sophisticated analytic approach. For surveys, these multiple planes can be conceived of pragmatically, as various nesting levels of: the survey interviewer, each call to a household, individuals within a household, the household, and the area (see Durrant and Maslovskaya's chapter). More epistemologically, a focus on multiple planes can raise knotty questions about the status of paradata, marginalia and fieldnotes. A review of the contributions in this collection raises intriguing, but perhaps unanswerable questions, about whether or not those of us who examine and explore paradata, marginalia and fieldnotes essentialise them in the process. Does the craft of study and analysis of these materials 'fix' them as bringing us close to what was actually going on at the time of their creation, or can we only access a somewhat flawed reconstruction of this? It also raises ethical questions since the interviewers could have no idea that their words would become analytic objects and, as ethical standards change over time, it is all too easy to appear anachronistically censorious.

Overall then, across varied disciplines and methodological traditions, paradata, marginalia and fieldnotes are legitimate and significant topics of interest that are able to make a valuable contribution to research understanding, not least because of their relationality as well as multi-dimensionality. Indeed the contributions that they enable make the notion of 'para'-data something of a misnomer. For far from simply sitting alongside of, resembling, or going beyond data in social research (to take the meaning of the prefix para-), the chapters in this book make clear that paradata are themselves important data that are all too often overlooked or given more limited attention than they warrant. One of the important developments over the last decade has been increasing recognition, as the result of various innovative pieces of work, of the fruitfulness of examining material that had previously been considered superfluous to academic endeavour or simply not seen (e.g. Couper, 1998; Jackson, 2002; Sherman, 2008).

A related development has been in digital technologies. Digitisation of materials has meant that the constraints of time and place in accessing and studying by-products have been overcome – multiple users can go online and explore digital documents from anywhere at any moment, as Jackson notes in her chapter. But there are other implications of fast developing digital technologies for the nature and even existence of paradata, marginalia and fieldnotes. On the one hand, technical developments mean that electronically captured survey by-products are likely to become more sophisticated, offering the promise of an extensive understanding and intervention in the quality and efficiency of the research process. On the other hand, when it comes to notations on documents, there are questions posed about 'what happens to marginalia in the age of the Kindle?' (O'Connell, 2012, unpaginated). While some see the future as a flowering of shared electronic observations within documents, others feel that calling up electronic note functions and inserting them into online text is impersonal and cuts across the potential spontaneity of written marginalia, making analysis of identities, for example, less possible. Moran (2011) suggests that electronic technology make it unlikely that people will assert ownership, of a Kindle for example, through marginalia. Similarly, as fieldnotes are kept electronically the technology to access them could either transcend time and place or render them inaccessible through redundant technologies. Katz (2012) suggests that this produces the paradox that, just as the potential fruitfulness of paradata is beginning to be more widely recognised, digital technologies might limit its possibilities.

> Among all the gifts of the electronic age, one of the most paradoxical might be to illuminate something we are beginning to trade away: the particular history, visible and invisible, that can be passed down through the vessel of an old book, inscribed by the hands and the minds of readers who are gone.
>
> (Katz, 2012, para. 15)

Returning to the present, implicit in the contributions to this volume is that the craft of studying paradata, marginalia and fieldnotes is fun; engaging as well as informative. We hope that this edited collection will help to stimulate research that considers and explores these by-products, in whatever form, well into the future.

REFERENCES

Brannen, J. and Edwards, R. (1998) 'Editorial', *International Journal of Social Research Methodology*, 1(1): 1–6.

Couper, M. (1998) 'Measuring survey quality in a CASIC environment', in *Proceedings of the Section on Survey Research Methods of the American Statistical Association:* http://www.amstat.org/sections/srms/proceedings/papers/1998_006. pdf [accessed 21 April 2016].

Jackson, H.J. (2002) *Marginalia: Readers Writing in Books*. New Haven, CT: Yale University Press.

Katz, A. (2012) 'Will your children inherit your e-books?' http://www.npr. org/2012/06/21/155360197/ will-your-children-inherit-your-e-books [accessed 24 April 2016].

Kristeva, J. (1980) *Desire in Language: A Semiotic Approach to Language and Art*. (Trans. T. Gora, A. Jardine and L. Roudiez) (ed. L. Roudiez), New York: Columbia University Press.

Moran, J. (2011) 'Why I write in the margin', *The Guardian*, 22 March. http:// www.theguardian.com/commentisfree/2011/mar/22/notes-in-the-margin-social-networking [accessed 24 April 2016].

O'Connell, M. (2012) 'The marginal obsession with marginalia', *The New Yorker*,

26 January: http://www.newyorker.com/books/page-turner/the-marginal-obses
sion-with-marginalia [accessed 22 April 2016].

Sherman, W.H. (2008) *Used Books: Marking Readers in Renaissance England.*
Philadelphia: University of Pennsylvania Press.

Wagstaff, K. (2012) 'The evolution of marginalia'. Unpublished paper. http://www.
wkiri.com/slis/wagstaff-libr200-marginalia-1col.pdf [accessed 24 April 2016].

Index